Private Palaces

Christopher Simon Sykes

Private Palaces

Life in the Great London Houses

VIKING

Viking Penguin Inc.
40 West 23rd Street,
New York, New York 10010, U.S.A.

First American Edition
Published in 1986

ISBN 0-670-80964-0
Library of Congress Catalog Card Number 85-40557 CIP data available

Design by Alan Bartram
Map by John Flower

Front endpaper: View of Bloomsbury Square, looking northwards, showing Southampton House.
Drawing by Edward Dayes, 1787.
Rear endpaper: The Hilton Hotel, Park Lane, London, with Londonderry House on the right.

Printed in Great Britain by
Butler & Tanner Ltd, Frome and London
Set in 11 on 13 Monophoto Ehrhardt

Title page:
Russell Square, looking south *c.* 1745. A coach approaches Southampton House (later Bedford House), to the right of which stands Montagu House.

Contents

IN MEMORY OF NORAH SMALLWOOD,
AND FOR LILY

This book would never have been written without the invaluable help of John Cornforth, who handed over to me without reservation all his notes for, and the manuscript of a book he had been working on some years ago for *Country Life*. For this, and for the fact that he made himself available at all times to answer endless tiresome questions and, at the end, to check through the manuscript for any glaring errors, I am eternally grateful.

Acknowledgements

Many people have helped me in various ways throughout the preparation of this book, and they all receive my heartfelt thanks. They are: The Marquess of Anglesey, the Dowager Duchess of Buccleuch, the staff of the Prints and Drawings room at the British Museum, Ms Carmen Callil, Mrs Sonia Cubitt, Lady Victoria Cuthbert, Mr Peter Day, Keeper of Collections at Chatsworth, the Duke and Duchess of Devonshire, the Marchioness of Douro, Mrs Marie Draper, archivist of the Bedford Estate Office, Ms Mireille Galinou, Assistant Keeper of Prints at the London Museum, staff at the Guildhall Library Print Room, Mr John Harris, Mr Gervase Jackson-Stops, the Marquess of Londonderry, Mr Douglas Matthews and the staff of the London Library, Lady Sophia Murphy, the Duke and Duchess of Northumberland, Mr Michael Pearman, librarian at Chatsworth, Mr A. J. Roberts, assistant archivist of the department of manuscripts and records at the National Library of Wales, Ms Mary L. Robertson, curator of manuscripts at the Huntington Library, San Marino, California, Mr Jacob Rothschild, Sir David Scott, the Earl of Shelburne, Mr Colin Shrimpton, archivist at Alnwick Castle, Ms Doreen Slatter, archivist at Bowood House, the Earl and Countess Spencer, Sir Tatton Sykes, Ms Jane Turner, Mr Ed Victor, Mr Alan Williams, Ms Sarah Wimbush and the staff of the National Portrait Gallery Archives, and last, but by no means least, my wife Belinda, for her sound advice and her constant support.

Illustrations acknowledgements

Abbreviations used below: BBC – BBC Hulton Picture Library, London; BL – British Library, London; BM – Trustees of the British Museum, London; Chatsworth – Devonshire Collection, Chatsworth, by permission of the Chatsworth Settlement Trustees; CL – *Country Life* magazine; Courtauld – Courtauld Institute of Art, University of London; GLC – Greater London Council Record Office; Guildhall – Guildhall Library, London; ILN – Illustrated London News Picture Library; NPG – National Portrait Gallery, London; NPG Edinburgh – Scottish National Portrait Gallery; NMR – Royal Commission on Historical Monuments (England), National Monuments Record; RIBA – The British Architectural Library/Royal Institute of British Architects, London; Soane Museum – Sir John Soane's Museum, London; V&A – Victoria & Albert Museum, London; Westminster – Westminster City Libraries Archives Department, London.

Colour plates
Plate 1 The Trustees of the British Museum; plate 2 from *Royal Residences . . .* by W. H. Pyne; plate 3 Soane Museum; plate 4 The Marquess of Anglesey; plate 5 Private Collection; plate 6 The Earl Spencer; plate 7 Paul Mellon Collection, Yale Center for British Art, New Haven, Connecticut, USA; plate 8 The Trustees of the Tate Gallery, London; plate 9 The Trustees of the British Museum; plate 10 Royal Institute of British Architects, London; plate 11 The Trustees of the British Museum; plate 12 His Grace the Duke of Northumberland; plate 13 Soane Museum; plate 14 from *Royal Residences* by W. H. Pyne; plate 15 Devonshire Collection, Chatsworth, by permission of the Chatsworth Settlement; plate 16 The Trustees of The Victoria and Albert Museum, London; plate 17 His Grace the Duke of Westminster, DL (photo: The Courtauld Institute of Art); plate 18 Private Collection; plate 19 Viscount Wimborne (photo: Eagle Star Insurance Company Ltd.)

Black and white illustrations
Front endpaper Guildhall; Half-title page CL; Title page CL; page 12 GLC; 15 Private Collection (photo: Courtauld); 17 GLC; 24 GLC; 25 top NMR Crown Copyright; bottom GLC; 26 Westminster; 27 The Provost and Fellows of Worcester College, Oxford (photo: Courtauld); 28 *Vitruvius Britannicus* by Colen Campbell; 31 left NPG; right The Royal Society, London; 32 top BM; bottom *Vitruvius Britannicus*; 33 left The Trustee of The Will of the 8th Earl of Berkeley deceased (photo:

Courtauld); right Chatsworth (photo: Courtauld); 34–5
Guildhall; 37 CL; 38 Warburg Institute, London (photo:
NMR); 39 CL; 40 Guildhall; 41 The Earl Bathurst
(photo: Courtauld); 42 private collection; 43 ML; 44 ML;
46 Earl of Bradford (photo: Courtauld); 48–9 Guildhall; 51
left The Collection of the Duke of Buccleuch and
Queensberry KT, at Boughton House, Kettering (photo:
NPG Edinburgh); right private collection (photo:
Courtauld); 52 CL; 53 Guildhall; 55 BM; 56 BM; 58 left
Sotheby's, London (photo: NPG); right Lord Montagu,
Beaulieu (photo: Courtauld); 59 Guildhall; 60 Guildhall;
61 BM; 64–5 top Guildhall; bottom Guildhall; 67 Soane
Museum; 68 Christie's, London (photo: NPG); 70
Christie's, London (photo: NPG); 71 ML; 72 ML; 73
ML; 74 Guildhall; 75 Barratt's Photo Press (S & G Press
Agency Ltd); 76 The Earl of Shaftesbury (photo: NPG);
78 CL; 79 NPG; 80 *Vitruvius Britannicus*; 81 Royal
Academy of Arts, London; 82 RIBA; 83 CL; 85 top left
Chatsworth (photo: Courtauld); top right NPG; bottom
ML; 86 *Vitruvius Britannicus*; 87 B. T. Batsford Ltd
(photo: NMR); 88 NPG; 89 top and bottom CL; 90 BM;
91 Guildhall; 92 Guildhall; 93 ML; 96 ML; 97 Brian
Sewell; 98 Chatsworth (photo: Courtauld); 99 top CL;
bottom Guildhall; 100 left and right ML; 101 left LM:
right D. A. Rumbelow; 102 From *English Decoration in the
18th Century* by John Fowler and John Cornforth (Barrie
& Jenkins, 2nd ed. 1978); 104 Chatsworth (photo:
Courtauld); 106 left CL; right GLC; 107 Soane; 108
Soane; 109 GLC; 110 CL; 112 Guildhall; 113 top and
bottom Guildhall; 116 top Guildhall; bottom left RIBA;
bottom right NPG; 117 Guildhall; 118 John Freeman &
Co Ltd; 119 CL; 122 NMR; 123 NMR; 124 NMR; 125
top NMR; bottom CL; 126 NMR; 127 NMR; 128 left
NPG, Edinburgh: Hamilton Collection; right Christie's,
London (photo: NPG); 131 Guildhall; 132 left Walker Art
Gallery, Liverpool; right His Grace The Duke of Norfolk
(photo: Courtauld); 135 NMR; 136 NMR; 137 CL; 138
CL; 140 CL; 141 CL; 142 Ashmolean Museum, Oxford;
143 NMR; 145 top and bottom CL; 146 top and bottom
CL; 149 top Guildhall; bottom BM; 150 CL; 151 left and
right private collection (photo: Courtauld); 155 The
Trustees of the Tate Gallery, London; 157 Reproduced by
gracious permission of Her Majesty The Queen,
Copyright HM The Queen; 159 top from *Royal Residences*
by W. H. Pyne; bottom BM; 161 From *Le Pâtissier
Pittoresque* by Carême (photo: Guildhall); 163 BBC; 164
National Trust, Erdigg, Wales (photo: Courtauld); 165
ML; 169 GLC; 172 left and right The Earl Spencer
(photo: Courtauld); 174 V&A; 175 Guildhall; 177 CL; 178
top and bottom CL; 179 NMR; 180 CL; 181 NMR; 182
CL; 183 NPG; 184 CL; 185 The National Trust/
Staffordshire County Council, Shugborough Hall (photo:
Courtauld); 186 GLC; 187 NMR; 188 top Sotheby's
(photo: NPG); bottom NMR; 189 Soane Museum; 190
NMR; 191 NMR; 192 The Marquis of Bristol (photo:

Courtauld); 193 ML; 194 V&A; 195 CL; 197 Collection of
the Marquis of Zetland (photo: NPG); 198 Soane
Museum; 200 Collection of the Marquis of Zetland
(photo: The Bowes Museum, Barnard Castle, County
Durham); 201 NPG; 204 top RIBA from *The Works in
Architecture of R. & J. Adam*, Vol 2; bottom B. T.
Batsford Ltd (photo: NMR); 205 top The Metropolitan
Museum of Art, Rogers Fund, 1932, NY; bottom NMR;
206 NMR; 208 top and bottom CL; 209 Courtauld; 210
B. T. Batsford Ltd (photo: NMR); 211 CL; 212 Guildhall;
214 CL; 216 top and bottom CL; 217 top and bottom CL;
219 NPG; 220 BM; 224 NMR; 225 NMR; 226 NMR; 227
RIBA; 228 Soane Museum; 229 (photo: NMR); 230
Chatsworth; 233 Sotheby's, London; 235 John Freeman &
Co Ltd; 236 NMR; 237 private collection (photo: The
Paul Mellon Centre for Studies in British Art); 239 ILN;
240 top Duke of Northumberland; bottom GLC; 241
ILN; 242 left private collection (photo: NPG); right NPG;
244 GLC; 245 CL; 246 top CL; bottom NMR; 247
NMR; 249 His Grace the Duke of Westminster DL (photo:
Courtauld); 250 top ML; bottom CL; 252 top BM;
bottom V&A from *Apsley House and Walmer Castle* by R.
Ford, 1853; 253 Guildhall; 254 NPG; 255 NMR; 258 top
and bottom private collection (photo: Courtauld); 259 top
and bottom ML; 261 CL; 262 NMR; 263 top and bottom
NMR; 264 NMR; 265 private Scottish collection (photo:
NPG Edinburgh); 268 ML; 270 CL; 271 NMR; 272
NMR; 273 ILN; 274 NMR; 275 NMR; 276 NMR; 277
top and bottom NMR; 278 NMR; 279 NMR; 280 NMR;
281 top and bottom NMR; 283 NMR; 284 NMR; 285 top
and bottom NMR; 286 ILN; 287 Wellcome Institute
Library, London; 288 RIBA; 289 NMR; 290 NMR; 291
NPG; 292 NMR; 293 CL; 294 NMR; 295 top and bottom
NMR; 297 top RIBA; bottom Guildhall; 299 Sotheby's,
London; 300 J. Rothschild; 303 left and right BL, from
The King magazine; 304 J. Rothschild; 305 BL, from *The
King*; 306 BM; 307 NMR; 309 NPG; 310 top and bottom
and 313 (all photos) reproduced from *The Duchess of
Devonshire's Ball* by Sophie Murphy, published by
Sidgwick & Jackson, 1984; 315 top NMR; bottom
Christie's, London (photo: NPG); 316 BL, from *The
King*; 317 NMR; 319 Messrs Knight, Frank & Rutley; 320
NMR; 324 Guildhall; 325 top and bottom *The
Architectural Review*, London; 327 NMR; 329 top and
bottom CL; 330 NMR; 332 Cecil Beaton photograph:
Sotheby's, London; 333 (photo: Sydney W. Newbery); 334
CL; 335 Courtauld; 336 NPG, (photo: Howard Coster);
337 CL; 338 CL; Rear endpaper NMR.

The poem by Henry Farjeon from *Nine Sharp and Earlier*
(published by J. M. Dent & Sons Ltd) is reprinted by
permission of David Higham Associates. The extracts
from Sir Henry Channon's *Diaries* are reprinted by
permission of Weidenfeld Publishers Ltd.

Aristocrats no longer keep up any state in London, where family houses hardly exist now. Here many of them have shown a sad lack of civic responsibility, as we can see by looking at poor London today. At the beginning of this century practically all the residential part of the West End belonged to noblemen and the Crown. A more charming and elegant capital city would have been far to seek. To the Crown – more specially I believe to King George V in person – and to two Dukes, Westminster and Bedford, we owe the fact that London is not yet exactly like Moscow, a conglomeration of dwellings. Other owners cheerfully sold their houses and 'developed' their property without a thought for the visible result. Park Lane, most of Mayfair, the Adelphi and so on bear witness to a barbarity which I, for one, cannot forgive.

Nancy Mitford in Encounter, *September 1955*

Key to map

The numbers of the map relate to the numbers and houses listed in sequence below. Black symbols represent houses which still stand, white symbols are for houses which no longer exist.

1 Aldford House, 26 Park Lane
2 Apsley House, Hyde Park Corner
3 18 Arlington Street (Pomfret Castle)
4 19 Arlington Street
5 22 Arlington Street (called Hamilton House & later Wimborne House)
6 Ashburnham House, Little Dean's Yard, Westminster Abbey
7 Barnato House, 25 Park Lane
8 Bath House, 82 Piccadilly
9 Bedford House, Southampton Street
10 5 Belgrave Square
11 44 Berkeley Square
12 Bridgewater House, Cleveland Row
13 Brook House, corner of Park Lane and Upper Brook Street
14 17 Bruton Street
15 Buckingham House (where Buckingham Palace now stands)
16 Burlington House, Piccadilly
17 Carlton House, Pall Mall
18 Carrington House, Whitehall Yard
19 Chandos House, Queen Anne Street
20 Chesterfield House, South Audley Street
21 Clarendon House, Piccadilly (also called Albemarle House)
22 Crewe House, Curzon Street
23 Derby House, 11 Stratford Place
24 Derby House, Grosvenor Square
25 Devonshire House, Piccadilly (formerly Berkeley House)
26 Dorchester House, Park Lane (replaced by hotel, 1930)
27 Dover House, Whitehall (later Fetherstonhaugh House and York House)
28 Dudley House, 100 Park Lane
29 Durham House, Strand
30 Egremont House, 94 Piccadilly

31 Ely House, 37 Dover Street
32 Essex House
33 1 Greek Street
34 Grosvenor House, Park Lane (demolished 1927)
35 5 Hamilton Place, Park Lane
36 Harcourt House, Cavendish Square
37 Hertford House, Manchester Square
38 Home House, 20 Portman Square
39 Lancaster House, Stable Yard, Pall Mall (earlier York House and Stafford House)
40 Lansdowne House, 44 Berkeley Square (formerly Shelburne House)
41 Leicester House, Leicester Square
42 Lichfield House, 15 St James's Square
43 Lindsey House, Lincoln's Inn Fields
44 Londonderry House, Park Lane (formerly Holdernesse House and Ulster House)
45 Marlborough House, Pall Mall
46 Melbourne House, Piccadilly (now Albany)
47 Monmouth House, Soho Square
48 Montague House, Great Russell Street
49 Montagu House, Whitehall Gardens
50 Newcastle House, Lincoln's Inn Fields (formerly Powis House)
51 Norfolk House, St James's Square
52 Northumberland House (also called Northampton House and Suffolk House), Strand
53 Ormonde House, 9–11 St James's Square
54 Pembroke House, Whitehall
55 148 Piccadilly
56 22 Portman Square (formerly Montagu House)
57 Powis House, Great Ormond Street
58 Queensberry House (now Uxbridge House), 7 Burlington Gardens
59 Richmond House, Whitehall
60 Russell House, 43 King Street, Covent Garden
61 20 St James's Square (Wynn House)
62 38 South Street
63 Southampton House (later called Bedford House), Bloomsbury Square
64 Spencer House, 27 St James's Place
65 Sunderland House, Curzon Street

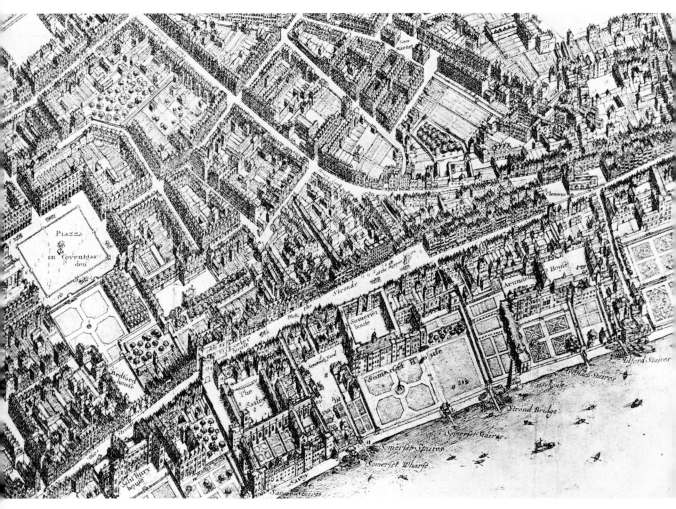

The Strand Palaces as
shown on Wenceslas
Hollar's map,
*A Bird's-Eye View of
West London.*

Prologue

The Magnetism of London

London is the garden of England, whear wee may all live together

Sir Anthony Denton to Thomas Isham, c.1601–5

Early in the spring of 1675, a traveller on the road from London to Woburn, in the county of Bedfordshire, may well at some stage in his journey have found the way barred by a splendid procession. Led by a magnificently attired master of the horse, a dozen or more outriders cleared the way for a richly decorated and gilded coach drawn by a team of six horses, with postillions and coachmen bright in orange livery. Its occupant, glimpsed through the open shutters, was Anne, Countess of Bedford, and the stately lord who rode alongside her, accompanied by his steward, was her husband William Russell, the fifth Earl. Behind them there rumbled a number of lesser coaches, carrying various members of their family, together with female servants, while more horsemen brought up the rear, keeping watch over a train of heavily laden wagons which stretched into the distance. Some of these were piled high with furnishings, bedding, and plate, and others with provisions and livestock; and they were the last of numerous similar loads which had been lumbering up to town for several days previously to help make ready Bedford House, the Earl and Countess's town residence, for their arrival there from their great country house at Woburn Abbey. Even as this cavalcade made its grandiose progress, the London housekeeper, Mrs Bruce, was putting the final touches to her own preparations to receive her master and mistress, having in the previous weeks paid sixpence 'for two pounds of soap to scour the great room', half-a-crown 'for six pounds of candles', six shillings for 'a woman six days for scouring and washing the rooms and cleaning the irons against the family's coming to town', and two shillings for 'a woman to help air the bedding when the family come to town'.[1]

In those days such a trip was a far cry from what it is today. The roads were little better than rough tracks, and were filled with deep ruts caused by the passing of endless heavy carts. In the summer they were covered with a smothering, suffocating dust; in the autumn and spring the ruts filled with water, leaving hard dry ridges which could, and often did, overturn a coach;

in the winter they were either transformed into a quagmire, or covered in ice. The servants who accompanied the family on these excursions carried bundles of ropes over their shoulders for the sole purpose of extricating those vehicles that got into difficulties. Their services would almost certainly have been required, for example, at a place called Hockley-in-the-Hole, only a few miles from Woburn, where the road, which was then referred to as being 'a sad road', full of sloughs and muddy holes, descended into a deep hollow, followed immediately by a steep ascent.

The coaches themselves did little to make the journey any more agreeable. There were no glass windows before the eighteenth century, curtains and wooden shutters being the only protection against wind and rain, so that in the winter passengers had the choice of being either stifled in the pitch darkness of the interior if the shutters were closed, or frozen if they were open. The springs were of a very primitive design, and the excessive jolting and swaying of the vehicle was not only unpleasant and tiring, but frequently induced among the passengers a nausea resembling sea-sickness. All this made even a journey as short as that from Woburn to London, a distance of only forty miles, a horrendous occasion which took two days to complete. It takes little to imagine how dreadful such trips must have been for families who lived further afield, such as the Duke and Duchess of Northumberland, who took well over a week to reach London from their home at Alnwick Castle on the north-east coast.

The destination of the Earl and Countess of Bedford on that spring day in 1675 was the Strand, that long street which runs along the north side of the Thames and which then linked the old walled City of London, England's economic capital, with the political capital of Westminster. For over a century it had been the fashionable place of residence in London for the nobility. As far back as the fourteenth century, politically ambitious bishops and priors from all over the country, eager to be close to the Court and the Abbey at Westminster, had bought estates along the banks of the Thames on which they had constructed noble mansions so grand that they were referred to as 'palaces' by numerous foreign visitors.[2] Here they had lived in the conspicuous luxury that had contributed to the eventual downfall of the pre-Reformation Church. With the fall of Wolsey and the suppression of the monasteries, these stately piles had been granted to some of the most powerful families in the land.

A voyage up the Thames from old London Bridge would have taken the seventeenth-century traveller past the riverside palaces of Essex House, Arundel House, Somerset House, Worcester House, Salisbury House, Durham House, York House and Northumberland House. Apart from the latter, which was the only one to survive as a private house beyond the eighteenth century, and which we shall be looking at later in some detail, very little is known about these 'Strand palaces'. The best impression of what they looked like can be got from Wenceslas Hollar's fascinating map, 'A Bird's-Eye View of West

London', published *c*.1648. This clearly shows how they were approached from the river, then London's main thoroughfare, and as important to its inhabitants as the Grand Canal is to Venice. A foreign visitor to London would leave the narrow and ill-kept roads at Gravesend or Greenwich and proceed to Westminster by water along what must have resembled a crowded highway according to a description by Cosmo III, Grand Duke of Tuscany, written in 1669:

The Thames, from York Watergate to Westminster Bridge.

> they began to sail down the Thames towards Greenwich: and all that space was crowded with ships of large size, and of every description: of these, it is said, that there are more than one thousand four hundred betwixt Gravesend and London Bridge, a distance of seventy miles, to which are added the other smaller ships and boats, almost without number, which were passing and repassing incessantly, and with which the river is covered . . .[3]

The Thames was wide and deep enough for the fleet to lie anchored close to the City, clean enough to swim in, and well stocked with an abundance of fish. 'What should I speak', wrote William Harrison, Canon of Windsor, in his description of England in 1577, 'of the fat and sweet salmons, daily taken in the streams, and that in such plenty as no river in Europe is able to excel it. What store also of barbels, trouts, perches, smelts, breams, roaches, daces, gudgeons, flounders, shrimps, eels etc. are commonly to be had therein.'[4].

Since there was as yet no embankment, access to the great houses was by a series of slippery river stairs, which are shown on the map as Essex Stairs,

Arundel Stairs, Somerset Stairs and so forth. These led up to imposing gateways or archways, the last surviving relic of which is the York Watergate, designed by Balthazar Gerbier in about 1625 and based on the Medici Fountain in the gardens of the Luxembourg Palace in Paris. It now stands in the gardens on Victoria Embankment and presents a rather melancholy sight, sunk in a hollow, far from the water upon which it once stood, and passed each day by thousands of people who are probably quite unaware of its grandiose origins.

Beyond these gates lay large and simple formal gardens, severely geometric in shape and often divided up by broad gravel paths. Within these divides, various features might be found – a bowling green, for example, can be seen on Hollar's map in front of Somerset House. Knot gardens were also popular, made from low, dense-growing plants such as thyme, hyssop, rosemary, germander, thrift and dwarf box, planted in interlacing, ribbon-like designs, with the intervening spaces filled either with flowers, to create a 'closed knot', or grass, sand, or brick paths to make an 'open knot'. Some gardens contained a wilderness, consisting of groups of trees and bushes cut into elaborate shapes by an arrangement of narrow alleys, or often a maze containing some central feature, such as a mount, an arbour, or a single rose-tree. At Somerset House the garden terminated 'in a grove of elms, divided in the usual manner into walks, for the convenience of promenading, and for affording a grateful shade to those who amuse themselves with looking at the boats which are continually passing and repassing on the water'.[5] Beyond these lay the palaces themselves which, with their halls and courts, were somewhat reminiscent of Oxford colleges.

As for Bedford House, it stood on the north side of the Strand, almost exactly opposite Worcester House, on part of a plot of land called Friars' Pyes, where Southampton Street, Tavistock Row, and the western section of Tavistock Street now stand. It had been built for the third Earl of Bedford in about 1586, and from the scant information we have it appears to have been a shallow timber-framed building of two storeys, with a gabled front some hundred feet long, from the western corner of which a long wing extended north. It had forty-five rooms, including a great chamber and a gallery, without which no large medieval house would have been complete, a 'turret room', located in an ogee-capped turret behind the western end of the main block, and at least one 'stoole room'. The family apartments were hung with tapestries, while the gallery, which overlooked the Strand, had green cloth and gilt leather on the walls. There were 'Turkey carpets' in many of the rooms and the furniture was upholstered in velvet or leather. The rest of the buildings, surrounding a courtyard, consisted of domestic offices, a laundry, and a large stable-yard, while to the north lay spacious gardens. At the front of the house, the courtyard gates opened directly onto the busy street, while at the back, beyond the garden wall, lay the beautiful Covent Garden Piazza, erected by the fourth

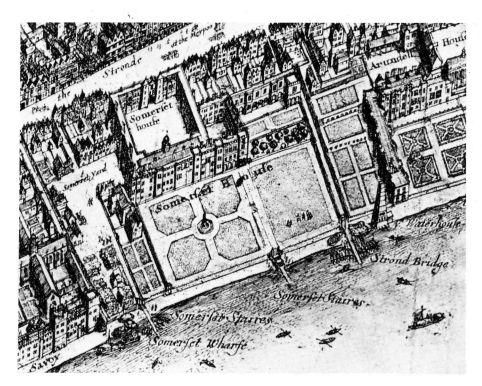

The gardens of
Somerset House.

Below:
Bedford House, in the
Strand.

Both illustrations are
from Hollar's map: see
page 12.

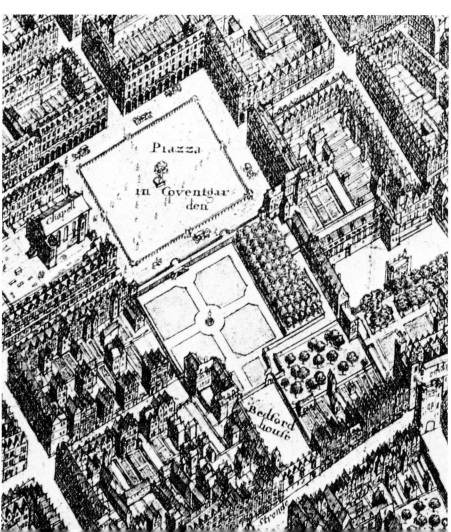

Earl in the 1630s. It was to this house that the family came on an annual migration which took place either in late February or early March, lasting till June or sometimes the late summer or early autumn, in which case they returned to Woburn in time for Christmas.

That they did so on a regular basis was indicative of the gradual emergence of a London season. Writing in the reign of Charles I, Margaret Lucas, Duchess of Newcastle, known to her contemporaries as 'Mad Midge of Newcastle', had recorded that her sisters and their husbands spent nearly every winter in London, engaging in pastimes which were to change little over the years:

As for the pastimes of my sisters, when they were in the country, it was to read, work, walk, and to discourse with each other. Commonly they lived half the year in London. Their customs were in Wintertime to go sometimes to plays or to ride in their coaches about the streets, to see the concourse and recourse of people, and in the Springtime to visit the Spring Garden, Hyde Park and the like places; and sometimes they would have music and sup in barges upon the water.[6]

By the 1660s and 1670s even people like the third Earl of Devonshire, who is known to have disliked London, were spending as much as seven months a year there.[7]

There were numerous reasons why the landed classes abandoned their estates for months on end to come to London. Many came purely for pleasure, to escape the loneliness and boredom of the country. For some time landowners had been waking up to the importance of land, not just as a symbol of power, but as a valuable means of income. As they subsequently let out bigger and bigger chunks of their estates, the resulting reduction in the day-to-day burden of management meant that many of them found time beginning to weigh heavily on their hands. 'I have not yet been a day in the country and I am as weary of it as if I had been a prisoner there seven year', wrote the Earl of Pembroke from Wilton, adding a month later, 'I have as little to do here as any man living.' From Yorkshire Lord Clifford complained loudly of having 'banished myself from all my friends and recreations this winter, being shut up among the mountains'.[8] In London, however, were to be found 'rich wives, spruce mistresses, pleasant houses, good diet, rare wines, neat servants, fashionable furniture, pleasures and profit the best of all sorts'.[9]

When they were not being entertained, either at Court, or in theatres, coffee-houses or gardens, or having their portraits painted by the fashionable artist of the moment, many of the aristocracy acted as agents of civilisation, taking the time to buy goods not generally available at home, and to note the new fashions in clothes and furnishings, and the latest methods of transport and building, so that they might return to their country residences full of new ideas about the ways in which life should be lived. William Douglas, Duke of Hamilton, for example, who made regular visits to London in the latter half of the seventeenth century, lost no opportunity to buy things there which would enhance his Scottish home at Hamilton Palace. So we find him on one occasion sending home 'a pair of silver candlesticks of the new fashion', 'a new fashioned screen', and 'four large double new fashioned beer and wine glasses'[10]; and on another 'six firkins of soap, six weather glasses, a tin box with tea in it, *The Scots Acts of Parliament*, two pamphlets, several pairs of shoes, a pound of chocolate, some harness, six maps of the Holy land, a quantity of sweetmeats, a looking-glass, an iron grate and Montaigne's *Essais* in three volumes'.[11] In London he placed his order for the very latest make of coach, bought cloth and spices from far-off lands, and hired superior kinds of servant – such as Daniel Gazeau, a French confectioner, who he was assured would 'learn you all to make dry sweetmeats, so the keeping of him it were but one year is worth something'. He also collected the most modern books and pamphlets giving advice on everything from medicine (*The Compend of Willis Physick*), and farming (*The Expert Farrier*) to manners (*The True Conduct of Persons of Quality*), and including 'a book of gardening' which, he told his wife, 'will teach us all to be good gardeners'.[12]

Others came on business, perhaps to settle some legal matter, such as the kind of land dispute which in earlier times might have ended in a pitched battle between neighbours, but could now be dealt with in the proliferation of courts which were making London the centre of justice. Year after year, for example, Lord Berkeley was seen 'with a milk white head in his irksome old age of seventy years, in winter terms and frosty seasons, with a buckerom bag stuffed with lawcases, in early mornings and late evenings, walking with his eldest son between the four Inns of Court and Westminster Hall, following his lawsuits in his old person'.[13]

At a time when the commercial prosperity of the country was rapidly growing, London was also the undisputed financial capital and the centre of speculative investment, the rewards of which were beginning to be seen by many of the nobility to be potentially enormous. Before the turn of the seventeenth century the Dukes of Leeds and Devonshire, the Earls of Pembroke and Bradford, Lord Edward Russell and the Marquis of Normanby were among the original proprietors of Bank of England stock.[14] When the Earl of Sunderland died in 1722 it was discovered that he had about £75,000 invested in stocks and shares. The Duke of Chandos was involved in speculations which varied from an oyster fishery and a soap factory to land in what would later form part of New York State.[15] Among the shrewdest were those who indulged in building schemes and real estate, men like Francis Russell, fourth Earl of Bedford, whose development of Covent Garden was the first planned layout of any importance in the expansion of London beyond the City; Thomas Wriothesley, fourth Earl of Southampton, who carried out a similar development on his Bloomsbury estate; and the first Earl of Clare, who by 1648 owned over two hundred tenements, bringing in a rental of more than £2,000 a year.[16]

There were other sources of riches in London as well. In an age when a judicious marriage was often the easiest way to a great fortune, there were those who came to arrange suitable unions for their offspring. The fifth Earl of Bedford cemented just such a match between his grandson, the future second Duke of Bedford, and Elizabeth Howland, the only daughter of a rich City draper. She was heiress not only to his estates of Streatham, Tooting Bec and Rotherhithe, but also to an even larger fortune from her maternal grandfather, Sir Joshua Child, a powerful London banker and East India merchant.

But of all the factors which contributed to making London so attractive to the landed classes, two were of outstanding importance and provided the real *raison d'être* for their maintaining great houses in London. The aristocracy inhabited a world in which the power of the individual was all-important, power which for centuries had been rooted in the ownership of vast tracts of land. They had never, however, underestimated the importance of keeping close ties with the Court and central government, both of which were by the end of the sixteenth century even more firmly established in London than they had been in previous centuries. Attendance at Court was not the mere social convention it was to become. It was essential for any great landlord who sought a wider field in which to employ his talents than the exercise of his authority over servants, tenants and local officials. It was the key to advancement and often to enduring wealth as well, for from it there flowed an endless stream of offices, favours and titles. 'All matters of importance have recourse to that place, all Princes and all persons of account ... make their repair thither,' Giovanni Botero had written in his celebrated essay *Treatise Concerning the Causes of the Magnificence and Greatness of Cities*. 'All such as aspire and thirst after offices and honours run thither overcome with emulation and disdain at others. Thither are the revenues brought that appertain unto the state, and there are they disbursed out again.'[17] Daniel Finch, second Earl of Nottingham, for example, who was Secretary of State for the South from 1689 to 1693, and again from 1702 to 1704, made a clear profit of over £50,000 on the office. By the 1750s even a relatively junior Court post such as Cofferer to the Household brought in '£2,200 a year, all taxes deducted', which was enough to enable George, first Lord Lyttelton, to 'build my new house without my being obliged to borrow'.[18] In 1726 a quarter of the active peerage held offices of administrative importance either in the government or about the Court, while most of the remaining positions were in the hands of their dependants or relations.

All the great houses about which anything is known were the property of ministers or courtiers or both. In the reign of Charles II, for instance, Southampton House in Bloomsbury was built by the fourth Earl of Southampton, then Lord High Treasurer; Clarendon House in Piccadilly, by the Lord High Chancellor, the first Earl of Clarendon; Arlington House in St James's, by the Secretary of State, Lord Arlington; and Montagu House in Bloomsbury, by

Lord Montagu, a prominent and ambitious courtier and Ambassador to Paris. .
Even when the London Season was at its most fashionable, and more and
more rich landowners were beginning to maintain large houses there, it was
invariably politics which was the main draw, and it is significant that many of
the greatest houses are still remembered for their political affiliations. Such
houses as Devonshire House in Piccadilly, Newcastle House in Lincoln's Inn
Fields, Lansdowne House in Berkeley Square and Bedford House in Bloomsbury were always thought of in this way, while their architectural character or
their contents were taken to be of secondary importance.

In spite of the ever-increasing flow of the nobility into London from the
seventeenth century onwards – which was large enough in the reigns of James
I and Charles I for both monarchs to attempt to limit it by royal proclamation
– great houses were still comparatively rare. One reason for this was the erratic
nature of parliamentary life which for many years was not regular enough to
justify maintaining a large London establishment as well as a similar one in
the country. In the first thirty-seven years of the seventeenth century, Parliament sat for a total of less than four and a half years. James I had four
parliaments, the first of which sat from 1604 to 1610, but did not meet between
July 1607 and February 1610, while Charles I had five, one in 1625, and
others in 1626 and 1628, but no more after that until 1640. Annual parliaments
did not start in earnest until the enormous cost of William III's wars against
Louis XIV forced the king to go to Parliament every year.

Building was also discouraged by the comparative rarity of freeholds, the
effect of which can be seen in the history of the first scheme for St James's
Square, which Henry Jermyn, Lord St Albans, wished to develop in 1663 as
a place of residence for courtiers. In his petition to the King, he requested
that a freehold should be granted: 'It is represented that unless Your Majesty
be pleased to grant the inheritance of the ground whereupon some thirteen or
fourteen houses that will compose the said Place are to stand, it will be very
hard to attain the end proposed, for that men will not build Palaces upon any
term but that of inheritance.'[19] Even though Charles II eventually granted his
request in 1665, the scheme for a square of palaces flopped, and the plots had
to be increased in number; this was largely due to a shortage of money, caused
by the long-term effects of the Civil War, and exaggerated by the disasters of
the Plague, the Great Fire, and the Dutch War. One hundred and seventy
years later Prince Pückler-Muskau also commented on the freehold problem,
writing home, 'You remember what I told you of the mode of letting land in
this country. As the builders of houses have only ninety-nine years to reckon,
they build as slightly as possible; the consequence of which is that one is not
very sure of one's life in some of the London houses.'[20]

When one examines the histories of those great houses which were built, it
seems very likely that it was lack of money, rather than inclination, which
prevented others from following suit. The building of Montagu House, for

example, was almost certainly connected with Ralph Montagu's marriage in 1673 to the Wriothesley heiress Elizabeth, Countess of Northumberland. Chesterfield House was probably partly paid for out of the fortune inherited by Lord Chesterfield's wife, and partly out of the handsome legacy he received from Sarah, Duchess of Marlborough. Again, her similar bequest to the Spencer family meant that they were suddenly much richer than they had been before, and could thus afford one of the most splendid houses in London. Thomas Anson, the builder of 15 St James's Square, was not able to build a fine London house until he inherited a fortune from his brother in 1762. The histories of Stafford House, Bridgewater House, Grosvenor House and Londonderry House are all bound up with phenomenal increases in estate income.

So it was that most of those aristocrats who came to London either lived in accommodation rented from some entrepreneur amongst them like the first Earl of Salisbury, who let out Little Salisbury House in the Strand to the Earl of Rutland, the Earl of Banbury, Lord Cottington, the Earl of Devonshire, Lord Howard of Escrick, Lord Paget, and the Countess of Carlisle in succession, or in modest houses bought on leasehold, first in such places as Lincoln's Inn Fields, Covent Garden, Queen Street, and Drury Lane, and later, as fashionable London moved further west, in the squares and streets which sprung up in St James's and Mayfair, in St Giles's, where the fields between St Martin's Lane and the lanes which were to become Regent Street were filled with streets and houses, and to the north of Holborn, where the first of the Bloomsbury developments began. 'Many a nobleman,' wrote James Ralph in 1734, 'whose proud seat in the country is adorned with all the riches of architecture, porticos and columns "cornice and frieze with bossy sculpture grav'n", is here content with a simple dwelling, convenient within and unornamented without.'[21] The exceptions were, however, magnificent, and it is the history of these that we shall be dealing with throughout this book.

1

The Rise of the Great Houses

'Upon Wednesday last', wrote John Evelyn to Lord Cornbury, in January 1665,

I went to London and spent the whole afternoon in viewing my Lord Chancellor's new House, if it be not a solecism to give a Palace so vulgar a name ... I went with prejudice and a critical spirit, incident to those who fancy they know anything in Art. I acknowledge to your Lordship that I have never seen a nobler pile ...It was without hyperbolies, the best contriv'd, the most useful, graceful and magnificent house in England.[1]

The house which Evelyn referred to, and which had inspired in him such praise, was Clarendon House, the newly built Piccadilly mansion of Edward Hyde, first Lord Clarendon, the Lord High Chancellor of England; and for its influence on English country houses such as Belton, near Grantham, and Combe Abbey, Warwickshire, it has long been recognised as one of the most important buildings in the history of English architecture. 'It was imitated', Sir John Summerson has written, 'large and small, well and ill, throughout Britain.'[2]

Before the appearance of Clarendon House, the history of London houses in the seventeenth century had been rather haphazard, largely owing to the political uncertainties of the time, and there is scarcely any link between it and the Strand palaces. One might have expected there to have been a phase associated with Inigo Jones, the darling of the Court aristocracy, whom they had taken up and encouraged in an effort to introduce classical architecture into England, and whose drawings, and the handful of buildings he did complete – the Whitehall Banqueting House, the Queen's House at Greenwich, and the Queen's Chapel in Marlborough Gate – showed such promise. Lindsey House, Lincoln's Inn Fields, built in 1641 for Sir David Cunningham, a truly classical house of stone and brick, with six Ionic pilasters supporting a central

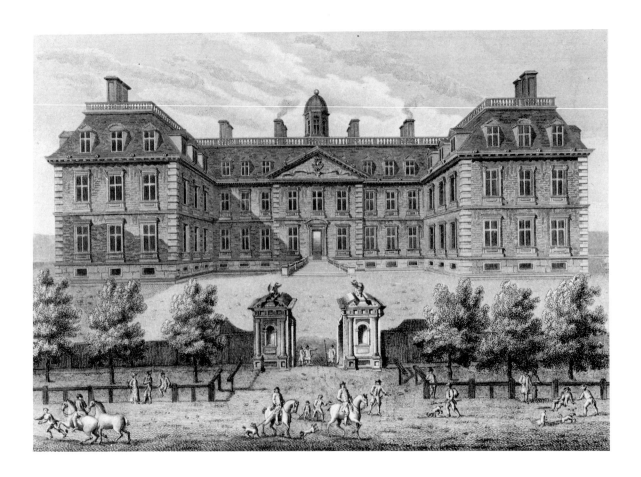

Clarendon House, Piccadilly.

Opposite, top: Lindsey House, Lincoln's Inn Fields.

Opposite, bottom: Goring House (later Arlington House), 1700.

pediment, certainly owes a great deal to his influence. On the other hand, as far as two of the grandest houses known to have been built in the 1630s are concerned, he might hardly have existed.

Despite its being built for a leading cavalier and courtier who is known to have spent as much as £12,000 on its embellishments, Goring House, erected by Lord Goring in 1633 on the site where Buckingham Palace now stands, appears to have been an old-fashioned gabled Jacobean building of the kind favoured by the Puritan gentry. It eventually passed into the hands of Lord Arlington who, according to Evelyn, filled it with 'the best and most princely furniture that any subject had in England',[3] and who was also to rebuild it. Leicester House, which stood on the site of the Empire cinema in Leicester Square, was built by Robert Sidney, second Earl of Leicester, another powerful man in the Court, and was a plain and austere edifice, with a hipped roof and broad brick surrounds to the windows.

Only one project for a really grand London house can be connected to Inigo Jones: Durham House, by his former pupil, John Webb, for the fourth Earl of Pembroke. The drawing of the entrance front shows a façade which, if

Leicester House.

realised, would have been 340 feet long, over three times the length of the Banqueting House at Whitehall. The courtyard around which the house was planned was to be bisected by a great cross gallery with screens of columns at either end, leading from a portico to the central room of the state apartment on the Thames front. To the left and right of this room were to be rooms of state with two complete private apartments at either end. No family would ever have been housed so grandly in London before, but the Civil War prevented the scheme ever coming to fruition. Court architecture was killed stone dead, and it was to be almost a century before Jones's legacy was to be realised.

The first of three great houses which rose to the north of Piccadilly as monuments to the new age, Clarendon House stood where Albemarle Street now runs, in a field called Pennyless Bank, facing south towards St James's Palace. As one of the architects of the Restoration, Clarendon had benefited enormously from it. This had included receiving, early in 1664, a grant by the king of £20,000, together with thirty acres of land north of Piccadilly. On this site, and that of additional land rented on a ninety-nine-year lease from the City of London, he made plans for the building of a palatial mansion where New Bond Street, Conduit Street, and Brook Street were to arise.

He chose as his architect Sir Roger Pratt, who had just completed Coleshill in Warwickshire for his cousin Sir George Pratt. He set to work without delay: '*May 2, 1664.* Paid to St Paul's of ye first stone – 60 tons.'[4] This entry in Sir Roger's notebook confirms that much of the stone for Clarendon House came from the medieval cathedral of St Paul's, which Inigo Jones had been commissioned to restore, since it was crumbling away and had already lost its

steeple. A considerable amount of stone had been bought for this work, which was halted by the outbreak of the Civil War. The stone was never used, and was subsequently acquired by Clarendon for his own building. This took just over a year to complete – which, considering the laborious building methods of the day, is a tribute to Pratt. The cost, however, went wildly over the estimate.

'Your Lordship was pleased to allow', wrote Pratt to Clarendon in February 1665, 'eighteen thousand pounds for ye finishing of your building, for which I told your Lordship I conceived it might be done ... This calculation was made by me upon this supposition, that nothing should fall out extraordinry in ye foundations of ye building, nor anything afterwards either be altered or repaired.'[5] Needless to say, things did not quite work out this way, and a list of unexpected expenses followed: three huge new lead pipes to replace the old ones, extra deep foundations for the chapel owing to marshy ground, 'the walls so wholly shattered by ye wet, and Frost of ye last winter, that both ends of ye house were forced to be taken up again, and much of ye stonework of ye fronts likewise, and ye other walls partly repaired everywhere'. Furthermore he complained that the price of timber had increased owing to the Dutch War, while the cost of bricks had been nearly doubled by the deaths from the plague of two master brickmakers and many of their servants. By the time the master carpenter had framed and raised the first floor, he 'professed himself to be utterly undone by so great an undertaking: refused to go forward and humbly submitted himself to your lordship's mercy, to deal with as you pleased'. No one suitable could be found to replace him, however, and so 'by fair words

John Webb's proposed plan for a house for the fourth Earl of Pembroke.

Belton House,
Lincolnshire.

and promises' and increased payments he was encouraged to continue, but his
accounts came to at least a third more than the agreed price. Finally, Pratt had
to cope with the whims of Lord Clarendon's son, Lord Cornbury, who 'desires
to have one foot added to ye height of ye rooms of ye first floor'.

All the trouble was worth while, however, for when it was finally completed,
the labour of 300 men and the expenditure of over £50,000 had indeed produced 'the first Palace of England',[6] and a worthy successor to the palaces of
the Strand. Glittering with tall windows, it was considerably larger than its
prototype, Coleshill, or Belton, which was modelled on it, and dwarfed Berkeley House and Burlington House, the neighbours which rose on either side
of it. Built on an H-plan, it was three storeys high, with a raised *piano nobile*
over the basement and a large courtyard in front of it. If we work on the
supposition that the layout of the inside was similar to what he had done at
Coleshill, and would do on his next project at Horseheath, Cambridgeshire,
there was probably a large entrance hall three bays wide in the centre, with a
saloon of the same width behind it, facing the garden – a plan derived from
Palladio, which was to become the core of both the Vanbrughian and the
neo-Palladian mansion.

Evelyn's admiration, however, was not universally shared, for Clarendon
was a violently unpopular man, and the hatred that was felt for him by so
many was vented against the house. Some said, quite unjustly, for he is known
to have opposed it, that he had engineered the King's marriage to a barren
wife, Catherine of Braganza, so that his own daughter and his son-in-law could

succeed to the throne. He was generally despised for having used the stones of old St Paul's to build his house, and for such enormous expenditure during a time of plague and an unsuccessful war. But the major cause of his unpopularity lay in his sale of Dunkirk to the French in 1662, both to raise money to help Portugal in her struggle against Spain, and to develop the port of Tangier, which was part of Queen Catherine's dowry. This sale was bitterly resented by many Englishmen, who also concluded that Clarendon had pocketed part of the money raised to finance his extravagant building. Henceforth the house was nicknamed Dunkirk House, or Tangier Hall. Andrew Marvell, amongst others, dipped his pen into the poison:

Lo! his whole ambition already divides
The Sceptre between the Stuarts and the Hydes,
Behold, in the depth of our Plague and our Wars,
He built him a palace that outbraves the Stars;
Which house (we Dunkirk and he Clarendon names),
It looks down with shame upon St James;
But 'tis not his golden globe will save him,
Being less than the Custom-house farmers gave him;
His chapel for Consecration calls,
Whose sacrilege plundered the stones from St Paul's.[7]

Clarendon had little time to enjoy his new home. In June 1667 public feeling against him erupted into violence when the Dutch fleet attacked the British navy in the Medway. A mob descended upon him, 'cut down the trees before his house and broke his windows, and a gibbet either set up before or painted upon his gates, and these three words writ: Three sights to be seen, Dunkirk, Tangier, and a barren Queen.'[8] In August the Great Seal was removed from him, and in November he was forced to flee the country after an impeachment for treason had been drawn up against him by his enemies, supported by the king. Evelyn visited him the day before he left, and painted a melancholy picture of the scene which met him: 'I found him in his garden at his new-built palace, sitting in his gout wheelchair, and seeing the gates setting up towards the north and the fields. He looked and spake very disconsolately. After some while deploring his condition to me, I took my leave. Next morning I heard he was gone.'[9] He is said to have told his second son, Lord Rochester, to tell all his friends 'that if they could excuse the vanity and folly of the great house, he would undertake to answer for all the rest of his actions himself'.[10]

Clarendon went into exile, where he died in 1674. His beloved 'great house' did not survive him for long. It passed first to his eldest son, Lord Cornbury, who, Evelyn tells us, filled it 'with the pictures of most of our ancient and modern wits, poets, philosophers, famous and learned Englishmen'.[11] During his tenancy, he was visited by Grand Duke Cosmo III who, travelling through England in 1669, has left us with a description of the garden.

From the inner part you descend into the garden, surrounded, in its whole extent, by walls which support flourishing espaliers, formed of various fruit trees; these render the view very agreeable, although the garden has no other ornament than compartments of earth filled with low and beautiful parterres and spacious walks; over which, in order to keep them smooth and level, they roll certain heavy cylindrical stones, to keep the grass down.[12]

Plagued by debts, Cornbury sold it on almost immediately to the second Duke of Albemarle for the paltry sum of £26,000. The Duke was little improvement on his predecessor, being a hard-drinking, high-living wastrel who was to die in Jamaica 'burnt to a coal with hot liquor'.[13] Having quickly run through his patrimony, he in turn sold it for £35,000 to John Hinde, a rich goldsmith and banker, who headed a syndicate who promptly demolished it for development.

As he had witnessed the rise of Clarendon House, Evelyn was also present at its fall. On one of the last occasions on which he was to set eyes upon the house, he was accompanied by Clarendon's son, then the second Earl. By that time it was a tragic sight, and tactful behaviour was called for to avoid distressing his companion. 'I returned to town in a coach with the Earl of Clarendon', he wrote in his *Diary*, 'when passing by the glorious palace of his father ... which they are now demolishing ... I turned my head the contrary way till the coach had gone past it, lest I might minister occasion of speaking of it; which must needs have grieved him, that in so short a time their pomp was fallen.'[14] Later he returned alone to take a final and closer look:

I walked to survey the sad demolition of Clarendon House, that costly and only sumptuous Palace of the late Lord Chancellor Hyde, where I have often been so cheerful with him, and so sad ... I was plainly astonished as at this demolition, so no less at the little army of Labourers and Artificers in levelling ground, laying foundations, and continuing great buildings at an expense of two hundred thousand pounds, if they perfect their design.[15]

The speculators who bought Clarendon House made more from the sale of materials after the demolition than they had paid for the whole property. On its site, and on neighbouring land, they then began the building of a whole network of streets which were to include Bond Street, Dover Street, Stafford Street and Albemarle Street.

Houses rose on either side of Clarendon House on land which had been surplus to Clarendon's requirements, and which he had sold. The most elaborate of the two was Berkeley House, which stood to the west, virtually where Berkeley Street and Stratton Street stand today, on the site of Hay Hill Farm, a name now immortalised in the nearby streets of Hay Hill, Hill Street, and Farm Street. John Berkeley, first Lord Berkeley of Stratton, had been one of the most eminent Royalist officers during the Civil War. Sometime before 1662 he married Christian Riccard, daughter of Sir Andrew Riccard, a rich merchant and governor of the East India Company. She was a considerable heiress whose

fortune, together with the salaries from various government offices which he held after the Restoration, enabled him to build himself a stately pile. Berkeley House was begun in 1664 to the designs of Hugh May, who was also employed by Clarendon at Cornbury House, Oxfordshire, and had just completed an important commission for Sir John Shaw at Eltham Lodge in Kent, the formula of which he repeated for the main block of the new house, with its pilastered and pedimented centrepiece. In linking it to flanking wings by building curved colonnades in the Palladian manner, he also came up with a design which was something of a novelty, not only in London, but throughout England, having been used only once before, by Inigo Jones, at Stoke Park in Northamptonshire.

This may have been the reason why Evelyn was so critical when he first saw it in 1672. 'I dined at Lord John Berkeley's', he wrote on 25 September,

newly arrived out of Ireland, where he had been Deputy: it was in his new house, or rather palace, for I am assured it stood him in neere thirty thousand pounds. It is very well built, and has many noble rooms, but they are not very convenient, consisting but of one Corps de Logis: they are all rooms of state without closets. The staircase is of cedar; the furniture is princely; the kitchens and stables are ill placed, and the corridors worse, having no report to the wings they join to. For the rest the forecourt is noble: so are the stables; and, above all, the gardens, which are incomparable by reason of the inequality of the ground, and a pretty piscina. The porticos are in imitation of a house described by Palladio, but it happens to be the worst in his book.[16]

He seems to have changed his mind, however, by 1684. The Clarendon House site was in the process of being developed, and the widow of Lord

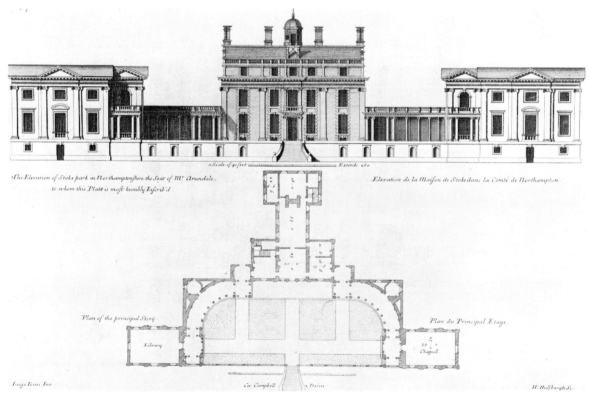

The Elevation of Stoke park in Northamptonshire. the Seat of Mr. Arundale. to whom this Platt is most humbly Inscrib'd

Elevation de la Maison de Stoke dans la Comté de Northampton.

a Scale of 40 feet   Extends 260

Plan of the principal Story

Library

Plan du Principal Etage.

Chappell

Inigo Jones Inv.   Co. Campbell Delin.   H. Hulfbergh Sc.

Top: Berkeley House,   Bottom: Stoke Park, Northamptonshire.
Piccadilly.   Design by Inigo Jones.

Left: John, first Lord
Berkeley of Stratton.

Right: Richard Boyle,
first Earl of
Burlington.

Berkeley, tempted by the high going rate for land in the area – up to £1,000 a year in ground rents – had decided to sell off some of her own gardens, which took in the whole of what we now know as Berkeley Square and the adjacent streets, and had called in Evelyn for advice. 'I went to advise and give direction about the building two streets in Berkeley Gardens', he wrote, 'reserving the house and as much of the garden as the breadth of the house. In the meantime I could not but deplore that sweet place (by far the most noble gardens, courts and accommodations, stately porticoes etc, anywhere about town) should be so much straightened and turned into tenements.'[17] Unfortunately Berkeley House was destroyed by fire in 1773 and no plan has survived. The only known view of Berkeley House, a nineteenth-century watercolour, suggests that it was a structure of great style and elegance.

Burlington House, which flanked Clarendon House on the east, completed the trio. It was begun in 1665 by Sir John Denham, the poet and an amateur architect, who had managed to get himself appointed Surveyor of the King's Works in 1660. This was much to the chagrin of John Webb, who complained that though Sir John 'may, as most gentry, have some knowledge of the theory of architecture, he can have none of the practice, but must employ another'.[18] Evelyn echoed these sentiments, calling him 'a better poet than an architect'.[19] What part he played in the design of the house is not exactly known, but his position allowed him to call upon his lieutenants in the King's Works, and in the light of what we know about him, it is quite likely that the work was theirs. For various reasons, both financial and personal, which included suffering from bouts of madness during which he believed he was the Holy Ghost, Sir John never completed the house, and in January 1667 he sold the unfinished carcass and the three-and-a-half-acre site on which it stood to Richard Boyle, first Earl of Burlington, for £3,300.

Burlington House, Piccadilly. From an engraving by Kip after Knyff.

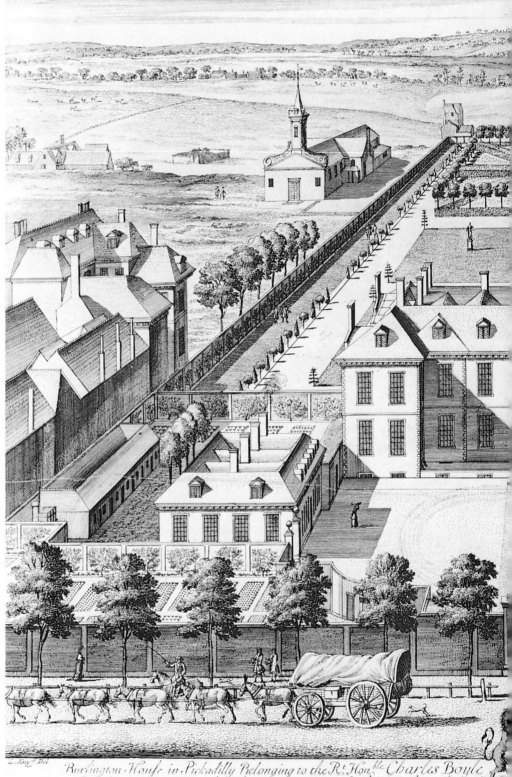

L. Knyff Del

Burlington House in Pickadilly Belonging to the Rt. Honble. Charles Boyle
& Bandon, Viscount Kynalmeaky, & Dungarvan, Earle of Corke in the Kingm.
County of the Citty of Corke, Lord high Treasurer of Ireland, Lord high Steward of

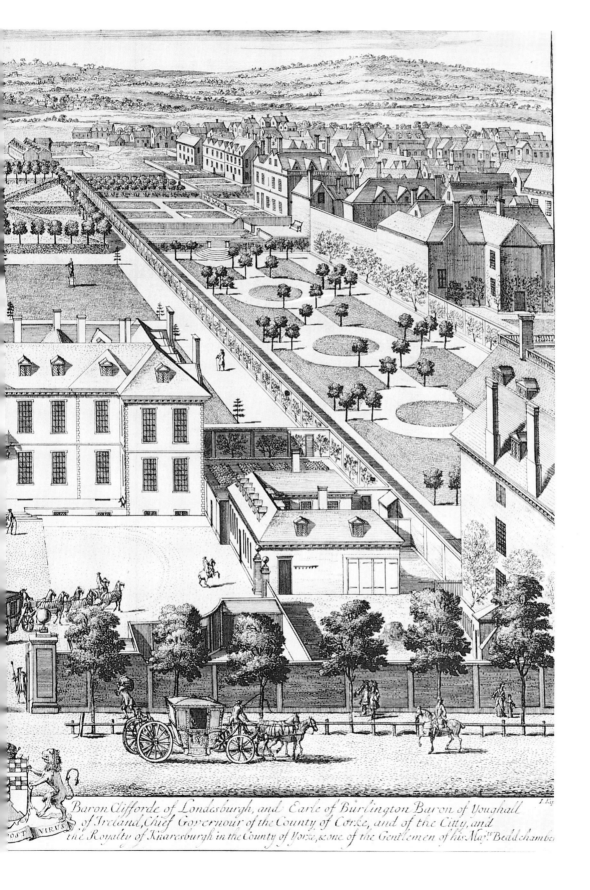

Baron Clifforde of Londesburgh, and Earle of Burlington Baron of Youghall
of Ireland, Chief Governour of the County of Corke, and of the Citty, and
the Royalty of Knaresburgh in the County of Yorke, & one of the Gentlemen of his Maj.ties Bedchamber

POST VIRUS

At this stage, although the exterior features of Burlington House were as good as finished, work had probably hardly begun on the outbuildings and the interior, and there was as yet no street wall. Burlington called in Hugh May to complete the task which, owing to the state of public affairs, took rather longer than expected. The City was in the throes of rebuilding after the disastrous fire of the previous year, and the Dutch War had also created a heavy demand for builders' materials. Letters to Lord Burlington from his wife and family, and from his agent, Richard Graham, on the progress of the house during this period, speak of the workmen being 'all much employed about ye King's work', while one from his son, Lord Clifford, reports that he and Mr Graham 'do all we can to quicken ye workmen, who in these unsettled times are generally very backward to work'. Planks for floorboards were scarce and prices high, though Burlington's sister, Viscountess Ranelagh, urged him not to wait in the hopes that peace would bring the price down, since the saving would be 'too trifling a thing to you to let it stop your proceeding'.[20] Burlington finally took up residence in April 1668. In his diary for that month he noted that the total cost of the house had been some £5,000, adding soberly, 'I beseech God, I may in it sense him constantly and that he will bless us in it, and confirm it to my family.'[21]

Kip's engraving of the view by Knyff shows Burlington House as it was at that time. It does not appear to have been a building of particular originality or distinction, but a typical Restoration house of good red brick, simply dressed with stone and wood, with a hipped roof, two rooms thick and with projecting wings to the front, similar to many others to be found in the country, such as Field Place in Sussex or Groombridge Place in Kent. Before it lay a courtyard, flanked by pavilions containing the stables and kitchens, and separated from Piccadilly by a high wall. Walled kitchen gardens can be seen on either side of these pavilions, while at the back large formal gardens stretched back to what is now Burlington Gardens and Vigo Street. As for the interior, no details have survived from this period, and one can only guess that it may have had some similarity to that of Clarendon House, since at one point May asked Lord Burlington to tell him 'if you remember any rooms in Clarendon House, which you would have imitated'.[22]

So far as great private houses are concerned, there is in fact only one noble interior that has survived from the reign of Charles II and that is at Ashburnham House, which is to be found on the north side of Little Dean's Yard in the shadow of Westminster Abbey. The main front has been so altered that it is now hard to guess that the house in fact dates from the early 1660s, though there is some good original brick detail on the north side. All that is known about its origins is that the site was leased to a William Ashburnham in 1662, but apart from the record of this there is nothing to show who his architect was, though in recent years the name of William Samwell, a gentleman architect of the same sort as Hugh May and Sir Roger Pratt, has been suggested on

Groombridge Place, Kent. The entrance front.

account of the similarity of the staircase at Ashburnham House to one he built for Sir Robert Henley at The Grange, Hampshire. It is a rather curious house since its architect was required to incorporate parts of a fifteenth-century Prior's house in the front part of his building, so that much to one's surprise one steps first into a late medieval hall. The most famous feature of the interior, the main staircase, lies behind double doors to the west of the back hall and is equally unexpected, for the doors lead straight onto the first short flight of the stairs. Since this is tucked away in a leg off the main area of the staircase, it is only when the first landing is reached that it is possible to take in the full splendour of the design. Three steps on the right lead to the second landing where the stairs turn, rising in two more flights to the first floor. Here Ionic columns create the effect of a porch, while over the centre of the stairs a small upper gallery is revealed beneath a circle of columns supporting a dome. Beyond the porch lie a handsomely panelled ante-room with fine architraves to its doors, and a 'great room' of four bays with a rich ceiling, but apart from these little survives. Even though what remains is a mere fragment, however, it still gives a sense of spatial excitement that is rare in early Restoration domestic architecture.

The staircase hall,
Ashburnham House.

Opposite: The upper
gallery, Ashburnham
House.

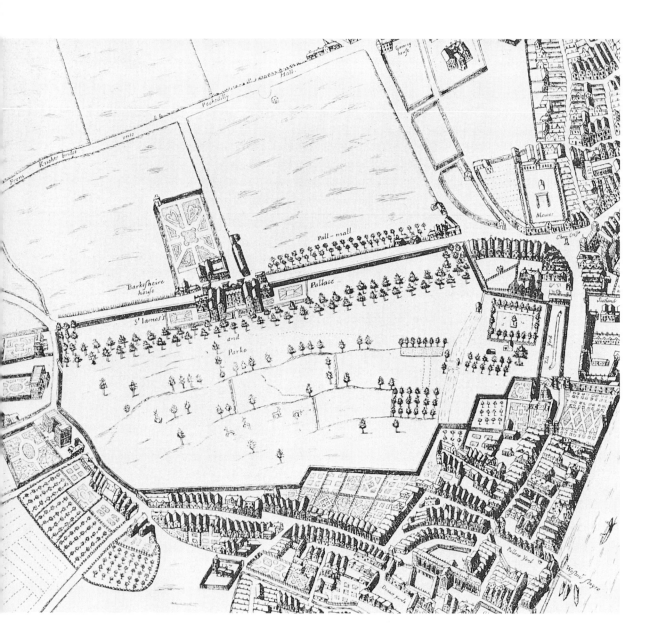

An extract from
Faithorne and
Newcourt's map of
1643-7 (published in
1658).

When Clarendon House, Berkeley House, and Burlington House were completed they were more like country houses conveniently situated for visits to
Court than town houses, for they stood on an open country road (now Piccadilly) that ran – according to Faithorne and Newcourt's 1658 map of London
– 'from Knightsbridge unto Piccadilly Hall', and was renamed Portugal Street
in 1664 in honour of the King's marriage to Catherine of Braganza. To the
west, nothing lay between them and Hyde Park, other than a cluster of mean
dwellings and a celebrated tavern, The Pillars of Hercules. To the north they

looked out over open country to the Highgate hills. Such an isolated position did not last for long, however, as their appearance at once established the area as the fashionable place of residence for the aristocracy, who were looking westwards after the disasters of the Plague and the Fire, which had finally broken all links between the Court and the City, and the abandonment by the King of a grandiose plan to enlarge and complete the Palace of Whitehall to designs by Inigo Jones. While Whitehall tended to become full of government offices, areas like the Strand were gradually abandoned to speculators like Dr Nicholas Barbon, as Daniel Defoe remarked when he visited London early in the eighteenth century:

All those Palaces of the Nobility, formerly making a most Beautiful Range of Buildings fronting the Strand, with their Gardens reaching to the Thames ... have had the same Fate ... in the Place of which are now so many noble Streets and Beautiful Houses, erected, as are, in themselves, equal to a large City and extend from the Thames to Northumberland House.[23]

Henry Jermyn (1604–84), Earl of St Albans. After Lely.

In the meantime the courtiers who had inhabited these areas started moving into St James's and Piccadilly, and streets and squares arose like magic.

One man, in particular, can perhaps claim the title of the 'Founder of the West End', and that was Henry Jermyn, Earl of St Albans, a leading courtier whom the French traveller Sorbière described as 'a man of pleasure, who makes little or no pretensions to the Prime Ministry, and entertains no other thoughts than to live at ease'.[24] On his return from Paris, soon after the Restoration, he was granted by the King a building lease of forty-five acres of St James's Fields, an area unoccupied by houses and bounded by Piccadilly on the north, by the Haymarket on the east, by Pall Mall on the south, and by where St James's Street now runs on the west, all of which were still little more than country lanes. The largest of these meadows was the Pall Mall Field, or Close, on which courtiers used to gather to play the French game of 'Palle Maille', and it was here that Jermyn planned to build a square of houses for noblemen, petitioning the King in August 1663:

Whereas the beauty of his great town and the convenience of the Court are defective in point of houses fit for the dwellings of noblemen and other persons of quality ... your Majesty hath thought fit for some remedy hereof to appoint that the place of St James's Field should be built in great and good houses.[25]

Such a scheme was well timed, for after years of civil war and general unrest the signs were that the Restoration had opened the door to a new, confident age – above all, an age of gaiety, in stark contrast to the sobriety of the Puritan era. This was reflected in many areas of life, but nowhere more so than in the lavish and flamboyant fashions adopted by the rich. It was, wrote Anthony à Wood in 1663, 'A strange effeminate age when men strive to imitate women in their apparel, *viz* long periwigs, patches in their faces, painting, short wide

The Riverside Gardens behind Somerset House, from a painting by a follower of Canaletto.

breeches like petticoats, muffs, and their clothes highly scented, bedecked with ribbons of all colours.'[26] Prosperity was on the increase, the arts and sciences were blossoming, and Charles II ruled over a glittering and extravagant court filled with gay and bawdy young blades, among whom Lord Rochester, Sir Charles Sedley, Lord Buckhurst and Harry Killigrew were the most celebrated, nicknamed as they were 'the Merry Gang' by Andrew Marvell. It is hard to imagine how the King dared to complain to Parliament, as he did in 1662, that 'the whole nation seemed to him a little corrupted in their excess of living. All men spend much more in their clothes, in their diet, in all their expenses than they need to do.'[27]

The nobility who flocked to the Court, and to sit in the newly recalled Parliament, brought with them their wives and families, who soon found that the town provided them with plenty of amusements. There was the Tower to visit, with the Crown Jewels and a collection of lions named after the kings of England, or the tombs and effigies at Westminster Abbey. There was the river to sail upon in highly decorated barges, or to walk beside in the Riverside Gardens behind Somerset House. For a person of quality no day would have been complete without a visit to Hyde Park or St James's Park, in either of which they might expect to meet the King and Queen. Writing in 1669, Grand

Duke Cosmo III described going one afternoon 'to one of the principal dancing schools of the metropolis, frequented both by unmarried and married ladies, who are instructed by the master, and practise, with much gracefulness and agility, various dances after the English fashion. Dancing is a very common and favourite amusement of the ladies in this country ...'[28] In the evenings there were visits to the theatre, invariably a comedy, at either the King's Theatre, Drury Lane, or the Duke of York's in Lincoln's Inn Fields, followed by supper and the inevitable cards at a private house. In his play *A Journey to London*, Vanbrugh satirised the corruption of a country lady newly introduced to the frivolous habits and agreeable vices of the West End: 'In short before her husband has got five pounds by a speech at Westminster she will have lost five hundred at cards and dice in the parish of St James's.'[29]

The demand for high-class accommodation which accompanied the ever-increasing flow of nobility into London was exactly what St Albans had anticipated. Though his original scheme had been to build a square of thirteen or fourteen 'palaces', he was hampered by a shortage of money, and was in the end forced to increase their number to twenty-two. These were mostly developed during the 1670s, and were built with frontages of varying widths. The house he built for himself in 1677, for example, at Nos. 9, 10, and 11, had a frontage of some one hundred and twenty feet, while No. 14, with only twenty-seven feet, was hardly wider than a normal terrace house: the average width was around fifty feet.

A good description of a house in the square is given by Lady Wentworth, who in November 1708 was looking for a home for her son, and set her heart on No. 31, also a former residence of the Earl of St Albans and the first house to have been erected in the square. 'My dearest and best of children,' she wrote on 23 November,

A typical house in St James's Square, by G. Shepherd.

I have been to see a very good house in St James's Square. It has three large rooms forward and two little ones backward, closets and marble chimney-pieces, and hearths to all the best rooms, and iron backs to the chimneys. There is two pretty closets with chimneys and glass over them, and pictures in the wainscoat over most of the chimneys, brass locks to all the doors, wainscoat at bottom and top and slips of boards for all the hangings. There will want little to be done to it. There is back stairs, two coach houses, and stable for 11 horses, rooms over for servants, very good offices, a yard for the drying of clothes, and leads for that purpose, a stable yard and a horse pond and back gate ... There is a handsome room all wainscoated for the steward to dine in, and another good room for the other servants to dine in even with the kitchen below stairs under the hall and parlours ...

A few days later, on the 26th, she was writing again:

... the man that showed me the house was a fool, he did not show me all the stables or coach houses ... Indeed it is a noble house, you may build a gallery over the offices ... He assures me none of the chimneys smoke and there is New River water in all

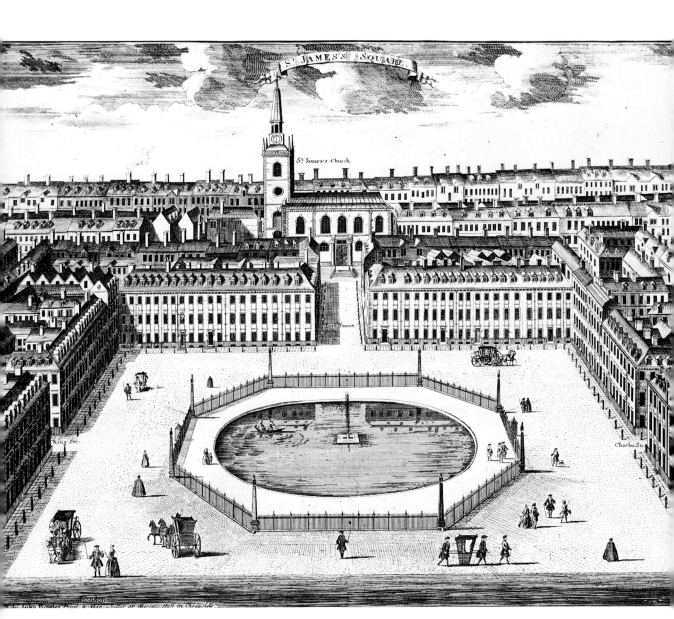

St James's Square,
c. 1722, by Sutton
Nicholls.

the offices and great lead cisterns in two or three places, the kitchen is one, and the brewhouse and wash house. There is a large chimney and grate and oven and five stoves in the kitchen ... it is a noble house and fit for you, and strong, no danger of its falling by great winds.[30]

In the end, Lady Wentworth's son, the first Earl of Strafford, moved into No. 5.

Ormonde House, the former home of the Earl of St Albans at Nos. 9, 10, and 11, was the largest house in the square, with some fifty rooms, including bedrooms on each of its four storeys. An inventory of 1685 shows it to have been a grand, though simply furnished, establishment. On the ground floor was a porter's lodge, and a hall containing fifty leather buckets bearing the Ormonde crest, coronet, and monogram. Most rooms appear to have contained only a single table and chairs of walnut, olive wood, prince wood or deal, some japanned furniture, or, as in the Duke's drawing-room, an ebony table inlaid with gilt work. They were usually hung with tapestry, though numerous paintings are mentioned, either hanging or in panels over doors and chimney-pieces, while some of the ceilings, such as those over the great staircase and in the Duchess's closet, were painted. The grandest furnishings appear to have been the curtains, upholstery, and bed furnishings. Many of these were of crimson and gold, while on the first floor there were more varied colours, with crimson, green and white brocade in the dining-room, white, green, and gold velvet in the Duke's drawing-room, and blue or crimson damask in the bedrooms.[31]

Here, according to an undated manuscript in the British Museum, either the first Duke of Ormonde or his son maintained an enormous establishment, consisting of forty-five household servants, a gentleman of the horse, two coachmen, a huntsman, eight stablemen, and seventeen watermen. The stables contained twenty horses, five coaches, and fourteen dogs.[32]

For the next fifty years or more, before the great extension of fashionable London westwards and northwards, St James's Square was the centre of political and social eminence. When the first Duke of Ormonde bought his house in the square in 1682, his son wrote to congratulate him, remarking 'how ill it would look now you are an English Duke to have no house there'.[33] His neighbours included the first Earl of Conway, a Principal Secretary of State; Sir John Ernley, the Chancellor of the Exchequer; the fourth Earl of Devonshire, Lord Steward of the Household; Lord Ossulston, Lieutenant of the Bodyguard; Lord Dartmouth, Master General of the Ordnance; the Earl of Ranelagh, Vice-Treasurer of Ireland; the third Earl of Suffolk, Earl Marshal of England; the first Marquis of Halifax, the Lord Privy Seal; and the first Earl of Essex, First Lord of the Treasury. By 1721 no fewer than six dukes lived there – those of Chandos, Dorset, Kent, Norfolk, Portland and Southampton – as well as seven earls, a countess, a baron, and a baronet. Only one other neighbourhood rivalled the new St James's Square in grandeur, and that was the work of another great aristocratic entrepreneur.

Thomas Wriothesley,
fourth Earl of
Southampton.
After Lely.

2

Rival Dukes

On Sunday, 2 October 1664, Pepys, on his way from church to pay a visit to Lady Sandwich, took a stroll 'through my Lord Southampton's new buildings in the fields behind Gray's Inn ... 'Indeed', he wrote, 'they are a great and noble work.' The following February, Evelyn 'dined at my Lord Treasurer's, the Earl of Southampton, in Bloomsbury where he was building a noble Square or Piazza, a little towne'. This ambitious development, begun in 1661 by the Lord High Treasurer of England, Thomas Wriothesley, fourth Earl of Southampton, on his Bloomsbury estate, had proved a great success, for not only had the presence of his own stately residence, Southampton House, acted as an attraction to many of the Earl's friends, but the area's comparative proximity to the City had drawn in a considerable number of the merchant class.

Southampton House itself, built *c*.1657, is thought to have been designed by John Webb. It was a long, low building of brick with a central block three storeys high, and two wings of two storeys, and stood on a site called the Long Field. In that it completely occupied the northern side of Bloomsbury Square, which arose around it, it set a new fashion in elegant layout, which was to be much copied. Sir Roger Pratt noted that the house was only forty feet high[1] which Evelyn, who visited it on 9 February 1665, considered far too low, though he was impressed by 'some noble rooms', 'a pretty Cedar Chapel', and 'the good air'. The principal rooms on the first floor, consisting of two 'great' drawing-rooms and a 'great' dining-room, looked out over a courtyard surrounded by a brick wall, 'a wall of singular beauty and elegance',[2] with a pair of wrought-iron gates in the centre. Most of the family apartments – bedrooms, dressing-rooms and the like – were on the first floor, though they spilled over into the attics, which were shared with the chief servants. The ground floor and the two wings were almost entirely given over to the domestic offices in which the work of running the household was done. The house dominated the square, while the grounds behind, which Evelyn then described as a 'naked garden', extended northwards so as to take in the southern part of Russell

Southampton House
and Bloomsbury
Square. Engraved by
Sutton Nicholls, 1754.

R BLOOMSBURY SQUARE

Highgate

Islington

Southampton Row

Russell Street

Square, and were famed for the views they commanded over open country towards Hampstead and Highgate. In that it was a perfect combination of town and country house, Southampton House encapsulated the aristocratic ideal.

Among the new streets which arose as part of Southampton's development was Great Russell Street, of which Strype was to write in glowing terms, calling it

a very handsome, large and well-built Street, graced with the best Buildings in all Bloomsbury, and the best inhabited by the Nobility and Gentry, especially the North Side, as having Gardens behind the Houses; and the Prospect of the pleasant Fields up to Hampstead and Highgate. Insomuch that this Place by Physicians is esteemed the most healthful of any in London.[3]

This was a major selling point, especially to those rich merchants who had previously lived within the walls of the City, exposed to the dangers of plague and pollution. 'It is an ill time for a fresh man to come to London', wrote Lady Grace Wynn in June 1660 to her son Richard, recently moved into Fleet Street; 'it is so crowded and has such close air.'[4] Over 500,000 people lived in densely-packed, timber-framed houses built about a web of cobbled streets so narrow that they might, to quote Sir William Davenant, have been 'contrived in the days of wheelbarrows'.[5] They were constantly jammed with traffic, and the tempers which flared as a result often led to violence and even murder. 'From thence to Westminster Hall,' wrote Pepys, on 27 November 1660, 'and in King Street there being a great stop of coaches, there was a falling out between a drayman and my Lord Chesterfield's coachman, and one of his footmen killed.' Down the centre or sides of these streets ran open gutters along which coursed rivers of filth.

The air too was polluted by the smoke which poured from the belching furnaces of a whole variety of industries that were carried on within the City walls, those of the brewers, dyers, lime-burners, salt and soap-boilers, to name but a few, whose furnaces were fired by sea-coal brought by sea from Newcastle. The resultant smog spread far and wide. In 1661 John Evelyn wrote to the King complaining that, while walking one day in the delightful grounds of Whitehall Palace, he had been overcome by 'a presumptuous smoke issuing from one or two Tunnels near Northumberland House, and not far from Scotland yard' which had so invaded the Court

that all the Rooms, Galleries and Places about it were filled and infested with it; and that to such a degree, as Men could hardly discern one another for the Cloud ... It is this horrid Smoke which obscures our Churches, and makes our Palaces look old, which fouls our Clothes, and corrupts the Waters, so as the very Rain, and refreshing Dews which fall in the several Seasons, precipitate this impure vapour, which, with its black and tenacious quality, spots and contaminates whatever is exposed to it.[6]

Of all the houses in and around Great Russell Street, one in particular

impressed Strype: 'But for stateliness of Building and curious Gardens, Montagu House hath the Preminence, as indeed of all Houses within the Cities of London and Westminster, and the adjacent Parishes.'[7] Montagu House was the most splendid house built in London in the 1670s and 1680s. Its builder, Ralph Montagu, was a man of commensurate ambition, who obtained both an earldom and a dukedom from different monarchs, and married in succession two of the richest widows of his day. He was, wrote Swift, 'as arrant a knave as any in his time'.[8] The second son of Edward, Lord Montagu of Boughton, a cavalier of the old school, he became heir on the death of his brother in 1665, and wasted no time in coming to Court, nor any opportunity of increasing his fortune or bettering his social position. In 1669 he was appointed ambassador to France, where he was to serve again in 1675, 1676, and 1677–8, and where his missions became noted for their spectacular extravagance. His marriage in 1673 to the former Lady Elizabeth Wriothesley, daughter of the fourth Earl of Southampton, and heiress to two fortunes – those of her father, and of her recently deceased husband, Joceline, Earl of Northumberland – enabled him fully to indulge the taste for splendour which he had acquired. He began by building himself a suitably grand house in Bloomsbury.

The site chosen by Lord and Lady Montagu for their new home adjoined the gardens of Southampton House, so that the two houses stood level with one another, each enclosed with a wall and with open country stretching out

Left: Ralph, first Duke of Montagu. From a painting by Gennari.

Above: Elizabeth Countess of Northumberland, first wife of Ralph Montagu. After Lely.

Southampton House
and Montagu House.
Detail from Samuel
Scott's painting of
Russell Square – see
title page.

behind. In drawing up the agreement with Lord Southampton, every care was taken that the new building should be worthy not only of a nobleman of the rank of Lord Montagu, but of its neighbour. As things turned out, it was to outshine the latter by far.

Montagu, an enthusiast for the French style, chose as his architect Robert Hooke, designer of Bedlam and the Royal College of Physicians, who had based his design for the former on the Palace of the Tuileries, a fact which is said to have so infuriated Louis XIV that he retaliated by commissioning an adaptation of St James's for 'offices of the vilest nature'.[9] There is sadly no record of Hooke's plan, which was begun in 1675 and stood only eight years, and it can be judged only by comparing views of the post-1686 house with a sketch on Ogilby and Morgan's map of 1682, which shows a clear division of the sections and high roofs, both of which features can be paralleled in other houses by him, such as Bedlam and Ragley Hall, Warwickshire. Contemporary accounts give only the vaguest idea of what it was like, though they do mention the many rooms painted by Verrio, whom Montagu had brought back with him from Paris in 1672, initially to make designs for the Mortlake tapestry factory. 'Went to see Montagu House', wrote Evelyn on 10 October 1683.

It is within a stately and ample Palace, Signior Verrio's fresco Paintings ... I think exceeds anything he has yet done, both for design, Colouring and exuberance of Invention, comparable certainly to the greatest of the old Masters: The garden is large and in good air, but the fronts of the house not answerable to the inside: the Court at Entry, and Wings for Offices seem too near the street ... which might have been

A section from Ogilby and Morgan's map of 1682 showing the first Montagu House before it was destroyed by fire in 1686 (looking north).

prevented, had they placed the house further into the ground, of which there was enough to spare: But in sum, 'tis a fine Palace, built after the French pavillion way ...

In January 1686, while Montagu was away in France, and the house was let to the Earl of Devonshire, disaster struck. It was witnessed from Southampton House by Lady Rachel Russell, who had been living there since the death of her father, the fourth Earl, in 1667. 'If you have heard of the dismal accident in this neighbourhood', she wrote to her former chaplain, Dr Fitzwilliam,

you will easily believe Tuesday night was not a quiet one with us. About one o'clock in the night I heard a great noise in the square, so little ordinary, I called up a servant, and sent her down to learn the occasion. She brought up a very sad one, that Montagu House was on fire, and it was so indeed: it burnt with so great violence, the whole house was consumed by five o'clock. The wind blew strong this way, so that we lay under fire a great part of the time, the sparks and flames continually covering the house, and filling the court. My boy awaked, and said he was almost stifled with smoke, but being told the reason, would see it, and so was satisfied without fear; took a strange bedfellow very willingly, Lady Devonshire's youngest boy, whom his nurse had brought wrapped up in a blanket.[10]

According to Evelyn, the blaze was started by some servants airing sheets over a fire.[11] For anything to have survived such a conflagration would seem to have been unlikely, yet an advertisement which appeared soon after in the *London Gazette*, offering a reward of £10 for the return of thirty-three Van

Dycks in grisaille, along with other pictures, suggests that there was some successful looting.[12]

According to Ackermann, 'The Duke of Montagu ... when receiving intelligence that his house was destroyed by fire, his spirits became greatly depressed, which induced Louis XIV to send artists to London to repair the losses.'[13] Exactly when these artists, La Fosse, Rousseau, and Monnoyer, actually arrived is open to question, but a manuscript history of the family which exists at Boughton House in Northamptonshire, the Duke's country seat, tells us that after the execution of his brother-in-law, Lord William Russell, in 1683 for his part in the Rye House Plot, Montagu went into voluntary exile in France 'and continued there till the latter end of King James's Reign, when he returned again to England; but forebore to appear at Court, living retired'. This surely suggests that he would not have ordered more than the basic repairs necessary after the fire, and may well have waited till the accession of William III in 1688 before undertaking elaborate redecorations.

In his celebrated architectural work, *Vitruvius Britannicus* – the first volume of which was published in 1715 – Colen Campbell claimed that the new house was designed by a French architect, 'Monsieur Poujet'. This may have referred either to Pierre Puget (1620–94), a notable baroque sculptor, or to his son François (1651–1707), a painter and architect, though the involvement of either of them is questionable since there is no record of their ever having come to England. The likelihood is, therefore, that it was the work of a certain Boujet, who is known only through some drawings in the Smythson collection at the RIBA. The basic layout almost certainly remained Hooke's, though he was not employed on the project. Visitors arriving from Great Russell Street would have swept through an imposing, pedimented gateway, crowned by a charming octagonal lantern, into a large forecourt. They were then faced by a single rectangular block, two rooms deep – a type known as double-pile – with a square central dome, and projecting end pavilions in the manner then popular in France. Wings containing the various offices, each one storey lower and graced by tall, stately chimneys, joined the house on each side, while on the south side a massive screen, fronted by an elegant colonnade, completed the quadrangle. They may have found the fusion of house and offices, possibly survivals from the fire, slightly awkward – as did Horace Walpole, who considered that the house lacked 'grace and beauty'. In his opinion, however, this was amply compensated for 'by the spaciousness and lofty magnificence of the apartments'.[14]

In the centre of the main block, two halls stood back to back, while the principal rooms lay over them on the first floor – a rather grander arrangement than in most country houses, where both hall and saloon generally occupied the ground floor. On either side of the north hall were apartments leading to the pavilions at either end. Although surviving inventories list all the rooms at

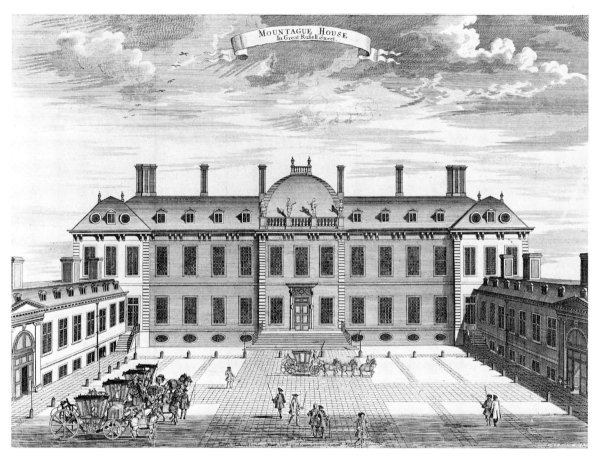

Montagu House, it is difficult to relate them to the plan of the house in *Vitruvius Britannicus*, as it is not accompanied by a key. The general impression, however, is one of great splendour.

The entrance hall was apparently called the 'painted stone hall', and contained five flower pieces by Jean-Baptiste Monnoyer. Round its walls were pairs of Ionic pilasters, and the ceiling was painted with allegorical figures. Two arches, filled with iron grilles, led to a vast painted staircase, with a wrought-iron balustrade; this must have been something of a novelty when it was put up, few if any having been used since Inigo Jones's 'tulip stairs' in the Queen's House in Greenwich. It rose up, through scenes of classical combat and architectural fantasy, to the vestibule, beyond which, occupying the central portion of the house and overlooking the gardens to the north, lay the saloon. This extraordinary room was entirely painted, from the Corinthian columns to the delicate floral swags and Elysian landscapes that covered the doorways – making them, according to Celia Fiennes, 'so well suited in the walls you cannot tell where to find the doors if a stranger'. She also noticed its strange acoustics, which were 'so contrived that speak very low to the wall or wainscot

Montagu House,
Great Russell Street.

See colour plate 1

in one corner and it should be heard with advantage in the very opposite corner across – this I heard myself'.[15] In suite with the saloon ran the state apartments – those to the west, with arched and painted ceilings, being the most important.

Opposite: The painted staircase at Montagu House, by G. Scharf.

Twice a week Montagu entertained on a lavish scale. 'If the poor Duchess of Mazarin had been yet alive', wrote Saint-Évremond, 'she would have had Peaches, of which she would not have failed to give me a share: she would have had Truffles, which I should have eat with her: not to mention the Carps of Newhall. I must make up the loss of so many advantages, by the Sundays and Wednesdays of Montagu House.'[16] Montagu's extravagance was colossal, for at the same time as he was lavishing so much money on his London house, he was doing the same in the country, where he was remodelling Boughton as a French château.

Montagu's first wife died in 1690 and, with so much money slipping through his hands, he lost no time in seeking out a new fortune to add to what was left of hers. It was to come from an unlikely source, for the widow upon whom he set his sights, Elizabeth, second Duchess of Albemarle, and the heiress to a great estate inherited from her father, the second Duke of Newcastle, was raving mad. Since the death of her husband, she had been in the charge of two sisters, Mary and Sarah Wright, with two physicians in constant attendance. Moreover, some ingenuity was required in order to obtain her hand, since she would consider marriage only to royalty. Suitably masquerading, Montagu represented himself to her as the Emperor of China, and in due time won her consent to become his Empress. They were married in September 1692. Rooms in Montagu House were set aside for her special use, and here she passed her life, humoured in every fantastic whim and served on bended knee with all the pomp and ceremonious ritual befitting her station. Apart from her special attendants and Montagu himself, no one was allowed to go near her, not even her closest relations, so it was not long before it was rumoured that she was dead. In fact she lived on long after the death in 1709 of her Emperor, by then the first Duke of Montagu, when she was transferred to the guardianship of her brother-in-law, John, Duke of Newcastle, who kept her in suitable apartments in Newcastle House, Clerkenwell. Here she lived till her death in 1734, at the age of ninety-four.

Montagu House saw some equally strange goings-on under Ralph Montagu's son and heir, John, second Duke of Montagu, who was best known in his lifetime as an efficient and serious soldier, being made Master General of the Ordnance in 1740 and a General in 1746. He also had an eccentric side, with an adolescent's taste for devising elaborate practical jokes. He gave a dinner for people who stuttered, another for those who squinted, and a banquet for serious professional men who, when they came to adjust their wigs in the mirrors later on in the evening, found themselves quite unknowingly looking into distorting mirrors, which made them think they were too drunk to see

Above: Elizabeth Duchess of Albemarle, 'The Empress of China', by Sir Peter Lely.

Right: John, second Duke of Montagu.

straight. At the age of fifty-two he was summed up thus by his mother-in-law, Sarah, Duchess of Marlborough: 'All his talents lie in things only natural in boys of fifteen years old ... to get people into his garden and wet them with squirts, and to invite people to his country house and put things into their beds to make them itch, and twenty such pretty fancies as these ...'[17]

Like his father, he enjoyed doing everything to excess and, while he lived at Montagu House, evidently did so in some style. Lady Anne Carew, writing to her stepmother, Lady Coventry, in February 1715, described a great ball given by the Duke:

I having no better news to send to Your Ladyship will trouble you with an account I heard of a Ball the Duke of Montagu gave at his house last week which was exceedingly fine. The Prince was there in Masquerade in a Dutch Bors habit. They say the King was there incog: There was several dresses, some running footmen, some Shepherdesses, and other dresses as is usual upon such occasions. Two hundred tickets was given to ye Prince and Princess to dispose of as they thought fit. The Entertainment was very fine, there being one long Table in the inner Room whereon was set two hundred and fifty Dishes of all sorts of cold things, and as soon as they were set off, the dishes were taken off and the same put whole on again. There was also another table where there was all sorts of rich Wines in great plenty. The Wax Candles that night came to two-hundred pounds. There was one gentleman who acted the part of selling Drams, which he did so natural that another Gentleman, to encourage him, tasted so often that he cast up his accounts in the Room amongst the Company! The

Duke himself had five changes of Clothes and said nothing vexed him so much as being disappointed of the sixth.[18]

So prodigal was his expenditure that, in the end, even an income as enormous as his failed to keep the second Duke out of debt. He sold an estate he owned in Kent in an attempt to straighten out his affairs, while his father-in-law, the first Duke of Marlborough, urged him to dispose of Montagu House and either buy a smaller residence, or move into rented accommodation. It was not, however, until 1733, ten years after the death of Marlborough, that he finally moved out, to a house in the Privy Garden, Whitehall, about which little is known. Montagu House then sat empty for another twenty years, when it was bought by the nation as a home for the British Museum.

The unstable political climate of the last years of Charles II's reign and that of James II, which had proved a difficult period for Ralph Montagu, seems to have been unconducive to building on a grand scale in London. There were, however, two ambitious schemes during this period. The first was that of James Scott, Duke of Monmouth, the eldest of Charles II's illegitimate sons, for a large house on the south side of Soho Square. Although little is known about its intended appearance, its importance lies in the fact that it was the first great house successfully designed to dominate a square and provide a focal point to the street pattern. This had been attempted in Bloomsbury Square, laid out in front of Southampton House, but the house, which Evelyn had

A view of the Thames from near Westminster Bridge showing Montagu House, Whitehall (left). From a painting by Samuel Scott.

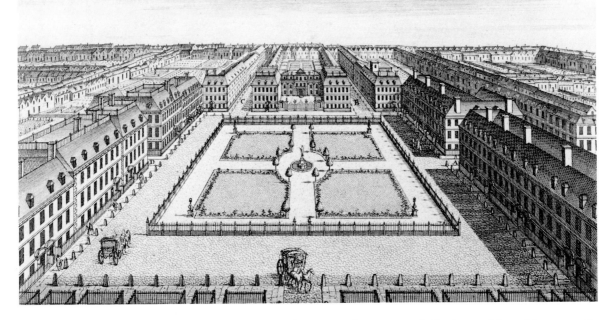

Monmouth House,
Soho Square, 1727,
looking southwards.
From an engraving by
Bowles.

Opposite: Newcastle
House, Lincoln's Inn
Fields.

criticised as being 'too low', was not large enough for its position. Monmouth's house was to be well set back from the frontage line of the flanking houses in the square, a deep forecourt giving it a palatial appearance. Monmouth leased the site in 1682, but his flight abroad in 1683 and his execution in 1685 after the failure of his rebellion against James II effectively prevented the completion of the fabric; and despite the efforts of his wife, the Duchess of Buccleuch, the house was still unfinished when she was obliged to sell it in 1714 to Sir James Bateman.

In 1686, William Herbert, first Marquis of Powis, the leader of the Roman Catholic aristocracy in the reigns of Charles II and James II, employed William Winde, a pupil of Balthazar Gerbier, to rebuild for him Powis House, which had stood since 1642 at the north-west angle of Lincoln's Inn Fields, on the corner of Great Queen Street, and which had been razed to the ground by fire two years previously. 'About five in the morning', wrote Luttrell on 26 October 1684, 'broke out a fire in the house of the Earl of Powis in Great Lincoln's Inn Fields, which in a very little time consumed that house, the family hardly saving themselves from being burnt, but lost all their things.'[19] Powis had little time to enjoy the imposing three-storey house which Winde had designed for him, with its fine large rooms overlooking the Fields, for in 1688 he followed James II into exile, upon which his home was forfeited to the Crown. That December, Powis House barely escaped destruction by the anti-popery mobs who scoured the streets seeking Roman Catholic property to destroy. On 11 December they gutted the popish chapel in Lincoln's Inn Fields, 'pulling down all the wainscot, pictures, books, etc. ... they would have plundered and demolished the houses of several papists, as Lord Powis, etc. if they had not been prevented by the trained bands which were out.'[20] In May 1705, the house was sold by the second Marquis to John Holles, first Duke of Newcastle, after which it was known as Newcastle House.

NEWCASTLE HOUSE
in Lincolns Inn Fields

If the building of great private houses in London had been on the cautious side during the 1680s and 1690s, in the country, where the aristocracy still felt most confident, the situation had been quite different, and had seen the development of a new direction in country house design through the work of a young architect called William Talman. At Thoresby in Nottinghamshire, Chatsworth in Derbyshire, and Hackwood in Hampshire, he had built on a scale not seen since the prodigious houses of Elizabethan days, dictating that the greatness of a nobleman should be reflected in his surroundings. This quasi-baroque style was not seen in London, however, until after 1700, when John Sheffield, Marquess of Normanby, soon to be Duke of Buckingham, employed Talman to design a house for him on the site of Arlington House, which he had bought in 1702 from the Duchess of Grafton, and which stood at the end of the Mall, where Buckingham Palace now stands.

Traditionally, Buckingham House is said to have been designed by William Winde, and started in 1705. In fact the setting out of the house and gardens was almost certainly begun three years earlier. A letter written from Vanbrugh to the Duke of Newcastle, complaining of Talman's arrogant and arbitrary behaviour, claims that 'my Lord Normanby has met with vexations too'.[21] Though there is no mention of where this trouble took place, it seems likely that it was at his new London house, since no record exists of his building anywhere else at the time. Not only does Talman seem much more likely than Winde to have attracted the patronage of a nobleman of the stature of Normanby, but the building had strong echoes of his previous work. The square main block of the house, with the roof suppressed in favour of an open balustrade, and the giant order, recall Thoresby and the south front of Chatsworth, while the linking of the flanking wings to the main house by colonnades had a precedent in his work at Hackwood. The truth may well be that when the 'vexations' with Talman got too much for his employer, he was dismissed and the less temperamental Winde was brought in to carry out his design. Perhaps Talman had, in this case, good reasons to be vexed, for there is a story that Winde, having taken on the job, became so frustrated, if not almost ruined, by his client's failure to pay his fees, that he induced him to come up onto the roof of the new house to admire the view. Once there, he locked the trapdoor onto the leads and threw the key over the parapet, threatening to throw himself after it unless Normanby agreed to pay his bill immediately. 'And what is to become of me?' asked the Marquess. 'Why, you shall accompany me!' replied Winde.[22] The account was promptly settled.

Buckingham, as Normanby had become by the time the house was completed, was totally delighted with the result. He expressed his feelings in a long letter to the Duke of Shrewsbury, who had accused him 'of singularity in resigning the Privy Seal with a good pension added to it, and yet afterwards staying in town at a season when everyone else leaves it', which, in his opinion, was tantamount to 'despising at once both Court and Country', and had demanded an explanation of how he spent his time.

'So many hours, that appear long to you', wrote Buckingham,

are but too short for me ... I rise, now in summer, about seven o'clock, from a very large bed chamber, entirely quiet, high, and free from the early Sun, to walk in the garden; or, if rainy, in a Salon filled with pictures, some good, but none disagreeable; there also, in a row above them, I have so many portraits of famous persons in several kinds, as are enough to excite ambition in any man less lazy, or less at ease, than myself. Instead of a little dozing closet, according to the unwholesome custom of most people, I choose this spacious room for all my small affairs, reading books or writing letters; where I am never in the least tired, by the help of stretching my legs sometimes in so long a room, and of looking into the pleasantest park in the world just underneath it. Visits, after a certain hour, are not to be avoided; some of which I own a little fatiguing (tho' thanks to the town's laziness they come pretty late) if the garden was not so near, as to give a seasonable refreshment between those ceremonious interruptions ... After I have dined (either agreeably with friends, or at worst with better company than your country-neighbours) I drive away to a place of air and exercise ... the company I commonly find at home is agreeable enough to make me conclude the evening on a delightful terrace, or in any place free from late visits, except of familiar acquaintance.

From his daily routine, the Duke now turned to a detailed description of his beloved house.

The avenues to this house are along St James's Park, through rows of goodly Elms on one hand, and gay flourishing Limes on the other, that for coaches, this for walking; with the Mall lying between them. This reaches to my iron palisade that encompasses a square Court, which has in the midst a great basin with statues and waterworks; and from its entrance, rises all the way imperceptibly, 'till we mount to a terrace in front of a large Hall, paved with square white stones mixed with dark-coloured marble; the walls of it covered with a set of pictures done in the school of Raphael. Out of this, on the right hand we go into a parlour thirty-three foot by thirty-nine, with a niche fifteen foot broad for a Bufette, paved with white marble, and placed within an arch, with pilasters of divers colours, the upper part of which as high as the ceiling is painted by Ricci. From hence we pass through a suite of large rooms, into a bed-chamber of thirty-four foot by twenty-seven; within it a large closet, that opens into a greenhouse.

On the left hand of the Hall are three stone arches supported by Corinthian pillars, under one of which we go up eight and forty steps ten foot broad, each step of one entire Portland-stone: these stairs, by the help of two resting places, are so very easy, there is no need of leaning on the iron baluster. The walls are painted with the story of Dido [by Laguerre] ... From a wide landing place on the stairshead, a great *See colour plate 2* double-door opens into an apartment of the same dimensions with that below, only three foot higher ... The first room of this floor has within it a closet of original pictures, which yet are not so entertaining as the delightful prospect from the windows. Out of the second room a pair of great doors give entrance into the Saloon, which is thirty-five foot high, thirty-six broad, and forty-five long. [By the time Pyne engraved it in 1818 the original layout of the stairs had been changed and the north wall had

Right: A view of
Buckingham House by
James Miller.

Below: The view from
Buckingham House
over St. James's Park,
by Rigaud, 1736.

been altered at first floor level, so that the double doors led straight into the Saloon.] In the midst of its roof a round picture of Gentileschi, eighteen foot in diameter, represents the Muses playing in consort to Apollo, lying along on a cloud to hear them. The rest of the room is adorned with paintings relating to Arts and Sciences; and underneath divers original pictures hang all in good lights, by help of an upper row of windows which drown the glaring.

Much of this seems appertaining to parade and therefore I am glad to leave it to describe the rest, which is all for conveniency ... a large and lightsome backstairs leads up to such an entry above, as secures our private bedchambers both from noise and cold. Here we have necessary dressing-rooms, servants rooms, and closets, from which are the pleasantest views of all the house ... These stairs, and those of the same kind at the other end of the house, carry us up to the highest story, fitted for the women and children, with the doors so contrived as to prevent all noise over my wife's head.

In mentioning the court at first, I forgot the two wings in it, built on stone arches, which join the house by Corridors supported on Ionic pillars. In one of these wings is a large kitchen thirty foot high, with an open cupola on the top; near it a larder, brew-house, and laundry, with rooms over them for servants: the upper sort of servants are lodged in the other wing, which has also two wardrobes and a store-room for fruit. On the top of all a leaden cistern holding fifty tons of water, driven up by an engine from the Thames, supplies all the water-works in the courts and gardens, which lie quite round the house; through one of which a grass walk conducts to the stables, built round a court, with six coach-houses and forty stalls. I'll add but one thing before I carry you into the garden, and that is about walking too, but 'tis on the top of all the house; which being covered with smooth mill'd lead, and defended by a parapet of ballusters from apprehension as well as danger, entertains the eye with a far distant prospect of hills and dales, and a near one of parks and gardens.

His description of the gardens brings to life a plan in the Soane Museum:

To these gardens we go down from the house by seven steps, into a gravel walk that reaches cross the whole garden; with a covered arbour at each end of it. Another of thirty foot broad leads from the front of the house, and lies between two groves of tall lime trees planted in several equal ranks upon a carpet of grass: the outside of these groves are bordered with tubs of Bays and Orange trees. At the end of this broad walk, you go up to a Terrace four hundred paces long, with a large semi-circle in the middle, from whence is beheld the Queen's two parks, and a great part of Surrey; then going down a few steps, you walk on the bank of a canal six hundred yards long, and seventeen broad, with two rows of limes on each side of it. On one side of this Terrace, a wall covered with Roses and Jasmines is made low to admit the view of a meadow full of cattle just under it, (no disagreeable object in the midst of a great city) and at each end a descent into parterres, with fountains and water-works. From the biggest of these parterres we pass into a little square garden, that has a fountain in the middle, and two greenhouses on the sides, with a convenient bathing apartment in one of them; and near another part of it lies a flower-garden. Below all this, a kitchen-garden full of the best sorts of fruit has several walks in it fit for the coldest weather.

'Only one thing I forgot', he concluded,

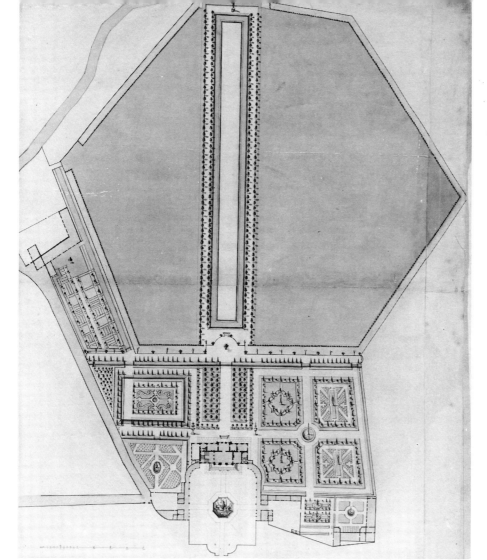

A plan of the gardens at Buckingham House.

though of more satisfaction to me than all the rest . . . 'tis a little closet of books at the end of that green-house which joins the best apartment; which besides their being so very near, are ranked in such a method, that by its mark a very Irish footman may fetch any book I want. Under the windows of this closet and green-house, is a little wilderness full of blackbirds and nightingales . . .[23]

In fact he also failed to mention what appears to have been another important room, a Japan closet, 'the chief part of which', according to an inventory of 1743, 'was lined with India Japan Boards, all the Japan finisht with carving and gilding and all the glass and picture frames the same – Eight carved and gilt flowers fixt in the lower panels';[24] and the statue of Samson and the Philistines by Giovanni da Bologna, which had belonged to the first Duke and is now to be found in the Victoria and Albert Museum. Nor does he refer to the inscriptions which he had placed on each side of the house. That on the east front, overlooking St James's Park, read: *Sic siti laetantur Lares* ('The household gods delight in such a situation'); that on the west front, facing the garden, *Rus in Urbe* ('The Country within a City'); that on the south side,

The Duke and
Duchess of
Buckingham, and their
son. Painting by
Enoch Leeman.

Spectator fastidiosus sibi molestus ('The too fastidious critic harms chiefly himself'); while that on the north side read *Lente suscipe, cito perfice* ('Be slow to undertake an obligation, and quick to discharge it').

According to his letter, most of the Duke's time was 'conjugally spent at home'. In 1705 he had married as his third wife a widow, Katherine, Countess of Anglesey, who was an illegitimate daughter of James II. She was obsessed about her royal descent, insisting on being treated as such, and was subsequently known as 'the haughty duchess'. It was after the death of her husband, however, in 1721, that she was able to indulge her eccentric whims to their fullest. She turned Buckingham House into an imitation court, and a hotbed of Jacobite intrigue. Neither her friends nor her attendants were allowed to sit in her presence. On each anniversary of the death of her grandfather, Charles I, she dressed in deepest mourning, bidding her 'ladies-in-waiting' to do likewise, and received her company in the great drawing-room, regally seated in a chair of state which was heavily draped in black.

Horace Walpole gives an especially good example of her behaviour. 'The Duchess of Buckingham,' he wrote to Sir Horace Mann,

who is more mad with pride than any mercer's wife in Bedlam, came the other night to the opera *en princesse*, literally in robes of red velvet and ermine. I must tell you a story of her. Last week she sent for Cori (the prompter to the opera) to pay him for her opera ticket; he was not at home, but went in an hour afterwards. She said did he treat her like a tradeswoman. She would teach him to respect women of her birth and bade him come the next morning at nine. He came, and she bade him wait until eight at night, only sending him an omelette and a bottle of wine. As it was Friday, and he a Catholic, she supposed he did not eat meat. At last she received him in all the form of a princess giving audience to an ambassador. 'Now', she said, 'she had punished him.'[25]

Even on her deathbed she could not forget the deference which she considered her due. 'Princess Buckingham', wrote Walpole,

is dead or dying. She sent for Mr Anstis and settled the ceremonial of her burial. On Saturday she was so ill that she feared dying before the pomp was come home. She said: 'Why don't they send the canopy for me to see? Let them send it though all the tassels are not finished.' But yesterday was the greatest stroke of all. She made her ladies vow to her that if she should lie senseless, they would not sit down in the room before she was dead.[26]

The Duchess left the house for his lifetime to one Charles Herbert, an illegitimate son of her late husband. When his lease of the Crown land upon which the house stood expired in 1761, it was bought off the family for £28,000 by George III, who wanted a private residence for himself and Queen Charlotte to which they could retire when the pomp and formality of St James's became too much for them. From then on it remained a royal residence, being altered and enlarged in the early nineteenth century to what we now know as

Buckingham Palace – in the process incurring the charge, from the Duke of Wellington, that 'notwithstanding the expense ... in building the Palace ... no Sovereign in Europe, I may even add, perhaps, no private gentleman, is so ill lodged as the King of this country'.[27]

The main façade of the original house was widely copied, in much the same way as Clarendon House had been years before. In the country there are several examples of its influence, ranging from Wotton and Chilton, both in Buckinghamshire, to Castletown in County Kilkenny, built as late as the 1760s. In London its most obvious imitation was Powis House at the north-west end of Great Ormond Street, which stood back from the street on the site of what is now Powis Place. Built in the latter part of the reign of William III by William Herbert, second Marquis of Powis, it had, like its namesake in Lincoln's Inn Fields, been burnt to the ground. At the time it was let to the French ambassador. 'After dinner at Lord Treasurers', wrote Swift to Mrs Dingley in January 1713, 'the French ambassador, Duke d'Aumont, sent Lord Treasurer word, that his house was burnt to the ground. It took fire in the upper rooms while he was at dinner ... We are full of speculations upon it, but I believe it was the carelessness of his rascally French servants.'[28] The French king, Louis XIV, subsequently employed Colen Campbell to rebuild the house. It was completed in 1714, and, to guard against the possibility of another fire, Campbell placed a large reservoir on the roof, which also doubled as a fishpond.

Following hot on the heels of the Duke of Buckingham, Sarah, Duchess of Marlborough also decided to build a town house, on land leased to her by Queen Anne, her close friend and confidante, on the eastern edge of St James's Palace. 'I mortally hate all Grandeur and Architecture',[29] she wrote to Sir Christopher Wren, to whom she had given the commission – an unremarkable statement from a woman who once said that her taste was 'always to have things plain and clean, from a piece of wainscoat to a lady's face'.[30] She insisted that he 'make my house strong plain and convenient and that he must give me his word that this building should not have the least resemblance of anything in that called Blenheim which I have never liked'.[31] The foundation stone was laid on 4 May 1709. Marlborough himself was unenthusiastic. 'I have no great opinion of this project', he wrote, '... you may depend on it that it will cost you double the money of the first estimate.' Being a devoted husband, however – he knew that his wife had set her heart on the project – he put her happiness first, and on 18 July he wrote: 'I am glad of the general approval your house meets with, since I am sure that it gives you pleasure, and, for the same reason, be not uneasy that it costs more money than you thought it would, for upon my word, I shall think nothing too much for the making you easy.'[32] Despite the Duke's fear of spiralling costs, the house was finished in midsummer 1711, for the not unreasonable sum of £50,000.

The house has been altered so much in the last two hundred years that it

Sarah, Duchess of Marlborough, by Sir Godfrey Kneller.

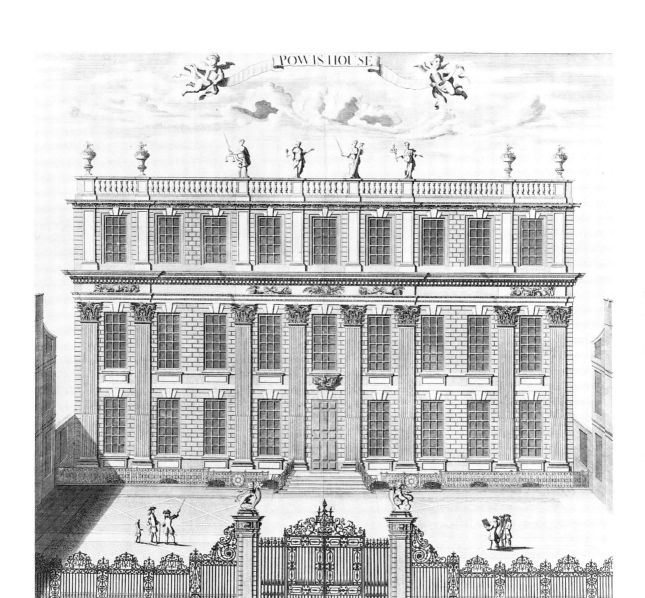

is hard to judge its original effect, even with the help of the engraving in *Vitruvius Britannicus*, though some idea of what it looked like may be gained from the present garden front, where the original height is marked by a heavy Portland stone cornice between the second and third storeys. Built of hard, rather small, Dutch bricks said to have been brought over by the Duke from Holland as ballast in the transports used in his campaign, thus saving any import costs, it consisted of a square central block, two storeys high, containing the hall or present saloon on the north and three square rooms on the south. This was flanked by slightly projecting wings, while on either side of the courtyard were lower wings, also of two storeys, the southern half of each wing

Powis House, Great Ormond Street.

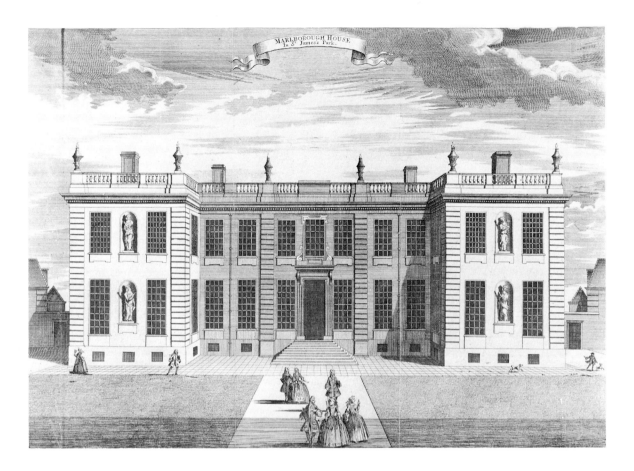

Marlborough House, St James's Park. An engraving of 1754.

having an open colonnade facing the courtyard. This arrangement is now largely obscured by the extensive nineteenth-century additions, in the course of which two extra storeys were added, the colonnade was filled in and a low addition was attached to the north side of the house, together with the *porte-cochère*.

Wren's original intention was undoubtedly more ambitious than it seems today, but it cannot be fully judged from the façade that is seen from the Park, which was of secondary importance. The main entrance was supposed to have been onto Pall Mall, so that the house was seen at the end of a forecourt, as in the case of Montagu House and Berkeley House. Unfortunately for the Duchess, she had quite underestimated the cunning and enmity of Sir Robert Walpole, with whom she had bitterly quarrelled. Solely in order to spite her, he bought up all the vital Pall Mall plots, which she needed to carry out her scheme, thus spoiling any chance of her home having an entrance in keeping with its importance and her dignity. Since he had also removed the privilege she had long enjoyed of going from Marlborough House through St James's Park in her coach, she was left with an approach from Pall Mall via a narrow passage through which a coach and six horses could barely squeeze.

For twenty-two years after the death of her husband in 1722, the Duchess Sarah held court at Marlborough House, an irascible old lady, deaf as a post, tortured by gout and rheumatism which kept her in a state of constant warfare with the world, and so grand that she used to refer to the King in St James's

The Mall in 1741.
Marlborough House
can be seen second to
the left. From an
engraving by
J. Maurer.

Palace as 'her neighbour George'.[33] She made biting criticisms of those who
came to wonder at her. 'There are many visitors', she wrote, 'but few have
sense, or are capable of friendship or truth.'[34] After the resignation and retirement of Sir Robert Walpole in 1742 she embarked on one more attempt to
improve the approaches to her home, and a plan of 1744 which exists at
Blenheim shows a proposed enlargement of the entrance by one hundred and
eleven feet by the demolition of four narrow houses which stood in the way in
Pall Mall. She died, however, the following year, and the plan was abandoned.

The Dukes of Marlborough occupied the house until their lease reverted to
the Crown in 1817, when it was designated a royal residence. During this time
it was enlarged by Sir William Chambers, who added an upper storey to the
main block of the house, and replaced the plain chimney-pieces so beloved by
the first Duchess with more elaborate ones – work which was carried out in
the midst of serious labour difficulties. 'I am obliged', wrote Chambers to the
Duke's agent,

to get the work done at Marlborough House when the workmen please and not when
I wish to have it nor when it ought to be done. The Slater was prevented by the
negligence of the Plumber from pointing his work more than a month and the Plasterer, under pretence that the slating was not done, neither sent in his stuff nor made
the least preparation for beginning . . . I was therefore compelled to make them all fall
to work at the same time or else God knows when it would be done.[35]

The house has little period feeling now, the character of Wren's original

Marlborough House in 1827, after the alterations by Sir William Chambers.

Opposite: The painted staircase at Marlborough House, with murals by Louis Laguerre.

interior and of Chambers's work for the third Duke having been largely lost as a result of additions and alterations made for Edward VII and George V, who both occupied it before they succeeded to the throne, and for Queen Alexandra and Queen Mary. However the basic plan of a two-storeyed hall with a pair of narrow staircase halls on either side of it still exists, as do Laguerre's grandiose paintings depicting Marlborough's battles and the cities he besieged. Perhaps the best features of the house are the ceiling in the hall, originally painted by Orazio Gentileschi for the Queen's House at Greenwich, and some fine elaborate chimney-pieces of the Chambers period.

The curious thing about Montagu House, Buckingham House and Marlborough House is that they really bore very little relationship to one another. Whereas the country houses built between 1660 and 1715 tended to be based either on the style associated with Pratt and May, or on the grander baroque style that was being adopted by some of the richer members of the aristocracy, no such pattern had emerged in London. One can only conclude that this slow and patchy development of the great town house was due to the instability of the English political scene, and a certain unwillingness of society, on economic grounds, to support it. The dawning of the eighteenth century, however, was to see all that change.

Anthony Ashley
Cooper, third Earl of
Shaftesbury, by John
Closterman.

3

The Palladian Influence

Yet Burlington's fair palace still remains;
Beauty within, without proportion reigns.
There oft I enter (but with cleaner shoes)
For Burlington's beloved by evr'y Muse.

John Gay, 'Epistle to the Earl of Burlington'

In 1712 the philosopher Anthony Ashley Cooper, the third Earl of Shaftesbury, published the stirringly patriotic *Letter Concerning the Art or Science of Design*, in which he suggested that the British people, having solved the fundamental problems of government, were now in the best possible position to develop the arts. 'For what I have observed of the rising Genius of our Nation', he wrote, 'that if we live to see a peace any way answerable to that generous spirit with which this war was begun, and carry'd on, for our own liberty and that of Europe; the Figure we are like to make abroad, and the Increase of Knowledge and Industry and sense at home, will render United Britain the principal seat of the Arts.'[1] He went on to say that 'As her Constitution has grown, and been establish'd, she has in proportion fitted herself for other improvements ... She has now the advantage of beginning in other Matters, on a new foot. She has her Models yet to seek, her Scale and Standard to form, with deliberation and good choice ...'[2] Three years later, with the War of the Spanish Succession over, the establishment of a Whig government, the peaceful acceptance of George I and the final collapse of the Stuart revolt, England really did seem to be approaching a new era of peace and prosperity.

At precisely this moment there appeared on the market two books, the publication of which was to have far-reaching consequences. The first was Volume I of *Vitruvius Britannicus* by the Scottish lawyer and architect Colen Campbell, a folio of one hundred engravings of classical buildings in Britain. It proclaimed the superiority of 'antique simplicity' over the 'affected and licentious' forms of the baroque, holding up for admiration the 'renowned Palladio' and the 'famous Inigo Jones'. Its appearance was followed closely by a translation of the first five instalments of *The Architecture of A. Palladio* by the Venetian Giacomo Leoni, a book long admired in England, and by none more than Inigo Jones himself. Together these two works were an inspiration

Elevation of Pembroke
House, Whitehall.

Opposite: Richard
Boyle, third Earl of
Burlington, attributed
to J. Richardson.

to the English nobility, sparking off a new Palladian movement, which began as a homage to the resurrected hero.

One of the early leaders of the movement was Henry Lord Herbert, the 24-year-old son of the eighth Earl of Pembroke, who, in 1717, obtained a lease of part of the site of the old Palace of Whitehall, which had been destroyed by fire in 1598, and on it built 'a very good house, of 58 feet 4 inches in front and 36 feet 7 inches in depth'.[3] Designed by Colen Campbell and overlooking the river, its main feature was a recessed portico on the first floor – an idea John Webb had used at Gunnersbury Park in Middlesex. Though Pembroke House was seldom copied, and was described by Horace Walpole as being 'madly built',[4] it was in fact a landmark in the history of English architecture, being the first completely Palladian villa. As such it was the forerunner of a style of house which, once established, was to last for close on half a century and be influential for a great deal longer.

Richard Boyle, the third Earl of Burlington, was a little younger than Lord Herbert, having come of age only in 1715; but having succeeded his father as early as 1704, he was in a stronger position to adopt the role of a patron. He was inspired particularly by *Vitruvius*, which also gave him the opportunity of

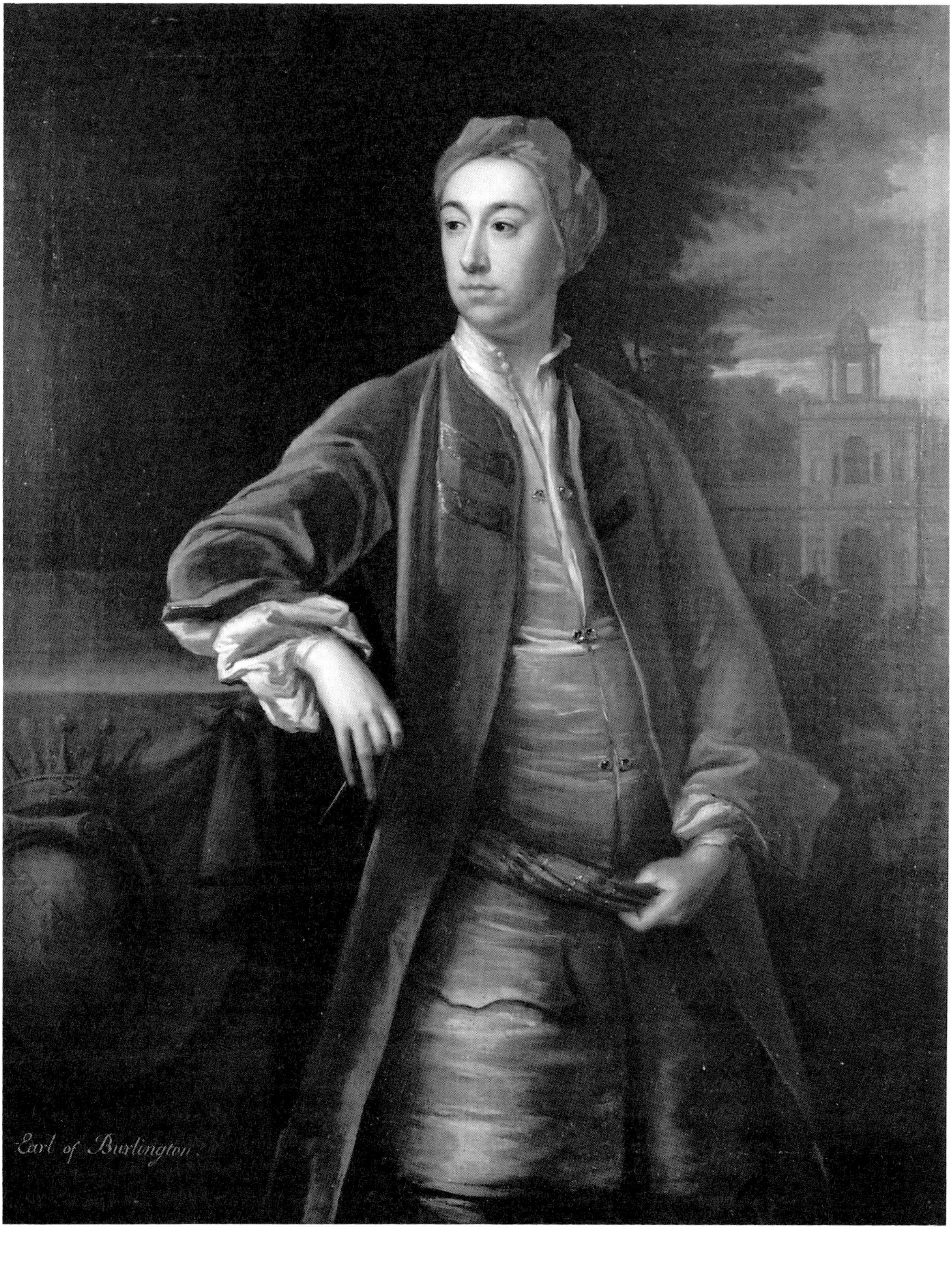
Earl of Burlington

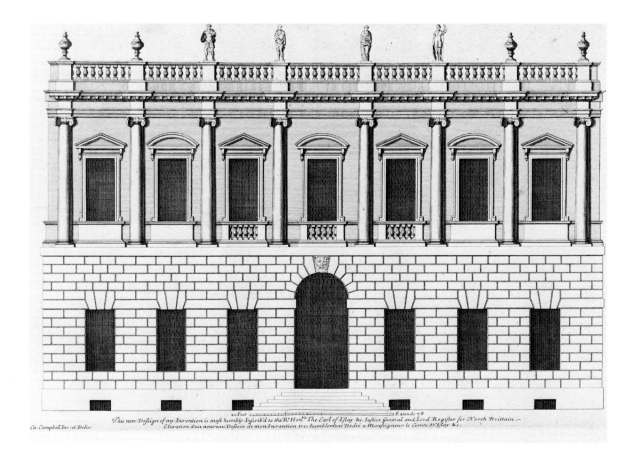

Colen Campbell's
'New Design for the
Earl of Islay'.

comparing the by now rather outmoded and simple front of Burlington House with the Palladian grandeur of Campbell's unexecuted 'New Design for the Earl of Islay'. Possibly under the influence of his mother, Juliana Lady Burlington, a woman of considerable character and taste, Burlington had already shown himself to be in the forefront of artistic fashion by employing the Venetian artists Giacomo Pellegrini and Sebastiano Ricci to decorate Burlington House some time between 1712 and 1713. Pellegrini had painted the hall which occupied the three central bays, work which is now lost, and Ricci the staircase, which lay to the right of it. The upper part of the latter, which is now the Council Room of the Royal Academy, still retains Ricci's ceiling, representing a scene in Olympus viewed through a *trompe-l'oeil* open dome. Burlington had also started on major architectural alterations there, including the construction of magnificent semi-circular Doric colonnades, designed by another Scottish architect, James Gibbs, and almost certainly inspired by those of Bernini, which form the approach to St Peter's in Rome.

See colour plate 3

Campbell's design for the Earl of Islay was a skilful adaptation of the rusticated basement and Ionic first storey of Inigo Jones's Banqueting House

Ricci's Olympus painted on the ceiling of the Council Room in the Royal Academy.

in Whitehall, which Campbell considered to be 'the first Structure in the World', and Burlington saw how it would be appropriate for refronting his own house. In spite of the splendour of the colonnades, Gibbs was dismissed and Campbell brought in, in 1717, to transform the south front of Burlington House from Restoration brickwork to Palladian stone. His façade still exists, though crushed by Sydney Smirke's top storey, added for the Royal Academy in 1872, and masked by his arcaded portico. Campbell also linked the colonnades with a noble gatehouse in the style of a triumphal arch, strongly reminiscent of the York House watergate, then revered as a work of Inigo Jones. Though stylistically of great significance, the remodelled Burlington House remained relatively unknown to the public at large until it was engraved in 1725, since it stood behind a 28-foot-high screen-wall which adjoined the gateway on either side. Only those lucky enough to have been passing when the gates opened to admit a carriage would have had a tantalising glimpse within.

Horace Walpole, for one, waxed lyrical when he first set eyes upon the colonnade. 'As we have few examples of architecture more antique and imposing than that colonnade', he wrote in his *Anecdotes of Painting*,

I cannot help mentioning the effect it had on myself. I had not only never seen it but had never heard of it, at least with any attention, when, soon after my return from Italy, I was invited to a ball at Burlington House. As I passed under the gate by night it could not strike me. At daybreak, looking out of the windows to see the sun rise, I was surprised with the vision of the colonnade that fronted me. It seemed one of those artifices in fairy tales that are raised by genii in the nighttime.[5]

Curiously enough, in spite of his enormous enthusiasm and a grand tour to Italy in 1714-15, Burlington did not actually see Palladio's original buildings at first hand until he made a second trip there in 1719, from which he returned with the young Yorkshire painter and architect William Kent, who had been living there since 1709. Though Kent took up residence at Burlington House, there is no surviving evidence of any architectural features attributable to him, other than the painted ceilings in the secretary's room and the saloon. The

Above: The saloon, Burlington House.

Opposite: A view into Burlington House showing Colen Campbell's great gateway and colonnades, 1718-19, destroyed 1866.

latter is the only complete room surviving from the Burlington period, and its decoration was probably designed by Campbell. Though it cannot be dated exactly, it is possibly the earliest, and certainly one of the finest, Palladian interiors in England.

The revamped house came in for much criticism. Hogarth, in *The Taste of the Town*, published in 1724, attacked its foreign influences, while an epigram said to have been written either by Lord Hervey or Lord Chesterfield is scathing of its discomfort - somewhat unfairly, one cannot help feeling, since the fashion of the period was to sacrifice everything for the grandeur of the reception rooms:

Possessed of one great hall of state,
Without a room to sleep or eat;
How well you build let flattery tell,
And all the world how ill you dwell.

Pope, on the other hand, wrote:

Who plants like Bathurst and who builds like Boyle?

and perhaps the last word should go to Gay:

Yet Burlington's fair palace still remains;
Beauty within, without proportion reigns.
There oft I enter (but with cleaner shoes)
For Burlington's beloved by evr'y Muse.[6]

During the lifetime of Burlington and his wife, whom he married in 1721 - she was the former Lady Dorothy Saville, the daughter and heiress of the Marquis of Halifax - Burlington House became known as a gathering-place for many of the most celebrated artists, musicians and writers of the day. As early as 1715, Burlington demonstrated his love of surrounding himself with genius and talent by returning from Italy accompanied by a sculptor, G. B. Guelfi, and a violinist, Pietro Castrucci, both of whom he installed in his home. He further celebrated this year of his coming of age by inviting Handel to stay, who was to occupy apartments there for the next three years, during which time he composed three operas, *Amadis*, *Theseus*, and *Pastor Fido* - no mean feat, since the house must have been crawling with builders and decorators during most of this time. Kent moved there in 1719. Pope, Gay and Arbuthnot were all regular visitors, as was Dean Swift, about whom Mrs Pilkington tells a story in her *Memoirs* (1748), which puts neither him nor his host in a very good light:

Being in London, Swift went to dine with the newly married earl of Burlington, who neither introduced his wife nor mentioned her name, willing, it is supposed, to have some diversion. After dinner the Dean said, 'Lady Burlington, I hear you can sing: sing me a song.' The lady thought this very unceremonious and refused, when Swift

General Wade's house at 29 Old Burlington Street.

said she should sing or he would make her. 'Why, madam, I suppose you take me for one of your poor hedge parsons; sing when I bid you.' The Earl laughed at this freedom, that the lady was so vexed that she burst into tears and retired. Swift's first words on seeing her again were, 'Pray, madam, are you as proud and ill-natured now as when I saw you last?' To which she answered with great good humour, 'No, Mr Dean, I will sing to you, if you please.' From this time Swift conceived a great esteem for the lady.[7]

'Never was protection and great wealth', wrote Walpole of Burlington, 'more generously and more judiciously diffused than in this great person, who had every quality of a genius and artist, except envy.'[8] Unfortunately such boundless generosity seems to have depleted his funds and by 1720, when he was most intent on decorating his house in the new style, he may have found it impossible to carry out all his schemes. In fact it is quite obvious that the house was never finished, for the Caroline garden front survived until 1812. He also became more and more absorbed in planning other houses, such as Richmond House in Whitehall, for the Duke of Richmond, one for Field-Marshal Wade at 29 Old Burlington Street, which was a faithful copy of a

The façade of 17 Bruton Street.

drawing by Palladio; and his own villa at Chiswick – with the result that by the time he withdrew from politics in 1733, he had really lost all interest in Burlington House, even going so far as to remove all his favourite pictures and objects to Chiswick.

Behind Burlington House, fronting directly onto the garden wall, was the third important essay in the new Palladian manner, and 'a very noble one', according to Macky in his *Journey Through England*.[9] This was Queensberry House, begun in 1721 for the first Earl of Darnley and completed for the third Duke of Queensberry who bought it in 1723, having given an undertaking to his landlord, Lord Burlington, that he would not let the house 'for a Butcher's shop or shop slaughter house poulterer's house or shop Tallow Chandler Melter of Tallow Soap-maker Tobacco Pipe Maker Brewhouse Distiller Farrier or Blacksmith'.[10] It was designed by Giacomo Leoni; his use of a giant order of pilasters to emphasise the central bays was soon quite widely imitated, while the façade became accepted as one of the basic designs for larger town houses, such as 17 Bruton Street, built by Isaac Ware in 1740. This house, which was the birthplace of the present Queen, was demolished in 1937 – a sad loss, since

See colour plate 4

it was noted not only for its impressive Palladian front, but for an interior which included a vaulted entrance hall, a fine saloon, and a number of richly decorated ceilings.

It took some time for the Palladian movement to become widely adopted. Robert Benson, Lord Bingley, for one, employed a stalwart of the English baroque school, Thomas Archer, the architect of St John's, Smith Square, when he wished to build himself a house in Cavendish Square. The only existing contemporary engraving of this shows it to have been a rather clumsy composition, though the accompanying inscription suggests that the fault might not have been entirely Archer's ('it was drawn by Mr Archer, but Built and Altered to what it is now by Edward Wilcox Esq'). It certainly did not impress the second Earl of Oxford who, on a visit to Lord Bingley's house in Yorkshire, Bramham Park, also the work of Archer, remarked that Lord Bingley 'may think it no great compliment to the architecture of it, to say that it makes a better appearance on the outside than that of his Lordship's in Cavendish Square'.[11] Occupying almost the whole of the west side of the square, its interior was elaborately decorated – in particular the ceilings, which were far richer than any that survive in an Archer house, being the work of the Italian *stuccatore* Serena, and incorporating paintings by Tillemans. When Horace Walpole dined there with the then owner, the second Viscount Harcourt, he wrote: 'I like the Hôtel d'Harcourt, it has a grand air and a kind of Louis XIV old-fashioned quality that pleases me.'[12] Other patrons of Archer were Sir James Bateman, who employed him on the refacing of Monmouth House, Soho Square, and the Earl of Orford, for whom he built Russell House, at 43 King Street in Covent Garden.

There was also little that was original in the plans for a veritable palace to be built by James Brydges, the 'princely' first Duke of Chandos, on the north side of Cavendish Square, and intended to complement his vast house at Cannons, Middlesex (a baroque edifice by John Price erected, according to Defoe, 'with such a Profusion of Expense, and all finished with such a Brightness of Fancy ... that it has hardly its equal in England').[13] However, owing to his extravagance and disastrous speculative investments, culminating in the South Sea Bubble ('all he got by fraud is lost by stocks', commented Dean Swift[14]), only the outer service wings were ever finished, one of which still stands on the corner of Harley Street. The only known record of this project, an engraving by its designer, John Price, shows that it was conceived in the tradition of William Talman as a massive flat-roofed cube; and though it might have looked splendid when seen from Hanover Square, it would soon have struck contemporaries as a rather old-fashioned pile. The two large houses with palatial stone porticos and Corinthian columns which can still be seen on the north side of the square were never, as often claimed, gate lodges to a drive which was to lead to Cannons, but were erected on the vacant site in 1769 as a speculation by a Mr Tufnell.[15]

James Brydges, first Duke of Chandos, by Herman Van der Myn *c.* 1725.

An interior of
Harcourt House,
Cavendish Square.

Below: The staircase
of Harcourt House.

A design by John
Price for a house for
the Duke of Chandos,
1720.

A natural conservatism on the part of some of the aristocracy was not the
only factor responsible for the slow spread of the Palladian movement. Equally
important, perhaps, was the comparatively slow development of the book trade.
After Leoni's *The Architecture of A. Palladio* and the first volume of *Vitruvius
Britannicus* had come out in 1715, there was a lull broken only by the appear-
ance of the next two volumes of *Vitruvius*, in 1717 and 1725 respectively.
These were followed by William Kent's *Designs of Inigo Jones* in 1727, and
James Gibbs's *Book of Architecture* in 1728. Moreover these books gave sur-
prisingly little attention to town house design. In his first volume Campbell
had included Old Burlington House, Montagu House, Marlborough House,
Powis House, Buckingham House, Lindsey House, and the proposal for Lord
Islay. In the second volume, however, there were no town houses, while the
third included only General Wade's house, Pembroke House, and the new
façade at Burlington House. Kent's book contained some interior details from
London houses, but no thought was given to planning. In Gibbs's book there
was nothing at all. The general lack of importance that still seemed to be
attached to grand London houses is well demonstrated by the fact that when
an engraving of Queensberry House was published in 1726, it was shown in a
country setting.

Yet this second decade of the eighteenth century saw building speculation
in West London reach a feverish level – 'a kind of Prodigy', as Daniel Defoe
called it.[16] 'I went away towards Hyde Park', he wrote in Applebee's *Weekly
Journal* in 1725,

being told of a fine avenue made to the east side of the Park, fine Gates and a large
Vista, or opening, from the new Squares called Hanover Square, etc. ... In the Tour

I passed an amazing Scene of new Foundations, not of houses only, but as I might say of new Cities. New Towns, new Squares, and fine Buildings, the like of which no City, no Town, nay, no Place in the World can shew; nor is it possible to judge where or when, they will make an end or stop of Building ... All the Way through this new Scene I saw the World full of Bricklayers and Labourers; who seem to have little else to do, but Like Gardeners, to dig a Hole, put in a few Bricks, and presently there goes up a House.[17]

A view of Hanover Square, looking south: the first of the new developments. Drawing by Edward Dayes, 1787.

This flurry of building can be attributed to the favourable political climate which followed the Peace of Utrecht and the crushing of the 1715 Jacobite rebellion, and also to a general desire on the part of the better-off members of society to escape the dangers inherent in the more crowded areas of the city. 'The City [the whole of London] does not increase,' commented Defoe, 'but only the Situation of it is going to be removed, and the Inhabitants are quitting the old Noble Streets and Squares where they used to live, and are removing into the Fields for fear of Infection; so that, as the people are run away into the Country, the Houses seem to be running away too.'[18]

Hanover Square, the first of the new developments, was built between 1717 and 1719. At the same time Lord Burlington was beginning to build up Burlington Gardens, Savile Row, and other streets behind his Piccadilly mansion. On the fields to the west of Bond Street, Grosvenor Square was laid out on a grand scale in the 1720s to form the nucleus of Sir Richard Grosvenor's estate. North of Oxford Street, Lord Harley and his wife, Lady Cavendish, commissioned a plan for the development of their estate, with Cavendish Square as its focal point, while at the south end of Mayfair, Lord Berkeley began the laying-out of Berkeley Square.

A view of Grosvenor Square. Drawing by Edward Dayes, 1789.

At the same time society was flourishing with a gaiety reminiscent of the brilliant days of the Restoration. It was no wonder, wrote Chesterfield, 'that pleasures pent up and in some measure incarcerated during two former reigns, should rush out with impetuosity in this; they did so "qua data porta", and every door was willingly open to them.'[19] John Macky, who came to London in 1714, certainly found it so. 'We rise by nine', he wrote,

and those that frequent great men's levees find entertainment at them till eleven, or, as in Holland, go to Tea Tables. About twelve the Beaumonde assembles in several Chocolate and Coffee-Houses: the best of which are the Cocoa-Tree and White's Chocolate-Houses, St James's, the Smyrna and the British Coffee-Houses: and all these so near one another, that in less than an Hour you see the Company of them all. We are carried to these places in Chairs (or Sedans) which are here very cheap, a Guinea a Week, or a Shilling per Hour, and your Chairmen serve you for Porters to run on Errands as your Gondoliers do at Venice. If it be fine Weather, we take a turn in the Park till two, when we go to Dinner; and if it be dirty, you are entertained at Picket or Basset at White's, or you may talk Politics at the Smyrna and St James's. I

must not forget to tell you, that the Parties have their different Places ... a Whig will no more go to the Cocoa Tree or Ozinda's, than a Tory will be seen at the Coffee-House of St James's ... the general way here is to make a party at the Coffee-House to go to dine at the Tavern, where we sit till six, then we go to the Play; except you are invited to the Table of some Great man, which strangers are always courted to, and nobly entertained ...[20]

A scene in St James's Street looking down towards White's Coffee House, from 'A Rake's Progress' by William Hogarth, 1735.

There can have been few more noble entertainments than that given in 1711 by the second Earl of Portland in his house at 31 St James's Square – the very house over which Lady Wentworth had so enthused, and onto which he had added a 'Great Room', thus realising her favourite scheme for a 'gallery over the offices'. The evening was given in honour of Prince Eugene of Savoy, and details of it have survived in a contemporary letter. Many parties were given for this great hero but, we are told, 'there has not been one that came to the twentieth part of what my Lord Portland did'. In style it was in the medieval tradition, with the men separated from the women, and it was 'the finest that ever was seen', not for its size, but for the richness of its accompaniments. Seventeen noblemen sat down to dinner at six o'clock, immediately following a sitting of the House of Lords, including the Dukes of Marlborough, Devonshire, and Bolton, and the Lords Sunderland, Hervey, Townshend, Dorchester, and Godolphin, and were waited upon throughout, not by servants in livery, but by

gentlemen that offered themselves, to have an occasion to see the feast.

The Linen and the Plate is the finest in England, the buffet for the gilt and silver plate as rich as any and for the china dishes and plates none in England come near my Lord's ... during the whole dinner, played in a room adjoining, Trumpets and Kettle-drums ... The dinner consisted in 26 dishes, the centre and four corners which was soups, being afterwards taken up and relieved by five others, so made it 31 for the first course. The Second Course was 33 dishes, both courses of the best that London could afford, and the best dressed, for there was eight cooks in the kitchen, and those Topping ones. What I observed most rare, being outlandish victuals, was at the first course a wild Boar's head from Germany, at the second 24 Ortolans ... The fruit was all served in china, 43 dishes large and set up in pyramids. It was a perfect garden to see, and like a beautiful landscape, the variety of fruit colours, glasses, and the gold and red and other colours of the china adding a new lustre to the whole; in short nothing could be more magnificent.

When dinner was over, at about nine o'clock, the whole company moved upstairs to the countess's apartments 'where several persons of quality of both sexes had been invited to cards with my Lady, and to hear the Symphony, which begun and lasted till about Ten. They were about 20 musicians of the opera, both vocal and instrumental music.' In the meantime, in the great room downstairs, the tables and buffet were cleared away and an orchestra was set up in an 'alcove on purpose contrived for the music', in preparation for a ball. This began as soon as the concert was over, and was opened by the Countess of Portland and the Ambassador to Venice dancing a minuet, Prince Eugene having declined the honour. Fifteen couples then 'exerted their legs and heels in a most eloquent manner' till three o'clock in the morning. 'After the Ball, they came down in my Lord's apartments where there was 2 Tables, one for the Lords, another for the Ladies. His Highness declining to sit down went behind my Lady Portland, the rest did the same to the other Ladies, and waited upon the Beauties, who on my Lady's invitation drunk the Prince's health.' This supper, which went on till five o'clock, consisted of fifty dishes served all at once 'meat and fruit, hot and cold', and was 'performed in the greatest order and magnificence imaginable so that the Prince said then, as he has done since, that he never was entertained so completely anywhere'.[21]

The diaries and letters of the day are filled with descriptions of such entertainments, and of the hectic comings and goings of the 'ton', as high society was then called. Sadly, few paintings and prints of this life survive which one can recognise as being set in London houses. Among the exceptions are 'A

Nobleman's Levee' by Marcellus Laroon; the nobleman in question is thought   *See colour plate 5*
to be John, second Duke of Montagu. Levees, which were almost exclusively
London events, were held each morning by the King and by all the great
noblemen, whose importance could be estimated by the number of people who
attended them. They took place while the King or nobleman was dressing, and
provided an opportunity for his subordinates to present petitions, or ask for
jobs and favours. While the truly favoured might be received in his bedroom
or dressing-room, the majority had to wait patiently until he deigned to appear
in an ante-room, probably still in the final stages of having his wig dressed by
his barber.

Long while we had not held Chit Chat,
Before his Grace appear'd
And with his ever pleasing Air
Our hearts and faces cheered
Then beck'ning us all one by one
He spoke to each so pat
That all rejoyc'd his Levee left
But I who smelled a Rat.[22]

Thomas Pelham-Holles, Duke of Newcastle, who was Secretary of State
under George II, was renowned for his levees at Newcastle House. 'His levees
were his pleasure and his triumph,' wrote Lord Chesterfield,

he loved to have them crowded and consequently they were so. There he generally
made people of business wait two or three hours in the ante-chamber, while he trifled
away that time with some insignificant favourite in his closet. When at last he came
into his levee-room, he accosted, hugged, embraced, and promised everybody, with a
seeming cordiality, but at the same time with an illiberal and degrading familiarity.[23]

Women too held levees, though of a more intimate nature, and concerned
not so much with politics and patronage, as with flirtation and amusement. In
Hogarth's *The Countess's Levee*, the Countess of Squanderfield receives a
mixed company while she has her hair dressed. An antique dealer has brought
some *objets d'art* for her perusal. A dandy in hair curlers sips chocolate, while
his neighbour affects to be entranced by the music of a flautist and a singer.
Behind him a squire up from the country has fallen fast asleep, riding whip in
hand. The Countess's fashionable friend appears to be too busy listening to
the singing to regale her with the day's gossip, so she turns instead to her
beau, Silvertongue, who has also bought her some tickets for a masquerade.
No doubt it consisted of the kind of tittle-tattle repeated by that arch-gossip
Lady Mary Wortley Montagu in her letters to her sister, the Countess of Mar:

All our acquaintances are run mad; they do such things! such monstrous and
stupendous things! Lady Hervey and Lady Bristol have quarrelled in such a polite
manner that they have given one another all the titles so liberally bestowed amongst
the ladies at Billingsgate.[24]

The Countess's Levee.
From Hogarth's
'Marriage-à-la-Mode'.

Lady Letchmere has lost such furious sums at Bath that it may be questioned whether all the sweetness the waters can out into my Lord's blood, can make him endure it, particularly 7001 at one sitting.[25]

Lord Teynham, we learn, has shot himself,[26] while Lord Denbigh is in Paris with his Dutch lady, 'who I am very certain is the produce of some French valet de chambre. She is entertaining enough'.[27] Lord Carleton has died

and disposed of his estate as he did of his time, between Lady Clarendon and the Duchess of Queensberry. Jewels to a great value he has given, as he did his affections, first to the mother, and then to the daughter. He was taken ill in my company at a concert at the Duchess of Marlborough's, and died two days after, holding the fair Duchess by the hand, and being fed at the same time with a fine fat chicken; thus dying as he had lived, indulging his pleasures.[28]

Another charming picture set out in a London house is *An Assembly at Lord Harrington's*, by Charles Phillips. Lady Mary Wortley Montagu wrote in 1723 that assemblies 'rage in this part of the world; there is not a street in town free from them, and some spirited ladies go to seven in a night',[29] and they formed the most important new type of entertainment in the eighteenth

See colour plate 7

century. They were mixed affairs which took place in the evening and, in that they involved several activities taking place at the same time, they represented a significant break away from earlier, more formal types of entertainment. In the first half of the eighteenth century they were inclined to be comparatively small affairs, involving no more than eight or nine couples, and usually taking place in one room. In that depicted at Lord Harrington's, for example, the ladies on the left, who include Lady Betty Germain and the Duchess of Montagu (fifth and sixth from the left), are taking tea. To the right of them the Duchess of Dorset and Lady Suffolk are playing cards, while the rest of the company indulge in conversation, more cards, and that most popular of eighteenth-century pastimes, flirtation. But as the century moved on they were to develop into vast and extravagant affairs, involving hundreds, even thousands of people.

A Musical Assembly. by Marcellus Laroon.

See colour plate 7

By the mid-eighteenth century assemblies began to merge with balls. 'Mr Howard', wrote Peter Wentworth to his brother, Lord Wentworth, in 1731, 'opens his assembly with a ball.'[30] These still remained relatively intimate gatherings, but took place in more than one room and were invariably accompanied by a supper. 'We was last night at the Duke of Devonshire', wrote Lady Wentworth to her father in March 1733,

Opposite, top: The front elevation of Devonshire House.

Opposite, bottom: A view of Devonshire House showing the great wall facing onto Piccadilly.

it was a ball, there was eight couples, *viz* Lady Caroline Cavendish and Lord Sunbury, Lord Hartington and Lady Mary Montagu, Lord Conway and Lady Harriet [Wentworth], Mr Walpole and Lady Lucy [Wentworth], Mr Conway and Miss Wortley, a Mr Webster and Lady Dorothy [Wentworth], Mr Whitworth and Lady Betty Cavendish, me and Lady Betty Montagu: and we had a very handsome supper, *viz:* at the upper end cold chicken, next to that a dish of cake, parch'd almonds, sapp biskets, next to that, a dish of tarts and cheesecakes, next to that a great custard, and to that another dish of biskets, parch'd almonds, and preserved apricots and next a quarter of lamb.[31]

Devonshire House, where this ball took place, was in fact none other than the former Berkeley House, at the westernmost end of Piccadilly, which the first Duke of Devonshire had bought in 1698, having abandoned a plan to build a house in Lambs Conduit Fields, a design for which exists by Talman. It is easy to understand why he preferred this site, for not only was it wonderfully convenient for the Court, but it was also so open, with a garden that extended behind it to the south end of what is now Berkeley Square. In October 1733, seven months after Lady Wentworth had attended the party, a fire broke out as the result of the carelessness of some workmen who had been carrying out alterations, and, in spite of exhaustive efforts to save it by a detachment of the Guards under Lord Albemarle, and other troops and firefighters marshalled by Frederick, Prince of Wales, who had come up from Carlton House, the house, with its beautiful painted staircase by Laguerre, was completely destroyed. One curious treasure which survived was the *trompe l'oeil* violin painted on one of the doors by John Vandervaart, which is now at Chatsworth.

A sketch of William Kent by Dorothy, Countess of Burlington.

The third Duke, 'plain in his manners, negligent in his dress',[32] wasted no time in planning its successor, and gave the commission to William Kent, who was fresh from completing Kew Palace for the Prince of Wales. Whether it was due to the influence of his employer, or simply that, as Chambers wrote, 'Mr Kent ... was fond of puzzling his spectators', the result was, by any standards, extraordinarily reserved, with no hint of the grandeur of his work to come, such as can be seen at Holkham Hall in Norfolk, or at 44 Berkeley Square. The new Devonshire House consisted of a long block of eleven bays, projecting slightly at either end and in the centre, and unadorned by a portico, or even by carvings in the pediment. Apart from stone window architraves, which offered some contrast to the simple brickwork of the walls, the only decorative feature was a double staircase leading up to the first-floor hall. 'It is spacious', wrote James Ralph in 1734, adding sarcastically, 'and so are the East India Company's warehouses; and both are equally deserving praise.'[33] The façade was, in fact, completely hidden from Piccadilly by a high wall, 'a horrid blank of wall, cheerless and unsocial by day, and terrible by night',[34] pierced by two entrances with solid doors, which gave it a fortress-like appearance and was generally bitterly resented. 'Would it be credible', wrote a com-

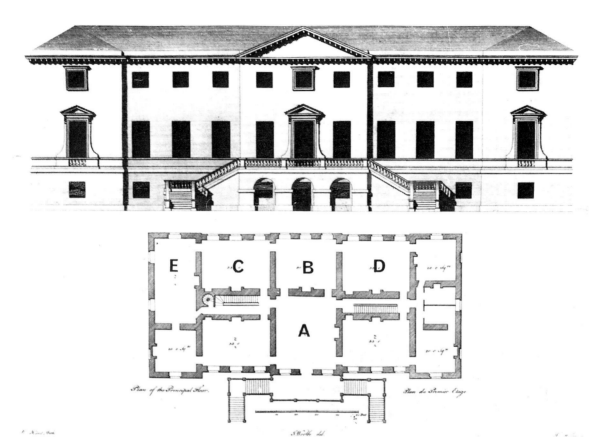

mentator in 1783, 'if the fact did not put it out of controversy, that any man of taste, fashion, and figure would prefer the solitary grandeur of enclosing himself in a jail, to the enjoyment of the first view in Britain, which he might possess by throwing down this execrable brick screen?'[35]

There was, however, good reason for such a wall, for outside it life was dirty, noisy and dangerous. The streets of London in the 1730s, Piccadilly included, were a far cry from those we know today. For a start, few were paved. They were rough thoroughfares, full of cavities harbouring water and filth; until the scavengers came to clear them out, the ditches which ran down either side of them became receptacles for heaps of garbage and rubbish 'of all hues and odours'. An endless procession of horses' hooves and the large iron wheels of heavy waggons and coaches did little to improve their condition, and covered anything in the vicinity with a shower of mud or dust. A survey published in 1739 reckoned that there were 2,484 private coaches in London, and 1,100 for hire, all of which contributed a continuous clatter to the already tumultuous street noises, the most noticeable features of which were the cries of a multitude of street vendors plying their wares:

a hundred voices screaming out, 'Brickdust! – Knives to grind – Scissors to grind! – Come buy my watercresses! New laid eggs, five a groat! ... Hot mutton pies, hot! – Buy my cod, dainty live cod! Coach! Coach! Coach! – You! Smouch! will ye have some pork? Crab! crab! will ye crab? ... The last dying Speech and Confession, both Parentage and Education, Life, Character, and behaviour of all the Malefactors that were executed this morning at Tyburn! ... Chestnuts! threepence a hundred chestnuts! Ground ivy! Come buy my ground ivy! – Cat's meat, or dog's meat! ... Buy my

Right: (L to R) 'Buy my fine singing Glasses':

'12 Pence a Peck Oysters';

'Knives Combs or Inkhornes'.

Far right: A caricature by Rowlandson of a typical watchman, 1800.

roasted pig! A long-tailed pig, or a short-tailed pig, or a pig without ever a tail! ... Hot loaves! ... Oysters! buy my oysters! – Sparrowgrass! buy my sparrowgrass! – Artichokes! fresh artichokes! – Potatoes! two full pound a penny, potatoes! Fine Kentish cherries, a penny a pound! – Swe-e-e-e-eeep![36]

At night out came the housebreakers and footpads, from whom none were safe.

Prepare for death if here at night you roam,
And sign your will before you sup at home

wrote Dr Johnson in his poem, 'London', and he did not exaggerate. Apart from the existence of bands of elderly watchmen, who invariably proved to be of little use, there was no police force to protect the citizens of London after dark, with the result that the activities of highwaymen were not restricted to the outlying areas of the town. Among countless similar accounts of robberies is one by Horace Walpole, witnessed from his dining-room in Arlington Street: 'The clock had not struck eleven, when I heard a loud cry of Stop thief! A highwayman had attacked a post-chaise in Piccadilly, within fifty yards of this house: the fellow was pursued, rode over the watchman, almost killed him, and escaped.' Another story tells of a highwayman who was pursued so hotly along Curzon Street that he could only escape by spurring his horse through the narrow walled passage dividing the gardens of Devonshire House and Shelburne House, and was so able to gallop unchecked to Berkeley Square and liberty.[37]

The interior of Devonshire House was far more successful than its façade.

The entrance hall at Devonshire House. Drawing (1811) showing Kent's interior.

Writing in 1819, Samuel Ware described it as being 'one of a continued range of eleven rooms equally well calculated for state, as domestic use, uninterrupted by passage or staircase ...'[38] Guests climbed the outer staircase at the south front and entered the grand entrance hall, two storeys high, and flanked by two drawing-rooms identical in size. There was no saloon as such, but beyond the hall, in the centre of the north front, was a great drawing-room, with two more rooms of similar size on either side, one of which was a library. The remaining accommodation on the principal floor comprised a dining-room, another drawing-room, and the Duke and Duchess's sleeping quarters. On either side of the hall were staircases, which rose between the two ranges of state rooms. This circuit was to remain virtually unaltered by later dukes with the exception that the sixth Duke, finding the outside approach to the *piano nobile* inconvenient, decided it would be better to turn the house round by making the grand hall into a saloon and building a new staircase on the north side of the house.

The limited amount that is known about them suggests that the contents were splendid – far more so than those at Chatsworth. Vertue had visited the latter in 1727 and found little to comment on apart from Holbein's cartoon for Henry VIII, while Thomas Martyn wrote in *The English Connoisseur* (1766) that 'Chatsworth has very little in it that can attract the eye of the Connoisseur. The grandeur with which it is fitted up, the magnificence of the marble portals, and the great quantity of rich carving, by the famous Gibbons, are all very striking ... The pictures are few in number and indifferent.'[39] This was reflected in a valuation of the two houses made in 1798, which put the total value of Devonshire House at £29,285 11s 1d, as against £22,321 10s 6d for Chatsworth, which included £4,760 13s 6d for farming stock and instruments of husbandry. A break-down of the totals shows that the greatest differences lay in the plate, linen, and china, which at Devonshire House came to £6,819 as opposed to £1,721 at Chatsworth, and in the books, prints, and pictures, which came to £13,311 in London as opposed to only £3,428 in Derbyshire. Devonshire House included some magnificent furniture designed for it by Kent, including a principal suite consisting of twenty-nine chairs, a sofa, three settees, a day bed and a stool, which can still be seen at Chatsworth.

But it was the picture collection that took pride of place at Devonshire House. It was, commented Martyn, 'surpassed by very few either at home or abroad'.[40] Horace Walpole wrote of the third Duke that 'No one knows pictures better', and there are several lists of paintings bought by him and his predecessor, of which the earliest published is that given by Dodsley.[41] He mentions several Van Dyck portraits now at Chatsworth, Rembrandt's *Old Man in a Turkish Dress*, Poussin's *Et in Arcadia Ego*, Rubens's copy of Titian's portrait of Philip II, as well as works by Bassano, Claude, Veronese, Tintoretto, Giordano, Le Sueur, Albano, the Carracci, and Salvator Rosa. Writing some years later, and before the sales of the Napoleonic period, when many other English collections were similarly enriched, Thomas Pennant considered that 'the collection of pictures by the great Italian masters, is by far the finest private collection now in England'.[42] Remarkably, considering the depredations caused by death duties, the greatest part of this collection is still intact, and at Chatsworth one can get a marvellous insight into the taste of an important collector of the period.

It is not known exactly when the new house was completed. Only one letter from Kent to the Duke survives, dated 22 July 1736, in which he writes:

The Building is gone exceedingly well on, and ye Season has been extreamly favourable for it, and now can come up to the Attick floor, the Brickwork of the principal floor is measured and comes to the sum of six hundred eighty two pounds five shillings and sixpence - I reckon at the same time will be required about two hundred pounds for the mason and one hundred for the carpenter ... by the time I hear your Grace to be in town the Building will be quite cover'd in ...[43]

After that there is but one receipt, dated 1 May 1740, for £1,000 to pay the workmen. The Duke was therefore probably living there intermittently from the early 1740s onwards, along with his wife Catherine and their children – four sons and three daughters, whose nicknames were Mrs Hopeful, Mrs Tiddle, Guts and Gundy, Puss, Cat, and Toe. 'The Duchess of Devonshire', wrote Horace Walpole, 'was more dreadfully vulgar than you could imagine:

William, third Duke
of Devonshire, by
J. Richardson.

3ʳᵈ Duke of Devonʃhire.

complained of the wet night and how the men would dirty the rooms with
their shoes, called out at supper to the Duke, "Good Lord, my Lord, don't
cut the ham – nobody will eat any!".[44] It was to be during the reign of a later
Duchess, when it was the unofficial headquarters of the Whig party, that
Devonshire House enjoyed the most splendid years of its existence.

As the Duke moved into his new residence, Kent was beginning work on
one of the masterpieces of the eighteenth century, a Palladian jewel which
many consider to be the crowning glory of his career. This time, however, it
was not a great family *hôtel* he was building, but a much smaller house for
a middle-aged spinster of noble birth and uncertain means. Lady Isabella
Finch, or Lady Bel as she was known to her contemporaries, was one of the
seven daughters, and seventeen children, of the second Earl of Nottingham

(and seventh Earl of Winchelsea), a powerful Tory politician and churchman whose dark complexion and air of religious gloom had earned him the nickname of 'Don Dismal'. Bel, who acted as lady-in-waiting to the two unmarried daughters of George II, the princesses Emily and Charlotte, was well known to Horace Walpole, who seems to have considered her rather a stiff woman, exuding snobbery and respectability: she refused to present her brother's illegitimate daughter to the two princesses, even though she had already been received by the King and Queen. He also made regular comments on the swarthiness which she and her sisters had inherited from their father, referring to them as 'the sable Finches'. On one occasion, writing to Lady Aylesbury from Strawberry Hill, he commented that if there were not soon some rain, 'I shall not have a leaf left. Strawberry is browner than Lady Bel Finch.'[45] If Walpole found her dull, Lady Pomfret certainly did not, and 'used to lug a half-length picture of [her] ... behind her post-chaise all over Italy, and have a new frame made for it in every town where she stopped'.[46]

Few respectable spinsters of the day can have been housed quite as magnificently as Lady Bel at 44 Berkeley Square. Kent had just completed Holkham in Norfolk for Thomas Coke, Earl of Leicester. With its noble, columned entrance hall derived from Roman basilicas and temples, it is one of the great monuments of the Burlington school; and to it the interior of No. 44 was closely related, if on a greatly reduced scale. On first setting foot in her friend's new home, Lady Pomfret may have been charmed but not impressed by the deceptively simple and small entrance hall, with an arch, aligned on the door, through which she could see the staircase hall and, beyond that, the dining-room. Once inside the staircase hall, however, she would have been a dull woman indeed had she not caught her breath at the palatial nature of what then faced her.

Until now staircases had been relatively unimaginative affairs, consisting essentially of flights of stairs rising round the inside walls of a square box, and occasionally made more interesting by bouts of sumptuous decoration. As features they were invariably subordinate to the great hall. None of this was true of the staircase Kent provided for Lady Bel and her friends to walk up. It rose from the very centre of the hall, causing the eye to gaze upwards through architectural forms of gathering complexity. Thirteen steps led up to a half-landing, there becoming a double flight rising into a concave screen of Ionic columns on the first floor, behind which another flight wound steeply upwards, emerging in an open gallery where the concave rhythms were repeated. All this was top-lit from a vaulted and delicately plastered ceiling which, like the plasterwork decorating the whole staircase, glittered with gilding. The whole effect was wonderfully theatrical, and inspired Horace Walpole, indifferent as he was to the charms of its owner, to describe it as being 'as beautiful a piece of scenery, and considering the space, of art, as can be imagined'.[47]

Above: The façade of
44 Berkeley Square.

Right: The entrance
hall, 44 Berkeley
Square.

Far right: Section of
the staircase, 44
Berkeley Square.

Drawing of the
staircase hall, 44
Berkeley Square.

Far right: The vaulted
and plastered ceiling
of the staircase hall,
44 Berkeley Square.

Kent contrived another surprise for Lady Bel and her friends in the saloon, or great room, which overlooked Berkeley Square. Here the dominant feature was the high coved and coffered ceiling rising up through the second storey of the house; the coffers were divided up by a bold honeycomb pattern of richly moulded and gilded ribs, and each one was painted with groups of classical figures in grisaille. This was a breakaway from the baroque, which favoured single large compositions, and made the ceiling much more architectural. It was an idea which derived from Italian ceilings of the High Renaissance, such as those at the Villa Madama in Rome and the Doge's palace in Venice, and Kent repeated it at 22 Arlington Street, a house he built for Henry Pelham during the same period. Glowing in crimson and gold, the saloon at 44 Berkeley Square gave an impression of great splendour, and guests must have felt that they were in the ante-room of some palace.

Quite why a woman like Lady Bel required such an exceedingly grand house remains something of a mystery, and one can only assume that it was for the occasional reception of her royal mistresses, and possibly even the King, as well as of her noble relations, such as her brothers-in-law, the Dukes of Somerset and Cleveland, the Marquis of Rockingham, the Earl of Mansfield, and Sir Roger Mostyn. On the whole, however, as Horace Walpole has led us to believe, her entertainments were inclined to be dull affairs, mostly small card parties: 'We had a funereal loo last night in the great chamber at Lady Bel Finch's.'[48] What a scene is conjured up of the effeminate Horace surrounded by Lady Bel and her gossipy cronies, among them perhaps the prim Lady Betty Germain, the rather sour Lady Mary Coke, and no doubt her ardent admirer Lady Pomfret, pushing cards gloomily round a table.

Kent was the only one of the first generation of Palladians to be a good decorator, a talent he probably owed to his training as a painter. He had a good colour sense and a feeling for rich effects, but his style was essentially a formal one, and he was at his happiest using heavy textured and patterned materials and splendidly carved and gilt mahogany, of which his work at Houghton and Holkham provide typical examples. At Lady Bel's, however, a new freedom was evident in his work – which was significant, because it happened to coincide, fortuitously or not, with the first rumblings of opposition to the rigidity of Burlingtonian Palladianism. This reaction was hardly surprising in a city like London, where fashions were quickly tired of. 'People are sick of Grecian elegance and symmetry, or Gothic grandeur and magnificence', wrote Mrs Montagu in 1749, and one only has to look at the way in which portrait painting was developing, and the appearance of the conversation piece, to see that a degree of informality was creeping into art.

Mark Girouard has traced the origins of this movement back to the mid-1730s, to a circle of artists who frequented Old Slaughters Coffee House in St Martin's Lane, and included Hogarth, Roubiliac, Francis Hayman, Nollekens and, above all, Hubert François Gravelot.[49] A young and rebellious crowd,

Opposite: The saloon, 44 Berkeley Square.

An engraving by Gravelot on sheet music: 'The Adieu to Spring-Gardens', a song of 1735.

Opposite: The Pleasure Gardens at Vauxhall. Top: Engraved for the *Universal Magazine* 1750. Bottom: A general view of Vauxhall Gardens.

they had little interest in the classical tradition, but were alive to new movements in France – and in particular the rococo, which was anathema to the Palladians. More than any of them, perhaps, Gravelot was responsible for introducing the sophistication and gaiety of the French style through his superb illustrations to such books as *Heads and Monuments of the Kings*, published in 1736, which contains some of the earliest important English examples of rococo design. More of his highly decorative work appeared in Birch's *Heads of Illustrious Persons*, and John Pine's *Tapestry Hangings of the House of Lords*, and undoubtedly inspired the impresario Jonathan Tyers to commission, from 1738 onwards, Gravelot and his contemporaries to produce paintings and sculpture for the supper-boxes, pavilions and temples at his Vauxhall Gardens, which soon became perhaps the most complete and convincing expression of the rococo in England. They were rococo not only in their decoration, but in the light-hearted and fantastic underlying concept:

The gardens at last, amid groves and avenues, arcades and colonnades, ... and brilliantly illuminated with innumerable vari-coloured lamps, boasted a magnificent orchestra, a pavilion called the Hall of Mirrors, which was the principal supper-room: a rotunda, a large handsome building for feats of horsemanship, and the performance of ballets, fitted with pit, boxes, gallery, etc – a Turkish divan – a Swiss cottage – a Gothic gateway – an Italian walk – a Dark walk, and a profusion of white statues glittering amid the dark and shady trees.[50]

The pleasure gardens at Vauxhall, later rivalled by those at Ranelagh, were among those grand public meeting-places which formed a curious eighteenth-century phenomenon, their existence owing much to the general increase in society and the love of parade which accompanied it. The 'ton' gathered there night after night, to dance and listen to music, to eat, to flirt and gossip, or simply to perambulate with their friends. 'I had a card from Lady Caroline Petersham', wrote Walpole to Montagu on 23 June 1750,

to go with her to Vauxhall. I went accordingly to her house and found her and the little Ashe, or the Pollard Ashe as they call her; they had just finished their last layer of red, and looked as handsome as crimson could make them ... We marched to our barge, with a boat of french horns attending and little Ashe singing. We paraded some time up the river, and at last debarked at Vauxhall ... Here we picked up Lord Granby, arrived very drunk from Jenny's Whim ... At last we assembled in our booth, Lady Caroline in the front, with the vizor of her hat erect, and looking gloriously jolly and handsome. She had fetched my brother Orford from the next box, where he was enjoying himself with his *petite partie*, to help us to mince chickens. We minced seven chickens into a China dish, which Lady Caroline stewed over a lamp with three pats of butter and a flagon of water, stirring and rattling and laughing, and we every minute expecting the dish to fly about our ears. She had brought Betty the fruit-girl, with hampers of strawberries and cherries from Rogers, and made her wait upon us, and then made her sup by us at a little table ... In short, the whole air of our party was sufficient, as you will easily imagine, to take up the whole attention of the Garden; so much so, that from 11 o'clock till half an hour after 1 we had the whole concourse round our booth; at last they came into the little gardens of each booth on the sides of ours, till Harry Vane took up a bumper and drank their healths, and was proceeding to treat them with still greater freedoms. It was 3 o'clock before we got home.[51]

Since Vauxhall Gardens was one of the most fashionable meeting-places of the day, its influence must have been considerable. It was not long before the first important rococo interior in London made its appearance, in the new house built by Lord Chesterfield.

4

The Age of Parade

I am at present in the process of ruining myself by building a fine house ... which will be finished in the French style with abundance of sculptures and gilding.

Lord Chesterfield to Madame de Monconseil

Philip Stanhope, fourth Earl of Chesterfield, was a far cry from the run-of-the-mill English nobleman from the shires who rolled up to London for the season and looked down his nose at everything foreign. For a start he hated the family seat at Bretby in Derbyshire, having spent long months there while his father was dying: repeated fits had left the old Earl 'entirely senseless', and his son had begun to fear for his own sanity, 'this place being the seat of horror and despair, where no creatures but ravens, screech owls and birds of ill omen seem willingly to dwell'.[1] He was, in addition, a passionate francophile, and had been strongly influenced, on his various visits, by Paris and by the life he witnessed at the Bourbon court, the 'sumptuous elegance, finished manners and conversational perfection' of which had impressed him as the epitome of civilised life.[2] Its realisation in his own country was a goal which he pursued for the rest of his life. It could certainly not, in his opinion, be achieved in the country. 'Congenial society', he wrote to his friend Madame de Monconseil in July 1747, 'is, in the end, the greatest joy in life, and it can only be found in capitals. It is on this principal that I am at present in the process of ruining myself by building a fine house here, which will be finished in the French style with abundance of sculptures and gilding.'[3]

More than any other great house built in London during this period, Chesterfield House was a monument to the taste and learning of its owner. Even the site reflected its individuality: for rather than build in the heart of the aristocratic enclave of St James's, Chesterfield chose a location which he described as being so remote 'and situated among a parcel of thieves and murderers' that 'I shall have occasion for a house-dog'.[4] It faced onto what is now South Audley Street, and its isolation can best be seen in a drawing made in 1750 by Edward Eyre. On the right stands the Mayfair Chapel, alongside buildings which look curiously like warehouses running down the south side of Curzon Street, while to the west and north there is nothing between the house itself and where Hyde Park led up to Tyburn. It is curious to reflect

Above: A view of
Chesterfield House
showing its remote
location.

Right: Isaac Ware and
one of his daughters,
by Andrea Soldi,
c. 1754.

Far right: Philip
Stanhope, fourth Earl
of Chesterfield, after
W. Hoare, *c.* 1742.

that while the great man of letters sat in his library, perhaps writing one of
those celebrated letters to his son, there might have come to him through an
open window, carried by the wind, the distant, drunken howls of the mob as
they gazed upon the still-living body of some unfortunate wretch who had
been cut down from the gallows before being drawn and quartered. It was
partly this rascally element which gave the area its unsavoury reputation, since
many of them must have thronged through Mayfair on their way home, and
partly the vast crowds that were attracted to the May fair which took place

The May fair.

annually on the site of Shepherd's Market, and where, wrote Strype, 'young people did use to resort: and by the temptations they met with ... did commit much sin and disorder. Here they spent their time and money in drunkenness, fornication, gaming and lewdness. Whereby were occasioned oftentimes quarrels, tumults and shedding of blood.'[5]

Building was begun sometime early in 1746-7; the exact date is uncertain. Chesterfield chose as his architect Isaac Ware, a protégé of Burlington's, who is said to have begun life as a chimney-sweep's boy, and to have owed his career to some benevolent gentleman who, walking down Whitehall, found him sketching an elevation of the Banqueting House with a piece of chalk. Until fairly recently Ware was considered a rather curious choice, since he was ostensibly an arch-Palladian, with a strong antipathy to the rococo and the French in general – a view which he forcibly expressed in his book *The Complete Body of Architecture*, going so far as to write, 'Let us rouse in every soul the national spirit against them; and no more to permit them to deprave our taste in this noble science than to introduce among us the miseries of their government, a foolery of their religion.'[6] We now know, however, that not only did he have many contacts with the artists associated with the English rococo[7], but he was also responsible for the elaborate French-style interior of Woodcote Park, Surrey,[8] and probably for that of Belvedere in Kent as well.[9] *The Complete Body of Architecture* was published in 1756 – the year in which the Seven Years' War broke out – and it is possible that its views were simply patriotic. They were certainly in direct opposition to the work he carried out at Chesterfield House.

Ware devoted a whole section of *The Complete Body of Architecture* to Chesterfield House, entitling it 'The construction of a town-house of the

The gardens at Chesterfield House.

greatest elegance', and in doing so has left us with a valuable commentary not just on the design of the house itself, but on the way various rooms were used. Addressing himself to 'the young architect', he writes: 'we shall here lay before him the construction of a house in the highest degree elegant, built for a nobleman of the most distinguished taste, and adorned at the greatest expense.'[10] After explaining that the house faces west, and has a spacious garden to the east approached by a double flight of stone steps – William Beckford was to describe it as 'the finest private garden in London'[11] – he gives a detailed account of its layout:

The principal building has before it a court 177 foot in length, and 94 in breadth, terminated each way from the house by a Corinthian colonnade, and flanked by the wings, containing the offices. At the back of this court, and in its centre, is to stand the house, and its front is terminated by a wall and gates. This wall, including the offices, and continued round the garden, gives the general outline of the ground ... In the centre of the front wall of the court, and directly opposite to the centre of the house, are placed the great gates of entrance; a law we have shown to be founded on reason, but often neglected in great and good buildings.

This gateway, to suit it to the edifice, must be decorated with piers, and within, on

each side, is to be allowed a small square room for a porter's lodge ... the boundary wall is to be continued entire to the right; but the wing to the left, containing the coach-house and stables, should have the convenience of an opening to the street. This will require a gateway near the corner; but as this is intended for use, not show, and is too remote to catch the eye at the same time with the house; the less decoration is employed on it the better. Its place is marked by an opening in the wall of the court, and a plain wooden pair of gates will best suit the purpose. Entering the court the wings are to be seen on each hand; in the centre the principal building, and on each side the colonnade ... Under the colonnades are arcades open to the east, which make a communication between the offices under the house, and the north and south wings. We have observed that the coach-houses and stables are placed in the left wing, that being the north; and in the opposite, which is the right, or south wing, are the kitchen, larders, pantry, scullery, warehouse, and laundry. Over the stables is a mezzanine floor, properly divided for a granary; and above these are lodging rooms for servants. In the same manner the upper part of the other wing is divided into lodging rooms for servants, and thus is the whole of this magnificent building constructed ...

The façade of Chesterfield House.

Taking us inside the house, he tells how 'The entrance must be into a hall', explaining its modest size in this case by the fact that 'in town a hall is a place of reception for servants; therefore, in this, neither magnitude nor elegance are needful: in the country where there are other ways into the house, the hall may be an elegant room.' To the right

the great stair-case ascends with three flights of steps; and is of white and veined marble, of a very uncommon size and degree of perfection ... On the left, in the same range, will be the dining-parlour; and it will be a handsome room according to the proportion there allowed ... with regard to the larger space behind the dining-parlour ... let it be made into ... a magnificent and well-proportioned ante-room ... Behind the hall and staircase there must be back stairs, for in such a house this cannot be wanting ... A dressing-room, not far from the foot of the stair-case, is a very requisite apartment in a house of this kind; and near it there should be a waiting-room ... A dressing-room in the house of a person of fashion is a room of consequence, not only for its natural use in being the place of dressing, but for the several persons who are seen there. The morning is a time many choose for dispatching business; and as persons of this rank are not to be supposed to wait for people of that kind, they naturally give them orders to come about a certain hour, and admit them while they are dressing ...

The architect will naturally say, that here yet want the two great apartments for such a house as this; these are a drawing-room and a library: they must be on this floor ... The plan of these two rooms must be laid with perfect regularity; they must correspond with one another in all respects, in length, breadth, and height; and they will then have every article of convenience and grace. The room to the right is to be the library, and at the corner of this should be an adjoining little building for a water-closet; that on the left should be the drawing-room ...[12]

For a period of three years, from the summer of 1747, the progress of his new home occupied Chesterfield's every waking moment. 'My new house is near opening its doors to receive me', he wrote to his friend Bristowe in December,

and as soon as the weather shall be warm enough, I shall get into the necessary part of it, finishing the rest at my leisure. My eating-room, my dressing-room, mon Boudoir, and my Library will be completely finished in three months. My court, my Hall, and my staircase will really be magnificent. The staircase particularly will form such a scene, as is not in England. The expense will ruin me, but the enjoyment will please me.[13]

This staircase of which he was so proud, described by Vertue as being 'all of marble, each step made of an entire block and 20 feet in length',[14] occupied a space quite out of proportion to the size of the main block and equally out of proportion to the size of the upper rooms. Its justification seems to have been the splendid balustrade, so conveniently incorporating a coronet (albeit that of a duke) and a C, and the marble screen separating it from the hall, which Chesterfield had been unable to resist buying at the demolition sale at the Duke of Chandos's house, Cannons, in 1747.

In his boundless enthusiasm for the fitting up of his house, Chesterfield had his friends scouring the Continent for all manner of suitable furnishings, hangings and pictures. He was particularly ambitious as far as paintings were concerned, though never forgetful of the money they might cost him. 'A propos of money', he wrote to Solomon Dayrolles, a friend for whom he had secured a diplomatic post in the Hague,

as I believe it is much wanted by many people, even of fashion, both in Holland and Flanders, I should think it very likely that many good pictures of Rubens, Teniers, and other Flemish and Dutch masters, may be picked up now at reasonable rates. If so, you are likely to hear of it as a virtuoso; and, if so, I should be glad to profit of it as an humble dilettante. I have already, as you know, a most beautiful landscape by Rubens, and a pretty little piece by Teniers; but if you could meet with a large capital history or allegorical piece, of Rubens, with the figures as big as the life, I would go pretty deep to have it, as also for a large and capital picture of Teniers.[15]

Dayrolles did not fail him, and when the Rubens arrived he was delighted, declaring it to be 'the best I ever saw of Rubens ... the figure of the Virgin is the most graceful and beautiful I ever saw.'[16] 'All the Rubenses in England', he was later to declare, 'must strike to mine.'[17] There was the occasional mistake: 'I must say, as most fools do, who would have thought it? My fine Titian has turned out an execrable bad copy'[18] – but they were few and far between, and by the close of 1748 Chesterfield was able to write, 'My great room will be as full of pictures as it ought to be; and all capital ones.'[19]

Long frustrating months passed before Chesterfield actually moved in, and when he finally did so, early in 1749, he could not wait to share his happiness with his friends. To Madame de Monconseil he confided: 'An affair of the heart, and several serious matters, keep me here; the affair of the heart is that of my new house, in which I have not yet fully rejoiced.'[20] To Dayrolles he wrote of his utter delight in both his house and garden, heading the letter triumphantly, 'Hôtel Chesterfield': 'I have yet finished nothing but my boudoir and my library: the former is the gayest and most cheerful room in England, the latter the best. My garden is now turfed, planted and sown, and will in two months more make a scene of verdure and flowers not common in London.'[21] The boudoir, which was probably that room described by Ware as the dressing-room, was one of the four rooms for which the house became famous, decorated, as Chesterfield put it to Madame de Monconseil, 'entièrement à la Françoise'. 'Its ceiling and woodwork are of a beautiful blue', he told her, 'with many mouldings and gildings; the tapestries and chairs are covered with a flowered design in petit-point, a splendid pattern on a white background; over the chimney-piece of Giallo di Sienna marble, there is much mirror and moulding and gilding, in the centre of which hangs the portrait of a very beautiful woman, painted by Rosalba.'[22] The three other elaborately decorated rococo rooms were the ante-room on the ground floor, a room on the first floor over the waiting-room, and a beautiful music room at the head of the stairs.

A view through to the staircase, Chesterfield House.

The great staircase, Chesterfield House.

Opposite: The boudoir, Chesterfield House

Above: The drawing-room, Chesterfield House

Left: The ante-room, Chesterfield House.

The music-room,
Chesterfield House

But it is with the library that one tends to associate the great man of letters most – a room which, stuffed as it was with 'easy chairs and easy books',[23] must have been one of the most delightfully comfortable of the age. Bookcases, filled with 'rich and classical stores of literature',[24] lined the walls up to the height of the tops of the doors, while above these hung, in 'stucco allegorical frames' so close together that they almost touched, the portraits of some of the most eminent men of English literature. Whether Chesterfield read, wrote, slept, or gossiped, he did so beneath the gaze of Shakespeare, Chaucer, Sidney, Spenser, Milton, Swift, Addison, and Pope. One of the most successful aspects of Chesterfield House was the contrasts of style and mode that were created. The library was solidly English – in particular the beautiful chimney-piece, of white marble below and white painted wood above, which so delighted Ware that he illustrated it in his book – 'I have determined to have no gilding at all in it', wrote Chesterfield to Bristowe, 'as the constant fire and candles in that

The library,
Chesterfield House.

room would so soon turn it black, whereas by having it new painted once in four or five years, it will always be clean and cheerful.'[25] Upon all the chimney-pieces and cabinets stood fine busts of old orators 'interspersed with voluptuous vases and bronzes, antique or Italian, and airy Statuettes of Opera Nymphs',[26] and the whole room was surmounted by a frieze inscribed, in foot-high capitals, with the Horatian lines:

Nunc veterum libris, nunc somno, et inertibus horis
Ducere sollicitae jucunda oblivia vitae.[27]

It was a retreat from the world in which, Chesterfield told his son, he expected to find 'uninterrupted satisfaction'.[28]

In contrast to the spaciousness and grandeur of the downstairs rooms, the bedrooms at Chesterfield House were bleak and uncomfortable, and considered unworthy of comment in contemporary descriptions. This was true of almost all the great houses of the day, and reflected the lack of importance attached to domestic life. All life was devoted to show. 'We see an addition of a great room now to almost every house of consequence', wrote Isaac Ware.

In houses which have been for some time built and which have not an out of proportion room the common practice is to build one on to them ... the custom of routs has introduced this absurd practice. Our forefathers were pleased with seeing their friends as they chanced to come and with entertaining them when they were there. The present custom is to see them all at once, and to entertain none of them; this brings in the necessity of a great room ...[29]

It became the ambition of every aristocrat of note to outdo the next in glitter and extravagance, and in this Chesterfield was no exception. In February 1752, he gave, Walpole wrote to Mann, 'an immense assembly ... to show the house, which is really most magnificent'.[30] Among the throng of fashionable society who graced this occasion was the Duke of Hamilton who, added the voracious gossip, 'made violent love at one end of the room, while he was playing pharaoh at the other end; that is, he saw neither the bank nor his own cards, which were of three hundred pounds each: he soon lost a thousand.' The object of his affection was Miss Elizabeth Gunning, who almost immediately after this became his Duchess, following a midnight wedding ceremony in the Mayfair Chapel in which a curtain ring had to double for the gold ring, which the Duke had mislaid in the excitement. She and her sisters – who were, according to Walpole, so beautiful that whenever they left their houses there were 'mobs at their doors to see them get into their chairs'[31] – were part of a large circle of distinguished men and beautiful women who often assembled at Chesterfield House during the lifetime of the fourth Earl.

Right: Elizabeth, Duchess of Hamilton, by Gavin Hamilton.

Far right: Charlotte, Marchioness Townshend, by Thomas Hudson.

1 The painted staircase at Old Montagu House, Bloomsbury, in the days when it was used to exhibit some of the British Museum's Natural History specimens. From a watercolour by G. Scharf, 1845.

2 Opposite: The painted staircase at old Buckingham House by J. Stephanoff, engraved by W.J. Bennett, 1818.

3 Below: The colonnade at Burlington House. From a watercolour of *c*.1806-8.

4 Below: Uxbridge House, formerly Queensberry House, *c*.1785. Artist unknown.

5 Opposite: *A Nobleman's Levee*, by Marcellus Laroon, *c*.1730.

6 View looking south across Green Park *c*.1760, showing the Piccadilly Reservoir of the Chelsea Waterworks Company, and Spencer House (fourth on the left), as well as Buckingham House (far right). English school.

7 Above: *An Assembly at Lord Harrington's*, by Charles Philips, 1739.

8 Right: *The Wedding Dance*, by William Hogarth.

If Chesterfield House was the first in which the rococo made its appearance, it was not long before it had an equally grand rival. 'The Duke of Norfolk's fine house in St James's Square is finished', wrote Mrs Delany to her sister in February 1756 'and opened to the grand monde of London; I am asked for next Tuesday.'[32] Even though this opening assembly appears to have been the most talked about social event of the year, the receiving of such an invitation was hardly exclusive since, as Horace Walpole wrote, 'All the earth was there. You would have thought there had been a comet, everybody was gazing in the air and treading on one another's toes.'[33] This greatly increased the insult to Lady Townshend who, for political reasons, was quite deliberately not invited. Her subsequent misery was parodied by Richard Owen Cambridge in his 'Elegy Written in an Empty Assembly Room':

> . . . to me alone no card is come,
> I must not go abroad – and cannot Be at Home.
>
> But when no Cards the Chimney-Glass adorn,
> The dismal Void with Heart-felt Shame we mourn;
> Conscious Neglect inspires a sullen Gloom,
> And brooding Sadness fills the slighted Room.
> If some happier Female's Card I've seen
> I swell with Rage, or sicken with the Spleen;
> While artful Pride conceals the bursting Tear,
> With some forc'd Banter or affected Sneer;
> But now grown desp'rate, and beyond all Hope,
> I curse the Ball, the Duchess, and the Pope.[34]

And what she missed as she sat alone at home in the darkness, with not a candle burning and the shutters tightly closed so that no passer-by should guess she was within!

'You never saw such a scene of magnificence and taste', commented Walpole. 'The tapestry, the embroidered bed, the illumination, the glasses, the lightness and the novelty of the ornaments and the ceilings are delightful. She [the Duchess of Norfolk] gives three Tuesdays, would you could be at one!'[35]

The importance of Norfolk House lay not only in its decoration, but in its layout. It was a house designed to cater for the ever-increasing demands of the new social life. No wonder poor Lady Townshend was so unhappy at the prospect of having to spend such an evening alone, when the sole aim of London society seemed to be to gather together in as large numbers as possible as frequently as possible from dawn to dusk. 'In the morning', wrote Madame du Bocage, a French visitor to London in 1750,

breakfasts, which enchant as much by the exquisite viands, as by the richness of the plate in which they are served up, agreeably bring together both the people of the country and strangers. We breakfasted in this manner today at Lady Montagu's . . . A long table covered with the finest linen, presented to the view a thousand glittering cups, which contained coffee, chocolate, biscuits, cream, butter, toasts, and exquisite tea. You must understand that there is no good tea to be had but at London. The Mistress of the house, who deserves to be served at the table of the Gods, poured it out herself . . .[36]

From then on a person of fashion spent the day in a round of occupations so frenzied that there was often scarcely time to get from one to another – and woe betide those who missed the attraction of the day. 'You scold me for going to see the ghost', wrote Walpole to Mann on one occasion, 'and I don't excuse myself; but in such a town as this, if a ghost is in fashion, one must as much visit it as leave one's name with a new Secretary of State.'[37] It was an exhausting life. 'One of the empresses of fashion', wrote Walpole of the Duchess of Gordon,

uses fifteen or sixteen hours of her four-and-twenty. I heard her journal of last Monday. She first went to Handel's music in the Abbey; she then clambered over the benches, and went to Hastings' trial in the Hall; after dinner, to the Play; then to Lady Lucas's assembly; after that to Ranelagh, and returned to Mrs Hobart's faro table; gave a ball herself in the evening of that morning, into which she must have got a good way; and set out for Scotland the next day. Hercules could not have achieved a quarter of her labours in the same space of time.[38]

If parade was the order of the day, then Norfolk House was certainly designed for it. It stood on the east side of St James's Square, on the site of old St Alban's House and its neighbour to the north, Belasyse House. Work on it was begun in 1748. The façade which overlooked the square was rather plain and uninspiring, moving a contemporary observer to comment: 'Would any foreigner, beholding an insipid length of wall broken into regular rows of windows . . . ever figure from thence the residence of the first Duke of England? "All the blood of the Howards" can never ennoble Norfolk House!'[39] Although he exaggerated somewhat, it is certainly true that the exterior in no way prepared visitors for the elaborate nature of what they found within. For Matthew Brettingham's genius was to have provided a top-lit staircase in the very centre of the building, around which, on the first floor, ran a circuit of magnificent reception rooms. Each of these had a different colour scheme, and most a different style of decoration, thus affording guests who had climbed the splendid stairs feast after feast for the eyes as they moved from room to room, making this indeed 'the floor of taste, expense, state and parade'.[40] Such a layout was then unique to London. One of the guests on that opening night was Captain William Farington, of the Indian Army – the brother of the famous diarist and Royal Academician, Joseph Farington – who wrote to his sisters Isabella and Mary that 'everyone who was there agreed that Norfolk House was infinitely superior to anything in this Kingdom . . . and to most things they had seen in Europe'.[41]

Farington has left us with a wonderfully detailed description of this party, which also serves as a tour of the house. 'There were', he tells us, 'in all eleven rooms open, three below, the rest above, every room was furnished with a different colour, which used to be reckoned absurd, but this I suppose is to be the Standard.'[42] The guiding hand behind the unusual decorative scheme was undoubtedly Mary, Duchess of Norfolk, a woman of intelligence, charm, and great taste, with a character formidable enough for Horace Walpole to have referred to her as 'My Lord Duchess'.[43] Like Chesterfield, she was also an incurable francophile, who had been received at the court of Louis XV, and whose taste in art had been fashioned on her many trips to that country. She was ultimately responsible for turning the sober Palladian hand of Brettingham to create, with the assistance of a Piedmontese architect, Giovanni Battista Borra, the extensive display of French-inspired rococo decoration which so amazed the guests that night.

Norfolk House (extreme right of picture), St James's Square, looking northwards to St. James's church. Drawn and engraved by T. Bowles, 1753.

Right: William
Faringon, by Edward
Penny.

Far right: Mary,
Duchess of Norfolk,
by J. Vanderbanck.

After getting out of his carriage, Farington stepped into an unusually large
entrance hall, soberly Palladian with as yet only a mere hint of the rococo in
the decoration round the central lantern. On the left, he noted, 'you enter a
large Room Hung and Furnished with a Green Damask, let in with a Handsome Gilt moulding, and several very Fine Paintings on the Hangings, through
this into a Wainscotted Room, with Pictures but not very Elegant.' From there
an arched doorway in the centre of the east wall led him to the staircase hall,
which was embellished with elaborate rococo trophies of arms and armour and
an enormous double scallop shell beneath the landing, all designed by Borra.
The stairs themselves, he wrote, were 'very large, and the Lights Beautifully
Placed, 'Twas entirely covered with a French Carpet, and in the Angles stood
Large China Jars with perfumes.' From the landing Farington moved through
an ante-room, the first room of the principal suite, into what was without
doubt the *pièce de résistance* of the whole house: 'The next Room is large,
Wainscotted in a whimsical Taste, the Panels filled with extreme fine Carvings,
the Arts and Sciences all Gilt, as well as the ceiling, which was the same
design, here the Duchess sat, the whole night that she might speak to everyone
as they came in.'

This was the music room, overlooking the square, and so white and gold
and mirrored, so reminiscent in fact of some grand Paris salon, that it might
have had any Palladian purists among the guests gasping for breath. It was a
room for parade, and the grand entrance into the main suite of state apartments. Its walls were lined with woodwork in a scheme of tall rococo panels
carved by one John Cuenot, an immigrant French craftsman, and designed by

Borra; but the finest decorative feature was a series of scintillating plaster panels on the ceiling representing Music, Painting, Literature, Sculpture, Architecture, Astronomy and Surveying. These charming trophies were almost certainly executed by the master plasterer Thomas Clarke, who was responsible for most of the other plasterwork in the house; preserved, along with the rest of the room, in the Victoria and Albert Museum, they are among the most fluent expressions of the rococo to be found in England.

'Having paid your regards', continued Farington, 'you then walk forwards; the next Room was Hung and Furnished with Blue Damask, covered with very Fine paintings, the Gerandoles, fixed in the Frames of the Pictures, which had an odd effect, and I can't think will be so good for the Paint.' An inventory of about 1756 in fact describes this room as the 'green damask room', so one can only presume that Farington was misled as to its colour in the candlelight. It had a diagonally-coffered ceiling by Brettingham, after William Kent's chapel at Holkham, and glorious carved and gilt pier glasses between the windows of the west wall, with 'mathematical trophies' by Cuenot, symbolic of architecture and composed with set squares, dividers and quill pens.

Referred to in the inventory as the 'flowered red velvet room', the adjoining drawing-room, into which the guests thronged next, had a fine ceiling copied from a plate in Robert Wood's *Ruins of Palmyra*, published in 1753 and destined to become a favourite source for ceiling designs. It was in the room at right angles to this, the 'great drawing-room' or 'tapestry room', that they were greeted by the Duke. 'You now enter the Great Room', wrote Farington,

... the Tapestry is the finest Picture I ever saw, chiefly with Beasts, it cost in France nine Pounds a Yard, the Hangings just cost nine Hundred Pounds, the Glasses a Thousand, being the largest Plates, I fancy that were ever brought over, but throughout ye whole House the Glass is thought the most remarkable furniture, there are two crystal branches, I don't know what they Cost, – but from what I have seen, imagine about three or four Hundred Pounds a Piece, the Furniture Crimson Velvet, in magnificent Gilt Frames, the Chimney Piece white marble, the Festoons as soft as Gibbons could work in wood, I don't suppose this room can be outdone in Elegance.

Borra was responsible for this chimney-piece, the finest in Norfolk House, as well as for another remarkable feature of this room – the elaborate doorcases topped by scrolled pediments on which stood grimacing monkeys holding heavy garlands of fruit and flowers.

Not only did the Duke receive his guests in the great drawing-room, but Miss Clifford, the Duchess's niece, stood there 'to fix those to Cards who chose to Play' – the sole mention by Farington of any entertainment during the evening. Inventories of 1756 and 1777 show that there were large numbers of card-tables in all the state apartments, suggesting that playing was in no way confined to a single room. The same went for dining and dancing. According to the 1756 inventory, there was a mahogany dining-table in the music room,

Opposite: The grand
staircase, Norfolk
House.

while that of 1777 refers to a series of them kept on the staircase and landing
outside. On grand occasions these would almost certainly have been moved
about quite freely, the company eating in the music room, the 'green damask
room', the 'flowered red velvet room', or the 'great drawing-room' as the mood
took them. Describing a ball given by the Norfolks in honour of the Duke of
Cumberland a few months later, Mrs Delany writes of 'suppers' having been
provided: 'there were two tables for the dancers, nothing hot but soups. The
Duke's supper was hot, two courses and dessert, lighted up with little lamps
in green cut glasses.'[44] This suggests separate dinners in different apartments.
So far as the dancing was concerned, since all the four main state rooms had
carpets, any number of them could have been adapted for dancing by rolling
these up. It was not till the nineteenth century that the 'great drawing-room'
was turned specifically into a ballroom.

The tour was completed by passing through what are termed in the inventory the 'state bedroom', the 'state dressing-room', and the 'china room', all of
which had light gilt rococo ceilings and looked out over the garden. The
provision of a state bedroom is surprising in a London house since, except
perhaps for the occasional eminent foreigner, people moving in London society
expected to be lavishly entertained, but not invited to stay. It seems likely that
these rooms were used by the Duchess as her own bedroom and dressing-room
– the so-called 'China room' becoming her closet – and that on grand occasions
they were thrown open to the general company to admire their fittings and
decorations. Thus Farington waxed lyrical about the embroidery on the State
Bed, 'upon a Peach coloured French silk ... neither Baptiste or Hondecoeter
could paint finer Birds or Flowers, than you'll find in the work' – work which
was actually carried out by the Duchess herself, considered to be one of the
finest needlewomen of her day.[45] He went on to enthuse about the decoration
of the dressing-room, which was 'entirely Chinese, the Hangings Painted either
upon Satin or Taffeta, in the most Beautiful India Pattern you can Imagine,
Curtains and Chairs the same ... on a Chinese Table stood a Basket of French
China Flowers, under which was Room for a Lamp to Burn Perfumes to
answer the Flowers,' and about the 'infinite number of Curiosities' to be found
in the closet. 'Then', he concluded, 'you have gone the round.'

Farington did not disappoint his sisters by failing to give them some account
of how people were dressed that night. 'There was a great blaze of Diamonds,'
he told them. In his opinion the finest belonged to Lady Granby, a woman of
celebrated extravagance who, according to Walpole, once 'squandered seven
thousand pounds ... in all kinds of baubles and frippery'.[46] Lady Rockingham,
on the other hand, 'had none on at all' – a far cry from a masquerade the
previous year at which she and Lady Coventry had appeared 'covered with
diamonds: the former represented Night, and the stars upon her dress, it's
said, were real jewels.'[47] Of this Farington took a dim view, 'as everyone
endeavoured to make themselves Fine':

The music-room,
Norfolk House

Opposite: A corner of
the ballroom, Norfolk
House.

The ballroom, Norfolk House

A Miss Vineyard was thought the prettiest woman there[48], as to fashions, there was not two Ladies Heads dressed alike, the more whimsical and absurd the better, the Clothes on them were all vastly rich; I heard one Single shop sold above a Hundred Suits, so you judge what Numbers were bought; mine was a Figured Velvet of a Pompodore Colour which is the Taste, an entire Silver Clinquant Waistcoat, with a loose Net trimming waved over the Skirts and my Hair dressed French, – don't you think your Brother is growing very youthful. There was several richer Clothes, but none I think prettier than my own, I dare say you'll like them – indeed it is thought a very fine suit – it is all lined with a white Satin.

'Now don't you dream of this Fairy Land', concluded Farington in his letter, 'for 'tis almost like it'; and that is exactly how Norfolk House, with its variety of styles, must have appeared to many of the guests on that dazzling night. Though neither Norfolk nor Chesterfield House had rivals on quite the same scale, others went some way to equalling them as far as the decor was concerned. At her house in Hill Street, for example, Mrs Edward Montagu, a

society hostess celebrated for her intellectual salons, sought diversity in fanta-
sies from the east and had her dressing-room 'lined with painted paper of
Pekin and furnished with the choicest moveables of China.'[49] 'It is like the
Temple of some Indian God', she described to her sister in a letter of 3
January 1750:

if I was remarkably short and had a great head, I should be afraid people would think
I meant myself Divine Honours ... The very curtains are Chinese pictures on gauze,
and the chairs Indian fan-sticks with cushions of japan satin painted: as to the beauty
of colouring, it is carried as high as possible, but the toilette you were so good as to
paint is the only thing where nature triumphs.[50]

This room was one of the first Chinese Rooms in London, and may well have
inspired that at Norfolk House. From the first day on which she showed it to
the world it was certainly rarely free of visitors. On 23 December 1752, for
example, Mrs Montagu wrote to Mrs Boscawen, that 'the Chinese Room was
filled by a succession of people from eleven in the morning till eleven at
night',[51] while the following May she told her husband, 'I had rather more
than an hundred visitants last night, but the apartment held them with ease,
and the highest compliments were paid to the house and elegance of the
apartments.'[52]

When Elizabeth Montagu tired of the Chinese, she amazed her guests with
new delights. 'If I had paper and time', wrote Mrs Delany to her niece on 28
May 1773,

I could entertain you with the account of Mrs Montagu's Room of Cupidons which
was opened with an assembly for all the foreigners, the literati, and the macaronis of
the present age. Many and sly are the observations how such a genius at her age, and
so circumstanced, could think of painting the walls of her drawing-room with bowers
of roses and jessamines entirely inhabited by little cupids in all their wanton ways ...
unless she looks upon herself as the wife of old Vulcan, and mother to all these little
loves![53]

Though few remnants can be seen today, it is likely that many other fashionable ladies had rooms decorated with 'paper of Pekin'. However, the Countess
of Pomfret, that old crony of Lady Finch's, had other ideas, though of an
equally fantastic nature. In 1760 she commissioned Sanderson Miller, who
with Horace Walpole was the acknowledged authority on Gothic, to build her
a Gothic folly in Arlington Street. Pomfret Castle, as it became known, must
have seemed a rather improbable structure in a street of otherwise rather plain
Georgian houses. A stuccoed building of three bays with a central pediment
and flanking turrets, it lay across a court and was approached through a single
storey gatehouse. The interior was its most remarkable feature, for several of
the rooms had elaborate perpendicular plaster panelling, and panelled or fan-
vaulted ceilings. The Ashmolean Museum in Oxford has a portrait of the
Countess and her husband in a wonderful Gothic frame which was made for,
and once hung in, the drawing-room of this curious house.

The gothic staircase, Pomfret Castle

The elaborate perpendicular plaster panelling in the staircase hall, Pomfret Castle.

Thomas, Earl of
Pomfret and his wife
Henrietta, by Thomas
Bardwell.

Opposite: The
drawing-room,
Pomfret Castle.

Of the more fantastic elements of eighteenth-century decoration in London houses almost nothing survives, apart from a small amount of rococo. Of this, probably the best interiors, other than those at the Mansion House, which do not fall within the scope of this book, are at No. 1 Greek Street, which was decorated in about 1755 for Alderman Richard Beckford, the brother of the builder of Fonthill in Wiltshire. Externally the house is very plain, and only its large size, with four bays onto Soho Square and five onto Greek Street, mark it out as a building of possible consequence. The front door leads straight into the staircase hall which, though Palladian in design, is filled with typically rococo plasterwork of scrolls and twisting leaves. Of special note are the elaborately framed medallions between the windows and to the left of the drawing-room – which is in a similar style, and has a particularly fine ceiling containing a large central oval of four cherubs symbolising the elements.

The scarcity of such decoration from the early 1750s is all the more regrettable since these were years of renewed activity and prosperity which saw not only the completion of Chesterfield House and Norfolk House, but also the building of Fetherstonhaugh House in Whitehall. Sir Matthew Fetherstonhaugh was the son of a former mayor of Newcastle, who had been left a fortune of £400,000 by his kinsman, Sir Henry Fetherstonhaugh, on the condition that he acquired both a country seat and a baronetcy. Having further increased his wealth by marrying a rich merchant's daughter, Sarah Lethieullier, he bought Uppark, in Sussex, which he remodelled and refurnished over a long period, so that it is still possible to follow there the gradual transition from rococo to neo-classical taste, the next important development in architecture. At the same time he commissioned James Paine – the builder of many fine houses in the north of England, such as Nostell Priory in Yorkshire – to design him a London house on a fine site he had acquired almost opposite the Banqueting House, overlooking Horse Guards Parade and St James's Park.

The house was set back at the end of a forecourt with a screen onto the street, and the range of offices facing the stables. The façades were plain, though that facing the park was originally intended to be rather more magnificent, with a giant order above a rusticated basement, and an elaborate entablature and balustrade capped with urns. From a modest entrance hall a door on the left led to the main staircase, which served the five principal rooms on the first floor: the ante-room, saloon, drawing-room, common sitting-parlour, and dining-room. There were no bedrooms on this floor, the six family rooms being in what Paine described as 'the Atticks'. The servants were housed either in lodgings in the roof lit by dormers, or over the coach house and stables. It was an unusual arrangement and suggests that it was becoming the fashion to give over the first floor entirely to public rooms. On Sir Matthew's death in 1774, his widow eventually sold the house to Prince Frederick, Duke of York, for whom Henry Holland added a columned portico and a circular hall. Since he had also recently executed the colonnade in front of Carlton House for the

Rococo plasterwork at
1 Greek Street.

Below: The staircase,
1 Greek Street.

An elevation of the east front of Fetherstonhaugh House, Whitehall.

Below: An elevation of the park front of Fetherstonhaugh House.

Prince of Wales, this prompted Lord North to remark that 'things were coming to a strange pass when the Duke of York was sent to the Round House and the Heir Apparent to the Pillory'.[54]

Paine's unexpected design for the park front was based on the north façade of Burlington's Chiswick House, but it also recalls the almost contemporary park front of the beautiful mansion built for Lord Spencer, begun in 1756. Since, however, we now find ourselves on the threshold of what was to be, so far as London houses were concerned, the period of their greatest architectural achievement, let us pause a while to look at what was involved in the running of these private palaces.

5

An Eighteenth-Century Household

My servants have all quarrelled in my absence, it seems to me, about the profits my indulgence left them. They had the produce of three cows, a great quantity of poultry, and the Kitchen Garden. They disputed about the divisions; each would have had it all.

Lady Mary Coke, 13 June 1772. The Letters and Journals of Lady Mary Coke, *vol. 4, p. 84*

'We have a vast old house in London', wrote the Duchess of Somerset in April 1749, 'not only to furnish from top to bottom but to lay new Floors put up new Ceilings, Chimneypieces, Sashes and Doors, for everything is gone into ruin. One thing my Lord is doing which gives me great pleasure and that is laying two rooms together to make a Neat Chapel without which so large a building appeared very incomplete.'[1] The house to which she referred in this letter was Northumberland House, a huge Jacobean pile and the sole survivor of the Strand palaces, which stood magnificently, if rather incongruously, where Northumberland Avenue now runs. Inherited the previous year by her husband, Algernon, the seventh Duke of Somerset, recently created Earl of Northumberland, it had been built between 1605 and 1609 by Henry Howard, the first Earl of Northampton, during whose lifetime it was known as Northampton House. According to George Vertue, it was the work of Bernard Janssen and Gerard Christmas, and consisted of three sides of a square, one of which faced the Strand while the other two extended towards the Thames, with towers at each corner surmounted by turrets. Along the street front ran a balustrade of letters, similar to that at Castle Ashby in Northamptonshire; the letters made up a Latin inscription containing the Earl of Northampton's titles, together with the builder's name. In his *Anecdotes of Painting* Walpole quotes a story, mentioned by Camden, according to which at the funeral of Anne of Denmark in 1619 a young man among the spectators was killed by the fall of the letter S, pushed down by the incautious leaning forward of sightseers on the roof.[2] From the street a large arched gateway led through into an inner quadrangle.

On the death of Northampton in 1614, 'eaten up by debts incurred in building his new house',[3] Northampton House had passed to his nephew,

Opposite, top: Old
Northumberland
House, then called
Suffolk House. From a
drawing by Hollar.

Opposite, bottom: The
south front of
Northumberland
House after the
alterations carried out
by the tenth Earl.
Drawn by S. Wale.

Thomas Howard, Earl of Suffolk, the Lord High Treasurer of England, becoming Suffolk House in the process. The builder of Audley End in Essex,
which James I described as being 'too large for a King, though it might do for
a Lord Treasurer', Suffolk added a new wing fronting the river, thus completing the square. This can be seen in a drawing by Hollar, which is the
earliest known view of the house. Considering the vast expense involved in
keeping up these two enormous houses, it is hardly surprising that Suffolk was
eventually suspended from office for embezzling treasury funds.

In 1642 Suffolk House became Northumberland House, when it was granted
to Algernon Percy, the tenth Earl of Northumberland, as part of the settlement
on his marriage to Suffolk's granddaughter, Lady Elizabeth Howard. He too
involved himself in a considerable amount of alteration and restoration. His
main contribution was to rebuild the south wing, and to move into it all the
principal rooms, which had formerly been in the north wing – a scheme which
involved the purchase of 221,000 bricks and 34,000 tiles, and cost well over
£6,000.[4] The reason for all this was given by Dodsley in his *Environs of
London*: 'When London became more populous, and the buildings about Charing Cross daily increased, 'twas found inconvenient to live in the apartments
which had been built by Lord Northampton; because they were greatly dis-
turbed by the hurry and noise of passengers and coaches in the street.'[5] In
1657 the Earl of Northumberland also added a massive stone staircase leading
from the house into the garden, which can be seen in a print published in
Dodsley's book. The surviving accounts show that this was completed by a
mason called Edward Marshall at a cost of £200 – probably to the design of
John Webb, who had been closely involved in the interior alterations.[6] When
Evelyn first saw these stairs, soon after their completion, while visiting the
house in June 1658, he was not impressed. 'The new front towards the garden
is tolerable', he wrote, 'were it not drowned by a too massy and clumsy pair
of stairs of stone, without any neat invention'.[7]

In the hundred years which had passed after the tenth Earl's improvements
Northumberland House had evidently fallen into a sorry state of neglect, most
probably because the family's attentions were concentrated on their many other
properties during this period. The new Earl, however, in 1749 employed Daniel
Garrett, a respectable architect of the Burlington school, to get under way a
series of major alterations and repairs. The following June the Countess was
able to write to Lady Luxborough,

My Lord will do a good deal to the front of the house, in order to make it appear less
like a prison; he builds a new wing on the right-hand side of the garden, which will
contain a library, bed-chamber, dressing-room, and a waiting-room. All the sashes,
doors and ceilings in both apartments must be entirely new, and the floors in My
Lord's ...[8]

Canaletto's painting of the house, carried out in 1753, shows just what

Canaletto's painting of Northumberland House showing Daniel Garrett's improvements

Garrett did to give the front a more charming and elegant appearance. He 'corrected' the proportions, inserted sash windows, and generally added new ornament, not only below the windows, but also in the design of the frontispiece – in particular at the top, where pilasters, a broken Palladian pediment and a great lead lion, six feet high and eleven-and-a-half feet long, presided over the legend 'ALG:D:S: 1749 C: N: REST'.

The restoration of the house was still incomplete when the Duke died in 1750, but luckily the new owners, his daughter Elizabeth and son-in-law, Sir Hugh Smithson of Stanwick Park in Yorkshire, were well equipped to carry on with the work. Elizabeth, whom Walpole was later to dub 'the Duchess of Charing Cross',[9] was not only immensely rich, having succeeded to the vast Percy estates on the death of her brother in 1744, but was a woman of great intelligence, whose strong interest in architecture and decoration was reflected in the extensive journals which she kept during her lifetime. Sir Hugh, who upon his marriage assumed the title of Earl of Northumberland, was, according to Dutens, 'one of the handsomest men in the kingdom' and possessed of 'more knowledge than is commonly found among the nobility'.[10] He had already made his mark before he became an earl, as the MP for Middlesex from 1746, and as a Fellow of the Royal Society and a member of the Society

Far left: Elizabeth, Duchess of Northumberland, after a painting by Reynolds.

Left: Hugh, Duke of Northumberland, by Daniel Gardner.

of Dilettanti. Already a very rich man himself – his great-grandfather had made a fortune from haberdashery – he was immensely proud of his wife's family and its history, and wasted no time in devoting his energies to improving and strengthening his new inheritance. 'They are building at Northumberland House, at Sion, at Stanwick, at Alnwick and Warkworth Castles!' wrote Walpole in 1752. 'They live by the etiquette of the old peerage, have Swiss porters, the Countess has her pipers – in short they will soon have no estate.'[11] But Walpole was wrong, for under the new Earl's able administration they grew richer. In 1749 the income from the family estates was £8,706 a year; by 1765 he had increased this to £25,000; by 1773 it was £31,000, and by 1778 £50,000.[12]

It seems likely that Northumberland House was the first project undertaken by the Earl, becoming a building 'so complete and stately as to be generally admired for its elegance and grandeur'.[13] His earliest contribution was a magnificent picture gallery, 160 feet long, 26 feet wide and two storeys high, the walls of which he covered with huge copies of famous masterpieces. It also doubled up as a ballroom. Needless to say, Walpole attended the opening in May 1757. 'Lord Northumberland's great gallery is finished and opened', he wrote to Mann, adding dismissively, 'it is a sumptuous chamber, but might have been in better taste.'[14] For the best description of this gallery, which must have been the noblest mid-Georgian room in London, we must turn to the diary of Count Kielmansegge who, on 6 November 1761, attended a party there to celebrate the coronation of George III at which six hundred guests were present.

The ceiling is decorated with gilt stucco, and divided into five parts, in which are painted Fame on the wing, a Diana, a triumphal chariot drawn by two horses, a Flora, and Victory with a laurel wreath. Over the nine windows on the garden side are small ones, which are hardly noticeable, and serve only to give more light to the ceiling. The opposite wall is divided into three parts by two valuable marble chimney-pieces, the corners being supported by figures of Phrygian prisoners, which are said to have been copied from those in the Capitol at Rome; over them are life-size portraits of our host and hostess in their Peer's robes ... Four large crystal chandeliers, each with twenty-five candles, light up the room even more brilliantly than is necessary, and I certainly think that it would not be easy to imagine a more splendid sight than this gallery presents when filled with people, all vieing with one another in the beauty of their dress.[15]

The Northumberlands threw a good many parties in this great room, and they soon gained the reputation of being one of London's gayest couples. Judging from contemporary descriptions, their entertainments were generally lavish affairs:

Lady Northumberland made a pompous *festino* ... t'other night; not only the whole house, but the garden was illuminated, and was quite a fairy scene. Arches and pyramids of lights alternately surrounded the enclosure; a diamond necklace of lamps edged the rails and descent with a spiral obelisk of candles on each hand; and dispersed over the lawn were little bands of kettledrums, clarinets, fifes, etc, and the lovely moon who came without a card ...[16]

They were also invariably crowded: 'you must be squeezed to death at my Lady Northumberland's in the evening', wrote Walpole to the Duchess of Grafton in January 1766,[17] while the *London Chronicle* of 5 June 1764 records that there were on one occasion '1,500 persons of distinction [at] a vast assembly at Northumberland House'. Judging by Count Kielmansegge's account of his attempts to leave a party attended by a mere six hundred guests, chaos must have reigned:

Nothing is perfect, not even in this house; the inconvenience of getting away is a very great drawback, the courtyard being too small for the quantity of carriages and sedan chairs, and everybody has to come in and go out by the one gateway, which is very narrow. The quantity of sedan chairs prevented any coach from getting into the court, consequently many people had to wait until two or three o'clock before they could get away.[18]

Apart from the small courtyard, however, everything else about Northumberland House was right for large-scale entertaining. The house and gardens together occupied a site of nearly four and a half acres: the façade stretched 162 feet along the Strand, while anyone who wished to stroll from there down to the end of the garden would have faced a walk of just over 500 feet. Count Kielmansegge counted over one hundred and forty rooms in the house, lit by three hundred windows. Of these rooms, the state and family apartments took up less than half. The rest consisted of endless domestic offices – the kitchens, the pantry, the servants' hall, the stewards' room, the still-room, the confectionery room, the housekeeper's room, the brewery, the wash-house, the laundry, the coal and wine cellars, and so forth – together with accommodation for the hordes of servants who played such a vital role in running these great homes, and who were collectively referred to as 'the family'.

The 'family' at Northumberland House, as at every other grand house in town or in the country, was headed by the house steward – in this case one John Lamb, who, on a salary of £80 a year, was in overall charge of the household. He hired the servants, paid the bills and wages, and kept all the accounts, as well as acting as a kind of private secretary to his master and looking after much of his personal business. He was not required to wear livery, which was indicative of his high standing in the house, and he was constantly on the move between all the family's residences. Among his most important responsibilities was to ensure that the household rules were carried out to the letter. At Northumberland House these were drawn up and signed by the Earl himself in a document entitled 'Rules for a Family', which was no doubt on prominent display in the servants' hall.

RULES FOR A FAMILY

The servant maids to be up at six in the morning & about their business in Summer, at seven in the morning in Winter; to Breakfast at eight in Summer; & nine in Winter for which is allowed half an hour.

To dine at half-past one Winter & Summer; & never to sit down to table unclasped but always neat and clean. One hour to be allowed for dinner.

The men servants to be about their business by six o'clock in Summer & seven in Winter & to breakfast at eight in Summer & nine in Winter for which half an hour is allowed them.

They are to dine at half-past one, Winter & Summer & none of them to sit down to table without being dressed clean and neat.

Each man servant, in turn, for a week is to see order kept in the Servants Hall, and these regulations obeyed, & is to answer to the Steward in case they are not.

viz each Person at the Servants' Hall table to have two plates set before them, a knife & fork & spoon; After dinner *A* shall go round the table & after putting the scraps out of each plate into an earthen pan, for the Dogs; Shall put all the plates into a Caldron of Boiling Water and wash them clean after which he is to put them in the place alotted for them.

The Maids all to sit at one end of the table where the eldest is to see proper decorum kept up & one to be helped first.

2 pound of meat is to be allotted for each servant per day but the Whole to be dressed at dinner time as the servants are to have nothing *hot* either for Breakfast or Supper; they are to have also at Dinner a large pudding & a dish of Vegetable every day. On Sundays roast beef and plumb pudding & to make up their breakfast and supper with bread & cheese, or while there is plenty Milk or anything of that sort, if they prefer it, they should be allowed but sufficient for each meal; & three times a week Ale; a Horn for each after Dinner, which they are to receive from Courvoisier.

After each meal *B* shall sweep the Servant's Hall & put the things all in their places.

The Upper Servants Nurses included shall dine in the Steward's Room after My Lord whose dinner they will have; but are not to have anything dressed for them, but what comes to his table, neither are they to have Hot suppers, but milk & fruit if they choose it; & there is sufficient for My Lord's Table.

My Lord to breakfast at ten; dine at half-past three or 4; drink tea at Seven; & sup at half-past ten.

The Young Ladies, and Gentlemen; to dine at one o'clock, & to be half an hour at table.

2 Housemaids; a Laundry Maid; a Kitchen maid; a dairy Maid; (& if wanted a Stillroom maid) the five first to be regulated by the Housekeeper who is to inform them, & me, of the business allotted them, & to be answerable to me for their industry, & good behaviour in the family. They must be told when hired that whatever they are required to do must not be refused, tho' it may not be the particular business for which they are hired; the Stillroom Maid must attend in the Nursery Laundry etc. if wanted; & on the Housekeeper of course. The Housekeeper is to take care of the Linnen, China, to make cakes, preserves, pickles; send up the Breakfast, Tea, take charge of the family if required, & see that the House is kept clean & that each particular room has all the necessaries in it.

The Steward is to see all the regulations of the family put into practice.

He is to inform me of the particular business allotted to each man Servant, & is to be answerable to me for their Honesty, Sobriety, Cleanliness, & good behaviour in the family & upon any complaint made by him unless remedied immediately; they must be discharged. He must see that they do their duty, & must allow of no waste or extravagance.[19]

The rules were strict and rigidly enforced, but in return those who adhered to them were, on the whole, well looked after. In a society in which the rich had all the advantages, servants had at least a measure of security. They were, as we have seen, well fed, and when sick they fared a great deal better than they would have done in the outside world. 'All my servants', wrote Horace Walpole in 1776, 'think that the moment they are useless I must not part with them, and so I have an infirmary instead of a menage.'[20] The first smallpox hospital in London, founded in Islington in 1746, was specifically intended for the domestics of great houses. When a servant of the fourth Duke of Bedford, a certain John Francis, went down with the disease in 1760, the Duke paid all his hospital bills and expenses in the 'Pest House'. Between 9 June and 15 July, he also sent in 54lb of lamb, 16lb of mutton, 16lb of veal, 7lb of beef, as

A servant girl plucking a turkey, by Henry Walton.

well as milk, vegetables, bread, beer, brandy and gin for the nurses and their patient.

Subordinate to the house steward, but each in charge of their own individual departments, were five male servants and one female. The groom of the chambers, John Augustus Corner, received visitors in the front hall, took their cards and announced them. His domain consisted of the main suite of reception rooms, where he was responsible for seeing that the furniture sparkled, the plate gleamed, the fires were lit, the lamps filled and the wicks long, and that all the desks were kept well stocked with paper, ink and sharp quills. He also saw to all new liveries. Important though his position was as the second manservant in rank, his somewhat lowly salary of only £28 a year suggests that it may well have been an honorary one, befitting perhaps someone of a higher social standing than the average servant. Such a possibility is strengthened when one looks at the household of the fourth Duke of Bedford, in which the groom of the chambers, one Richard Branson, was assigned an extra duty: when they were in residence in London he played nursemaid to the Duke's two young children, Francis, Marquess of Tavistock, born in 1739, and Lady Caroline Russell, born in 1743. His 'Bills of Disbursements for Lord Tavistock and Lady Caroline' show that he spent most of his time keeping them entertained. On various occasions in 1753, for example, he 'paid for fireworks for Lord Tavistock', 'paid for battledore and shuttlecocks for Lord Tavistock', 'paid for whips and tops for Lord Tavistock', 'paid for a book of drawings for Lady Caroline', and 'paid for the print of Miss Bellamy and Mr Garrick for Lady Caroline'. From time to time he and Lord Tavistock would slip out alone, on expeditions no doubt considered quite unsuitable for young ladies: 'paid for seeing the rhinoceros and alligator with Lord Tavistock', and, on another occasion, 'paid for seeing the Russia man with Lord Tavistock'. Branson also looked after the children's pets. In February 1752, he 'gave the dog doctor 5s 0d for coming to Bounce'; in May he 'paid Isaac Smith a bill for bird cages for Lord Tavistock and Lady Caroline'; in July he 'paid for three peewits for Lord Tavistock'; while in April 1753, he 'paid for a new door to the dormouse's cage'.[21]

The butler, William Hall, who received a salary of £60 a year, was responsible mainly for the wine cellar, for all the silver and plate, for the serving of meals in the dining-room, and for the conduct and efficiency of the footmen. In the servants' hall he sat at the head of the table, from where he doled out the allotted rations of home-brewed beer. He was invariably the last of the household to bed since it was his duty to go round the house after the family and their friends had retired to ensure that all the doors and windows were fastened, and that there were no servants left in the servants' hall or elsewhere. The Earl's gentleman, Ralph Bell, sometimes referred to as the valet or valet de chambre, was also prone to long hours, since it was his duty not only to wait upon his master at all times, but to dress and undress him, for which privilege he earned himself £40 a year.

At Northumberland House two of the most important positions in the household were filled by Frenchmen. Louis Lamanche was the clerk of the kitchen, and though no salary is given for him, it would have been about £60 a year. He was responsible for ordering all the provisions, which was a mammoth task. The staggering weekly consumption of food in Northumberland House is evidence of the large number of people employed there. In the week ending 26 March 1757, for example, there were consumed 52 stone 6lb of beef, 26 stone 5lb of mutton, 9 stone 6lb of veal, 2 stone of pork, 2 lambs, 5 sweetbreads, 6 calves' feet, 1 ox tongue, 4 palates, 8lb of middle bacon, 16lb

of lard bacon, 11lb of lard, 7lb of Epping butter, 58lb of lump butter, 160 dozen eggs, 3 34lb cheeses, 12 rabbits, 6 pigeons, 1 pheasant, 6 pullets, 1 turkey, 2 ducklings, 2 capons, 1 wild duck, 3 chickens, 6 snipe, 2 tame pigeons, 6 squabs, 2lb of sausages, 8lb of salmon, 4 large perch, 50 crayfish, 3 pints of oysters, a 23lb ham, 130 loaves of bread, as well as various vegetables, fruit and confectionery.

Much of this food was brought in carts every day from the farm at Syon,

Dessert being served at a dinner party, by Marcellus Laroon.

the Northumberland residence just outside London. This was normal procedure for families who had a great country house as well as one in town. The Earl of Shelburne, for example, had estates at Bowood in Wiltshire and Wycombe Abbey in Buckinghamshire which were meticulously organised so as to provide all the food for Shelburne House in Berkeley Square (built in 1761), where the family lived when in London. The Earl's clerk of the kitchen worked out that this was undoubtedly cheaper than buying their foodstuffs in town. Beef and mutton came from the Park at Bowood; butter, bacon, hams, lard, cheese, from the farm there. There was a Menagerie which 'must furnish the House in Town and Country with Turkeys, Pheasants, Ducks, Guinea Fowl and Pea Fowl, Geese, etc – must preserve the best breeds of the Common Fowl, and may assist in regards to the Fish'. The Bowood Garden supplied root vegetables only. The lighter vegetables, being more perishable, came from the garden at Wycombe, the closer of the two properties to London, which also provided fruit and fish.[22]

Between 24 November and 22 December 1781, the following deliveries were made by cart to Shelburne House:

November 24:	6 Fowls, 2 Ducks, 2 Geese, 1 Turkey, 3 Hares, Giblets from Bowood Park.
November 27:	1 Hare, 6 Woodcocks and 2 Partridges from Wycombe. 2 Hares, 5 Woodcocks and Garden Stuff from Bowood Park.
December 1:	1 Hare, 6 Woodcocks, 7 Snipes, 2 Turkeys, 1 Goose, 2 Ducks from Bowood park.
December 5:	Hamper of Garden Stuff from Bowood Park.
December 8:	1 Pig, 12 Fowls, 2 Turkeys, 2 Ducks, 1 Goose, 2 Hares, 1 Woodcock, and 5 Snipes from Bowood Park.
December 12:	1 Hare, Asparagus, and 12 Bottles of Preserved Gooseberries from Wycombe.
December 14:	2 brace Carp and 1 brace of Tench from Wycombe and Garden Stuff.
December 15:	1 Sheep, Side of Bacon, 12 Fowls, 2 Turkeys, 1 Goose, 2 Ducks, 2 Hares, 3 Woodcocks, and 4 Snipes from Bowood Park.
December 18:	Truffles and Asparagus from Wycombe.
December 20:	1 brace of Carp and 1 brace of Tench from Wycombe and Garden Stuff.
December 22:	1 Sheep, a side of Bacon, 12 Fowls, 2 Turkeys, 1 Goose, 2 Ducks, 2 Hares, 3 Woodcocks, 4 Snipes from Bowood Park.[23]

'To be a good Clerk of the Kitchen', wrote Lord Shelburne's clerk, 'you must have been a good cook.'[24] Joseph Dufour was the cook at Northumberland House and his wages were equal to those of the clerk of the kitchen. Lord Chesterfield, whose dinners at Chesterfield House were celebrated, had started the vogue for French chefs by employing La Chapelle, a descendant of the great chef who had worked for Louis XIV, since when they were to be found in all the grandest houses. Among the most famous was Monsieur Cloe, chef

Above: The kitchen at
St James's Palace,
c. 1800.

Left: The Duke of
Newcastle and his
chef, Monsieur Cloe.
The Duke's words:
'O! Cloe if you leave
me, I shall be Starv'd
by G-d'
Cloe's words: 'Begar,
me can no relish dis
dam English
Proclemacion!' (Cloe
holds a paper:
'Proclamation against
Papists'.)

to the second Duke of Newcastle who, according to Walpole, lived in daily fear that he might leave, and was thus ruled by him. Judging from this description by Horace Walpole of a dinner at Northumberland House, Monsieur Dufour must have been a man of infinite patience to have put up with the rather erratic arrangements of the Countess. 'Now for my disaster', he wrote to the Earl of Hertford in April 1765:

you will laugh at it, though it was woeful to me. I was to dine at Northumberland House, and went a little after four. There I found the Countess, Lady Betty Mackenzie, Lady Strafford, my Lady Finlater, who was never out of Scotland before; a tall lad of fifteen, her son; Lord Drogheda and Mr Worsley. At five arrived Mr Mitchell, who said the Lords had begun to read the Poor-Bill, which would take at least two hours, and perhaps would debate it afterwards. We concluded dinner would be called for, it not being very precedented for Ladies to wait for Gentlemen; – no such thing, six o'clock came, – seven o'clock, – our coaches came, – Well! we sent them away and excuses were we were engaged. Still the Countess's heart did not relent, nor uttered a syllable of apology. We wore out the Wind and the Weather, the Opera and the Play, Mrs Cornelys's and Almanacks, and every topic that would do in a formal circle. We hinted, represented in vain. The Clock struck eight; my Lady, at last, said she would go and order dinner; but it was a good half hour before it appeared. We then sat down to a table for fourteen covers; but instead of substantials, there was nothing but a profusion of plates striped red, green, and yellow, gilt plate, blacks, and uniforms! My Lady Finlater, who had never seen these embroidered dinners, nor dined after three, was famished. The first course stayed as long as possible, in hopes of my Lord's arrival, so did the second. The desert at last arrived, and the middle dish was actually set on, when Lord Finlater and Mr Mackay arrived! Would you believe it! – The desert was remanded, and the whole first course brought back again! – Stay, I have not done; – just as this second course had done its duty, Lord Northumberland, Lord Strafford, and Mackenzie came in, and the whole began a third time! – Then the second course and the desert! I thought we should have dropped from our chairs with fatigue and fumes! When the clock struck eleven, we were asked to return to the drawing-room, and drink tea and coffee, but I said I was engaged to supper, and came home to bed. My dear Lord, think of four hours and a half in a circle of mixed company, and three great dinners, one after another, without interruption . . .[25]

There was only one female servant of any importance in a household dominated by men, and that was the housekeeper. At Northumberland House her name was Mary Bell, and she earned £30 a year. She was one of the few servants who did not move with the family when they changed residence: each of their homes having a separate housekeeper with a skeleton staff. She was in overall charge of all the female servants, and her particular domains were the still-room, in which she made all kinds of cakes and pastries, preserves and pickles, etc, and the china and linen closets. She was particularly busy immediately before the family came to town, when it was her responsibility to see that the whole house was scrubbed from top to bottom – a treatment that was also meted out to the state rooms before any great ball or entertainment. Hence

Horace Walpole, describing a 'numerous and magnificent' ball at Bedford House in April 1759, wrote, 'Then I said, "This room feels very cold ... I'll not stay here; this room has been washed today".'[26]

Beneath these six important individuals was a complicated hierarchy of other servants, many of whom considered themselves a cut above the rest. No doubt the confectioner, Monsieur Louch, felt contemptuous of the roasting cook, James Gibbs, even though their matching salaries of £34 show that they were considered of equal standing. Elaborate desserts were very much the fashion, and were often works of art. 'All the geniuses of the age', wrote Walpole to Mann in February 1750, 'are employed in designing new plans for desserts. The Duke of Newcastle's last was a baby Vauxhall, illuminated with a million little lamps of various colours.'[27] Joseph Farington described one he saw at a dinner with the Duke and Duchess of Norfolk:

after a very Elligant Dinner of a great many dishes ... The Table was Prepar'd for Desert, which was a Beautiful Park, round the Edge was a Plantation of Flowering-Shrubs, and in the middle a Fine piece of water, with Dolphins Spouting out water,

'All the geniuses of the age are employed in designing new plans for desserts.' From a book on desserts by Carême.

and Deer dispersed Irregularly over the Lawn, on the Edge of the Table was all Iced Creams, and wet and dried Sweetmeats, it was such a Piece of work it was all left on the Table till we went to Coffee.[28]

At a ball at Bedford House, Walpole noted, 'the Wilton Bridge in sugar almost as big as the life . . .'[29]

The position of the under-butler, Geoffrey Smith, lay somewhere between the butler and the footmen; although his salary of between fifteen and twenty pounds was the same as those of the latter, he ruled autocratically over their ranks, and often had the title of first footman. The jobs of footmen were various and numerous. They waited at table; they looked after the fires; one was constantly on duty waiting in the hall; they fetched and carried for all and sundry; they accompanied their master or mistress whenever they went out. At all times they wore full-dress livery with knee breeches, silk stockings and powdered hair. They were always specified as either 'my lord's footman' or 'my lady's footman', and their numbers varied from year to year. We do know, however, that the Countess of Northumberland had a penchant for footmen, for in December 1764 Walpole, who considered her a 'great vulgar Countess',[30] wrote to Hertford: 'Lady Northumberland has added an eighth footman since I wrote to you last'; and he never forgave her the time she paraded 'before the Queen with more footmen than her Majesty'. 'That was impertinent!' he added.[31]

There were perks to being a footman – one of which was that, apart from his salary, he could always expect some extra income in the shape of tips for such jobs as escorting a guest home or for helping out at the house of a friend of his master and mistress. For example, when the Duke and Duchess of Bedford gave a ball in May 1759, they borrowed fifteen such footmen from various friends; three from Lord Sandwich, three from the Duke of Grafton, two from Lord Gower, two from Lord Bolingbroke, and five others from unspecified employers. For this work they were paid a guinea each. There was also the chance that a footman might catch the eye of his mistress. In her diary of 26 October 1764, for example, the Countess of Northumberland recorded that

Lady Harriet Wentworth youngest sister to the Marquess of Rockingham a girl of admirable good sense and an unblemish'd Character eloped with John Sturgeon a lad of about nineteen who was her own Footman so illiterate when he came into her Service that he could not even write his name but she had taught him Mathematics, Writing, Music, etc. She parted with all her fine Cloths, she should for the future wear only Washing Gowns as was fit for his Wife.[32]

This so upset her aunt, our old friend Lady Bel Finch, that she had to be blooded.[33] Some years later, Lady Elizabeth Craven was driven abroad after rumours had circulated that she had conducted 'a low amour with one of her own servants'.[34]

A footman snatching a kiss off a maidservant.

In addition to the regulars, there were also two 'running footmen' at Northumberland House, whose job was to carry messages between one house and another. Such servants frequently carried a tall cane topped by a silver ball. This contained a mixture of white wine and egg, which they drank to sustain their energy. Those with particular fleetness of foot were much prized by their masters, and it was not unusual for them to be raced against one another, with heavy betting on the result. One of the last recorded contests of this kind took place, some time before 1770, between a celebrated running footman and the Duke of Marlborough. The wager was that the footman could run to London more quickly than the Duke could drive there in his carriage and four; both were to start at the same time. The Duke was the winner by a hair's breadth; the poor footman died, as much from chagrin, it was said, as from exhaustion.[35] 'I have always thought a running footman', wrote Walpole, 'as meritorious a being as a learned man. Why is there more merit in having travelled one's eyes over so many reams of papers, than in having carried one's legs over so many acres of ground?'[36]

Besides the footmen, there were two ushers – the usher of the hall, who laid the table for meals in and generally looked after the servants' hall, and the usher of the stewards' room, who did the same for the stewards' dining-room. Two blacks were also mentioned on the Northumberland House wages list for 1764 – the same ones Walpole refers to in his description of the nightmare dinner-party. They would have been purely for show.

A Negro coachboy in the 1730s.

At the very bottom of the scale, so far as the indoor staff were concerned, were the various female servants, the majority of whom were little more than skivvies. The two exceptions to this rule were the Countess's chambermaid, who was the female equivalent of the valet, and the nurse, both of whom earned salaries of £20 a year; after whom there came, in rapidly descending order, the woman cook, who cooked for the servants and did all the less important cooking jobs, the still-room maid, who was really the housekeeper's assistant, the laundry maids, and finally the house and kitchen maids. None of the latter was paid more than £10 a year.

The remainder of the household, the outdoor staff, were also numerous and equally important, and their domain was the stables. Here the head coachman, Jonathan Cammack, reigned supreme for a salary of £30 a year, driving the main coach and keeping all the stabling accounts. The stable yard was situated in the east wing of Northumberland House, and consisted of four coach-houses, a livery-cleaning room, harness and saddle rooms with hay and corn lofts above, and stabling for eight coach horses and ten saddle horses, with bedrooms for the coachmen, grooms and stable helpers above them. The stable accounts for 1756 show that one landau, two chariots, one four-wheel post-chaise, one two-wheel post-chaise and one two-wheel chair were kept at Northumberland House. All of them were elegantly painted with the family coat-of-arms, as were various carts and waggons.

A lady's maid preparing her mistress's wig, by J. Gillray.

Short journeys, such as that from London to Syon, would have been made in the post-chaise, a light travelling carriage which had come into use since the establishment of a turnpike trust had led to a gradual improvement in the roads, and had much reduced travelling times. For example, when the fourth Duke of Bedford's grandparents, William and Rachel Russell, had left Bedford House in Bloomsbury for Woburn Abbey, their heavy coach lumbering down Great Russell Street into the Tottenham Court Road and so over the Highgate Hills, it had taken them, depending on the weather, between twelve and sixteen hours non-stop travelling to complete the journey.[37] Though there are no exact records of how long it took the fourth Duke or his household to make the journey, his grandson accomplished the same journey by post-chaise in only four hours. When the Northumberlands moved to one of their more distant country residences, such as Stanwick in Yorkshire, it was a considerable business. They travelled in a much heavier travelling carriage, accompanied by a retinue of servants riding saddle-horses. The journey took six days, with stops at Baldock, Huntingdon, Colsforth, Tuxford, Ferrybridge, and Burrowbridge. The carriages were lined with hard-wearing cloth, and they often carried with them a bed or beds, rolled in leather, to offset the appalling discomfort they were liable to meet in the various inns in which they were obliged to stay *en route*. The baggage went ahead by waggon, taking eleven days to make the 230-mile journey.[38]

Immediately below the head coachman came the second coachman, who was responsible for the cleaning of the carriages and harness; various grooms; the first and second post-chaise men, who drove the post-chaises; and the postillion, who rode one of the carriage-horses to help to control them. If greater show was needed, a second postillion was hired. Like the indoor footmen, the postillions, coachmen and post-chaise men all wore fine liveries. A surviving account from Bedford House shows just how elaborate these could be.

April 15, 1757

To making a Postillion's Suit, richly laced with gold and velvet lace.	£2.12.6*d*
Sleeve linings and pockets.	2.6*d*
Body lining.	2.6*d*
Velvet stand-up collar.	1.0*d*
Breeches linings and pockets.	4.6*d*
Silk garters.	2.0*d*
4 dozen gilt coat buttons.	10.2*d*
4 dozen 7 breast buttons.	5.9*d*
Twist and sewing silk.	12.0*d*
Buckram and stays.	4.0*d*

£4.16.11*d*[39]

Last in the Northumberland House 'family' – but by no means least, since no visitor could enter without their permission – came the porters, John Huggins and William Jones. They shared day and night duty, doubling up as watchmen, and had their office in the main gatehouse, beneath the Percy lion. One of their main tasks was to vet all callers thoroughly. By the time the Earl of Northumberland was created first Duke in 1766, the procedure for getting an appointment to see him had become extremely complicated, and those who failed to adhere to the strict etiquette involved, including close acquaintances of the family, were liable to find themselves in difficulty. Just such an occurrence took place one day when John Cowslade, a gentleman companion to the Duke's brother-in-law, Lord Beauchamp, and known as 'the Cow', turned up unannounced. 'A Gentleman, viz myself', he wrote, 'knocked at the gate and enquired, "Is the Duke of Northumberland at home?"'

Porter: No Sir.

Gent: I want to speak to him.

Porter: His Grace is not at home.

Gent: Does not the Duke go to the levee?

Porter: Yes.

Gent: Is he dressed?

Porter: No, but he will go into his dressing-room as soon as he comes home.

Gent: It is very late if he is to dress before the levee.

Porter: His Grace is at his retirements . . . I will go into the House and acquaint Mr Parker, his Grace's Secretary, that you want to speak to his Grace.

[In about seven or eight minutes Mr Parker enters . . .]

Gent: Pray Sir, are you the Duke's Secretary?

Parker (bowing conceitedly): Yes, Sir, I am his Grace's Secretary, but you cannot see His Grace.

Gent: Will you only let the Duke know that I am here, and that I wish to speak to him for a very few minutes.

Parker: Sir, you *cannot* possibly see him.

Gent (pulling a card with his name on it out of his pocket): Well, Sir, only show this card to the Duke, tell him that I am here, that I wish to speak a few words to him, not to detain him, but that if it is extremely inconvenient to him I will call another time.

Parker: I dare not do it. I have lived with his Grace above a twelvemonth. I am well acquainted with his Grace's temper. He would be very angry if he knew you had been let in. I wonder how the Porter came to let you in.

Gent: Sir, you don't know me, you don't know who I am, you don't know the particular connection I have had with the Duke during the whole course of my life. I have myself lived long enough in the house with him to be as full acquainted with him as you can be, or anybody else whatever. Therefore all I desire of you is to show this card to the Duke, and then if his Grace wishes to see you, he will appoint a shall say no more.

Parker: Sir, I cannot possibly carry in your card.

Gent: Not carry in my card?

Parker: Sir, the *Etiquette* of this house, indeed of all great houses of the same kind, is this. You are to enquire for his Grace at the Gate, and leave your name. The next day you are to call again, and then if his Grace wishes to see you, he will appoint a time for your admission, when he will be prepared for what you may have to say.

Gent: Sir, I am full as well acquainted with the world and the customs of great families as you can be, and though that Etiquette you have mentioned may be a general rule, it cannot, I am fully persuaded, hold good with regard to me. All I desire is that you would show my name to the Duke.

Parker: I dare not do it. I must obey orders . . .

The result was that 'the Cow' never got to see the Duke.[40]

Judging from the wages lists at Northumberland House, and from other houses of a similar size, such as Bedford House, Devonshire House and Shelburne House, the average size of a 'family' was around forty, and this was to remain so up to the outbreak of the First World War. Of these, a certain number were permanent. Northumberland House, for example, had its own housekeeper, still-room maid, three housemaids, and porters. The rest moved around between residences. '£27.9.5d for 20 servants to Chatsworth' runs a bill which has survived from Devonshire House, suggesting that this was generally the case.

In addition to those listed above, all of whom lived within the house and grounds, there were a number of other regular employees from outside, each of whom played a very important role in the running of the household. Chairmen, who carried sedan chairs, appear from time to time on the Northumberland House wages list, while on other occasions they were simply hired when the family were in town. They seem to have been used for various other tasks as well – for example, there exists a 'Chairmen's Bill for Cleaning and Beating Carpets' from the Michaelmas quarter of 1788, when the family would have been in the country. Likewise when the Duke of Bedford gave a great Ball at Bedford House in May 1757, and was obliged to borrow plate from his friends to supplement his own, it was brought to the house and taken away by their chairmen, each of whom received a tip for the service.

Paid for bringing and carrying the Plate home:

The Duke of Marlborough's Chairman	5s.0d
Lord Bolingbroke's Chairman	5s.0d
Lord Gower's Chairman	4s.0d
Lady Ossory's Chairman	4s.0d
Lady Betty Waldegrave's Chairman	4s.0d[41]

At another ball, in April 1759, various chairmen were paid five shillings each for 'cleaning of knives'.[42]

In an age when the most primitive forms of central heating were still at the experimental stages, and there was as yet no gas lighting, three vital tasks were performed by the charcoal man, who kept the house supplied with firewood, the lamplighter and the oil man. Working in the lamp room, the lamplighter was in overall charge of all the lighting in the house: he checked the wicks and polished all the lamps, and scraped the wax from the candelabra and cleaned them. The oil man manufactured and supplied all the lamp oil. A letter sent from Woburn Abbey to the Steward at Bedford House suggests that he was also responsible for supplying oil to the country: 'Sir, we have no lamp oil in the house and as I am in expectation of my Lord's being at home soon beg the favour of you to order Ten or Fifteen Gallons of the best Lamp Oil to burn in the house to come by Partridge's Waggon next Saturday.'[43]

The other important outsiders were the tin man, who looked after all the coppers etc in the kitchen, and the ice man, who kept the ice house filled. 'Charges for Filling the Ice House at Northumberland House: Geo: May Cart Carriage. 6 loads of Ice at 2/6*d* per load, 15*s*.'[44] One of the ice cutters had the wonderfully appropriate name of John Frost. Ice houses went back to the Restoration: what appears to have been the first in the country was built in St James's Park in October 1660, 'as the mode is in some parts of France and Italy and other hot Countries for to Cool wines and other drinks for the Summer Season.'[45] The event was celebrated by Edmund Waller in his poem 'On St James's Park as Lately Improved by His Majesty':

Yonder the harvest of cold months laid up,
Gives a fresh coolness to the Royal Cup;
There Ice like Christal, firm and never lost,
Tempers hot July with December's frost,
Winter's dark prison; where he cannot flie,
Though the warm Spring, his enemy grows nigh.
Strange! that extreames should thus preserve the Snow
High on the Alpes, and in deep Caves below!

Six ice houses were built at about this time – five for the Royal household, and one for the Duchess of Cleveland. The latter was discovered in 1956 during excavations for a new building on the site of 21 St James's Place. It consisted of a deep pit measuring 12 feet 11 inches from ground level to the deepest part of the sloping floor, the base being 7 feet 3 inches in diameter

An ice house discovered in 1956 on the site of 21 St James's Place.

and the top 13 feet 5 inches. It was lined with brick, and an arched drain, towards which the floor sloped, was cut in the south side, following the natural decline of the land. Just above the drain the brick lining projected to form a circular ledge on which the timber-slatted floor probably rested. This acted as a sieve for any melted ice, which would then drain through the brick culvert. This was essential since, for the ice house to be effective, it was necessary to keep the ice as dry as possible.[46] As soon as there was a frost, the ice men would be out in force scouring the lakes for whatever they could find. 'Be pleased to inform my Lord Duke', wrote the Woburn ice man to the steward at Bedford House, 'that I have got the ice house at Woburn Abbey almost full of ice by a short frost on Thursday night last, but the ice was so thin was obliged to skim it off the water with nets.'[47]

One final browse through the household bills from Northumberland House, Bedford House, Shelburne House and Devonshire House reveals a veritable swarm of other tradesmen who relied on them and their kind for a living. The wax and tallow chandlers provided candles; the brewer brewed beer for the servants; the scavenger took away the rubbish; the ratcatcher killed the rats; the newsman brought the papers; the soap boiler boiled up the soap; the glassman blew the glasses; the cork cutter cut the corks; the cutler made their knives, while the sword cutter sharpened them; the tailor, woollendraper, laceman, and buttonmaker produced liveries; the bellhanger hung the bells; the stationer provided quills, ink and paper; the miller ground flour for the still-room; the apothecary sold not only weird and wonderful drugs, but also gum-dragon, isinglass, gum arabic, cream of tartar and cochineal for the confectioners, and the muffin man delivered muffins – not to mention the grocer, the fishmonger, the butcher, the purveyor of sweetmeats, the wine merchant, and the whole industry which surrounded the stables and included the corn merchant, the saddle-maker, the trunk-maker, the sedan-chair-maker etc. And when the family left town, in moved the upholsterers and carpenters to take up the carpets, take down the tapestries, swaddle the walls and pictures and furniture in dust sheets, and beat and clean and sweep and mend. There was no time when these houses were free from an endless hustle and bustle.

6

The Neo-Classical Triumph

When do you come? If it is not too soon, you will find a new town. I stand today at Piccadilly like a country squire: there are twenty new stone houses; at first I concluded that all the grooms that used to live there, had got estates and built palaces.

Walpole to Montagu, November 1759

Shortly before Christmas 1755, Althorp House in Northamptonshire, the home of the Spencer family, was the scene of great gaiety and rejoicing. 'No one in the house is sober,' wrote one of the guests, Anna Maria Poyntz, to a friend.[1] The reason for this state of affairs was two days of festivities, on 19 and 20 December, in celebration both of the coming of age of John Spencer, and of his marriage to Miss Georgiana Poyntz, his fiancée of several years standing, which took place on the following day. For some reason known only to herself, for all the guests were well aware of what was going on, Spencer's mother, the Countess Cowper, insisted that the whole ceremony be performed in secret in her dressing-room, in the middle of a ball which was going on in the rooms below. This was the cause of enormous embarrassment to the poor bride, who hardly dared show her face for fear of 'the jokes of some of the gentlemen, particularly of a Mr Robinson who is mostly agreeable and very ridiculous, but more to be dreaded for those kind of things than anybody else.'[2] All in all it was, however, a splendid affair, befitting a man who had at least £30,000 a year, and news of it was not slow to reach London. 'One has heard of nothing for sometime past,' wrote Lady Hervey to Mr Morris, 'but the magnificence, or rather the silly vain profusion on account of Mr Spencer's wedding ...'[3]

The Spencers' journey up to London, shortly afterwards, bore all the trappings of a royal procession. 'They came to Town from Althorp ... with three coaches and six horses, and two hundred horsemen,' continued Lady Hervey:

the villages through which they passed were put into the greatest consternation: some of the poor people shut themselves up in their houses and cottages, barricading themselves up as well as they could. Those who were more resolute, or more desperate, armed themselves with pitchforks, spits, and spades; all crying out it was the *invasion* which was come; and, to be sure, by the coaches and six horses, both the Pretender

Right: Georgiana,
Countess Spencer.

Far right: John, first
Earl Spencer.

Miniatures by Jean
Etienne Lisotard.

Right: Georgiana,
Countess Spencer.

Far right: John, first
Earl Spencer.

Miniatures by Jean
Etienne Lisotard.

and King of France were come too. In short, great was the alarm, and happy they
were when this formidable cavalcade passed without setting fire to the habitations, or
murdering the inhabitants . . .[4]

Nor were the bridal pair any less conspicuous when, having arrived in
London, they went to pay their respects to the Prince and Princess of Wales
at Leicester House:

The procession consisted of two carriages and a chair. In the first carriage were the
bridegroom and Lord Cowper, with three footmen behind, the bride followed in a new
sedan-chair, lined with white satin, a black page walking before, and three footmen
behind, all in the most superb liveries. The diamonds worn by the newly-married pair
were presented to Mr Spencer by Sarah Duchess of Marlborough and were worth
£100,000. The shoe buckles of the bridegroom were alone worth £30,000.[5]

Such ostentatious behaviour aroused not a little envy among the great ladies
of London society, and for some time poor Georgiana Spencer was the victim
of much back-biting. 'It is now the fashion to pull Mrs Spencer to pieces',
wrote Mrs Delany to Mrs Dewes in February 1756 'for not returning her visits
faster than she possibly can and for some blunders her servants have made; it
is well they can find no other fault; but some fault there must be.'[6] Mrs Delany
quite rightly considered this unreasonable, especially since Georgiana had been
in London only five weeks, during which she had twice been confined with a
cold, and had received six hundred people. Lady Mary Coke, however, knew
of a fault that was not quite so forgivable. 'The terrible custom at Lord
Spencer's of making the servants drunk', she wrote on one occasion after a
dinner at their estate in Wimbledon,

exposed me to great danger, and had not the footman been a little soberer than the postillion, nothing could have saved me. As I soon found out how very drunk he was, I ordered him to go a foot's pace, but when I came to a little bridge between Hammersmith and the Acton road, he turned short about, and drove me down into a place where I have seen water enough to have drowned me, and how the Chaise stood I can't imagine. I then considered a moment if it would be more dangerous to walk home or remain in the Chaise, but as it was near ten o'clock, I thought I should run a greater risk in walking, and therefore desired the footman to go at the head of the horses, and hold the postillion on, if he could, and in that way I at last arrived home.[7]

At the time of the marriage, the Spencers were living in a house in Grosvenor Street, bequeathed to the family by Sarah, Duchess of Marlborough, John Spencer's great-grandmother. This was a modest affair in comparison to Sunderland House, their former residence, which stood east of Burlington House, on the site of the Albany, and had been sold in 1745. With all the comings and goings, coupled with a growing awareness of his own importance, it was not long before John Spencer decided that he needed something much grander. So, in May 1756, he bought a ninety-nine-year lease of a site at the south-west end of St James's Place, on which the architect John Vardy had planned a house for Lord Montfort, who had committed suicide the previous year.[8] To begin with he kept on Vardy, a member of the Palladian group, and set to work without delay.

By the end of September 1756, Mrs Delaney, walking in Green Park, was able 'to see Mr Spencer's House, which is begun and the ground floor finished. *See colour plate 6* One front is in St James's Place, on the left hand as you go up the street, and another front to the Green Park. It will be superb when finished.'[9] The key to Spencer House was John Spencer's membership of the Society of Dilettanti, a club founded in 1734 by certain gentlemen who, having completed the Grand Tour, wished to encourage a taste in England for the artistic styles and objects which had fascinated them during their wanderings. It was the art and culture of the classical age which particularly interested them, and they tended to lack sympathy for the contemporary Frenchified rococo and Walpole's sham gothic. At the time of Spencer's election in 1756, the Secretary of the Society was General George Gray, a celebrated amateur of architecture, who in 1751 had published *Proposals for publishing an Accurate Description of the Antiquities of Athens* by James Stuart and Nicholas Revett, two English architects in the vanguard of the neo-classical movement, to whom he had been introduced by his brother, Sir James Gray, the British Resident at Venice. Seeing an opportunity to further both the aims of the Society and the career of Stuart, in whom he was greatly interested, the General persuaded Spencer to allow him to supervise the erection of his new house. Since building was already well under way according to the plans and elevations of Vardy, Gray retained him until the ground-floor rooms were completed and then, in 1758, on some unrecorded pretext, replaced him with Stuart, who set to work on decorating the state rooms on the first floor.

Although the initial stages of Spencer House had been completed with some speed, from now on things slowed down. This was due to a number of factors. First of all Spencer's early enthusiasm had resulted in a greater expenditure than he had expected, so that for a while there was a shortage of money. Equally important, however, were the health and character of Mr Stuart, who suffered from gout, had a fondness for the bottle, and was incurably lazy. As late as May 1763, Lord Villiers was writing to Lady Spencer, 'Other news I heard none yesterday except that Stuart has got the gout and that the estimate of the plastering work alone of the ceiling intended for your Great Room amounts to £480,'[10] while in August Mrs Howe commented, 'I am sorry to hear your house is yet no forwarder – it is horribly provoking.'[11] There was better news the following February, though by then poor Lady Spencer might have been forgiven for losing interest. 'I called the other day in St James's Place,' Lord Villiers informed her,

James 'Athenian' Stuart, after George Dance.

and had the pleasure to find the ceiling in the Great Room quite finished and ready for the gilders. The rest of the works go on with as much expedition as possible ... they have been very unlucky in their weather for the drying of the ceiling which will have delayed the gilding a little but that will be only of a few days. The other rooms go on too and as far as can be seen of them, the ornaments appear rich and in good taste.[12]

In spite of all the delays Spencer House, completed two years later, emerged as one of the most charming and successful of all eighteenth-century London houses. The west front overlooking the park was especially effective, with a bold Doric order rising above an arcaded and rusticated basement to support a pediment over the five central bays, surmounted by classical figures. 'I do not apprehend there is a house in England of its size,' wrote Arthur Young in 1768, 'better worth the view of the curious in architecture, and the fitting up and furnishing great houses, than Lord Spencer's in St James's Place. Nothing can be more pleasing than the park front, which is ornamented to a high degree, and yet not without profusion; I know not a more beautiful piece of architecture ...'[13]

As for the interior, it was in no way, to quote Young, 'inferior to the beauties of the outside'. His tour took in first Vardy's ground-floor rooms:

We were shewn first into Lord Spencer's Library, which is 30 feet by 25; the ornaments handsome. The chimney-piece very light, of polished white marble. On one side of the room hangs a capital picture of the nature of witchcraft ... From hence you enter the dining-room, 46 by 24; the decorations in the finest taste, and the richest of their kind; the ceiling and cornice of white and green, beautiful, the slabs of Siena marble, large and finely veined. The chimney-piece, a basso relievo, of white marble well polished. On one side of it is a landscape, the killing of a dragon ... On the other side is another yet more pleasing ... the figures are a centaur carrying off a naked woman ... Next we entered the drawing-room, which is 24 by 21, clear of a bow-window, parted from the room only by two pillars of most exquisite workmanship;

they are carved in leaves, the thick foliage of which bends round in a fine arch from one to the other, in a taste that cannot be too much admired; on each side, in a semi-circular cove in the wall, an urn of white marble with basso relievos. Nothing can be more elegant than the chimney-piece; a border of Siena marble with a festoon of flowers upon it in white; the ceiling, cornice, and ornaments of green and white and gold, and in a delicate style. Over the chimney, a picture of two usurers . . .[14]

The park front of Spencer House. This aquatint was drawn and engraved by Thomas Malton, 1800.

Now Young ascended the staircase, with its unique painted metal drapery balustrade by Vardy, to the first floor – to find, beyond the Spencers' private apartments, Stuart's exquisitely decorated state rooms, reflecting his love of the classical antiquities of Rome and Greece. First

the dressing-room 25 by 23, which is fitted up with great taste; scarce anything can be more beautiful than the mosaic ceiling, the cornices and all the ornaments: the chimney-piece is finely designed and admirably executed; it is of white marble wrought with the utmost taste, and beautifully polished; over the cornice are festoons of the lightest carving, and two eagles, with a very fine basso relievo of carving in the centre: the pictures are disposed with great elegance, and hung up by ribbons of gilt carving in a pretty taste . . .[15]

Opposite: The
entrance hall, Spencer
House.

Many of these pictures were by Rubens, and indeed the room was often
referred to as the Rubens Room. 'Out of this room,' he continued, 'you enter
the saloon 45 by 30, than which I never beheld one fitted up and furnished in
a more pleasing taste.'[16] This room, the 'great room' referred to by Lord
Villiers in his letter, was almost a double-cube; and with its high coved ceiling
giving it the princely air of a Roman palazzo, it must have been one of the
noblest in London. It was painted green, white and gold, with gilt medallions,
representing Music, Hospitality, Venus, and the Three Graces, supported by
amorini, griffins and leopards, let into the ceiling; the red damask walls were
hung with huge paintings of the Italian school – two Guercinos of *King David*
and *The Samian Sybil* on one end wall, and two large Salvator Rosas flanking
the very grand chimney-piece. Opposite this, between the windows, were 'two
slabs very large of the finest Siena marble, the frames carved in the most
exquisite taste and richly gilt. The pier-glasses of a large size, single plates,
and the frames of the lightest workmanship ...'[17] The room also contained a
huge set of seat furniture, comprising four sofas, eighteen single chairs, and
twenty-six armchairs.

See colour plate 9

It comes as no surprise that the next room thrilled Arthur Young most, for
this, the painted room, was Stuart's masterpiece, and the first complete neo-
classical room in Europe. 'The next room is to me a Phoenix,' he wrote;

... on one side is a bow window ornamented with the most exquisitely carved and gilt
pillars you can conceive; the walls and ceiling are painted in compartments by Mr
Stuart in the most beautiful taste; even the very scrolls and festoons of the slightest
sort, which are run between the square and circular compartments, are executed with
the minutest elegance: the ground of the whole is green; and the general effect more
pleasing than is easily conceived. Nothing can be lighter or more beautiful than the
chimney-piece ... Remember to observe the peacock's feathers over one of the glasses,
the turtles on a wreath of flowers; and the magpies on bunches of grapes: they are
beautiful, and the deception of the first extraordinary; the bold relief of such light
strokes does honour to the pencil of the artist.[18]

The furniture was as splendid as the decoration: six massive armchairs, four
sofas with winged lion ends, and a pair of *torchères*, supporting candle-sconces
and incense burners, thought to be the earliest pieces of neo-classical furniture
decorated with painted panels. Arthur Young was not alone in waxing lyrical
over this extraordinary room. A later visitor, Mr Edwin Beresford Chancellor,
was entranced: 'When we enter this apartment', he wrote in 1908,

we seem to be stepping back two thousand years; we are no longer in a London
reception-room; we are in the *tablinium* in the house of Marcus Lucretius, or in one
of the remarkable painted chambers in the dwelling of Meleager; that red light in the
sky is not the sun setting over the trees of Green Park, but the afterglow of some great
eruption of Vesuvius! If a door open, surely Glaucus or Diomed or the blind Nydia
will appear! It is truly a room in which to dream of the past ...[19]

Above: The bow-window of the drawing-room, Spencer House.

Right: The dining-room, Spencer House.

Opposite: The great room, Spencer House, photographed when it still had its superb set of seat furniture.

Another view of the great room, Spencer House.

Stuart's fantastic painted room, Spencer House.

The bow-window in the painted room, Spencer House.

The period which saw the building of Spencer House was one of great activity. 'When do you come?' wrote Horace Walpole to Montagu in November 1759: 'If it is not too soon, you will find a new town. I stand today at Piccadilly like a country squire: there are twenty new stone houses; at first I concluded that all the grooms that used to live there, had got estates and built palaces.' Despite the Seven Years' War, it was a time of much greater prosperity than the 1730s and 1740s. It was also more stimulating artistically – including the publication of a number of beautifully illustrated and influential books, of which Robert Wood's *Ruins of Palmyra* came out in 1753 and his *Ruins of Balbec* in 1757, Chambers's *Treatise on Civil Architecture* in 1759, Volume I of Stuart and Revett's *Antiquities of Athens* in 1762, and Adam's

July 13th 1793

Geo Dance

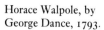
Horace Walpole, by
George Dance, 1793.

Ruins of the Palace of the Emperor Diocletian at Spalatro in 1764. At the same
time, a new generation of talented architects was setting up – in particular Stuart,
William Chambers, and, most important of all, Robert Adam. Stuart, as we have
seen, was the first to get his chance, largely because of his connections with
the Society of Dilettanti, and it was this which led to his next two commissions.

The first was for the sixth Earl of Holdernesse, a prominent member of the
Society and a cultivated patron of the arts with a distinguished career as a
courtier and diplomat. Holdernesse House, which later became better known
as Londonderry House, stood on the corner of Park Lane and Hertford Street,
and was notable for three splendid ceilings, in the two drawing-rooms overlooking Park Lane and in the boudoir on the Hertford Street front; while that

in the central drawing-room was highly reminiscent of the 'painted room' at Spencer House. It is not certain whether Stuart actually built the house from scratch, or merely decorated or redecorated an existing one, for his accounts show only that work was going on there about 1765-6, £50 being paid to him on 10 May 1765, and £625 to Joseph Rose, the plasterer, on 7 May and 5 December 1766.[20] The work must have been completed that year, when the architect and draughtsman John Carter sketched details of its decoration. Lady Mary Coke attended the opening in 1767. 'The hangings, chairs and window curtains of the Great Room', she wrote, 'are of the three coloured damask, but I think the finest I have ever seen. The glasses are magnificent. Four rooms were open, but not many people; three tables however at loo. . .'[21]

Thomas Anson, in the manner of Vanderbanck.

Opposite: Stuart's Saloon at Holdernesse House.

At Lichfield House, 15 St James's Square, James Stuart created for Thomas Anson, a fellow Dilettante, the first Greek-style façade in London. Anson, an elderly bachelor squire, had had a long-standing interest in and knowledge of the different phases of classical art, which he had put to good use over the years in the remodelling of his house and park at Shugborough in Stafford-shire.[22] It was not, however, until he inherited a fortune from his younger brother, Admiral Lord Anson, in 1762, that he was able to contemplate build-ing a town residence. Being thoroughly up to date on all the latest develop-ments, he naturally wished to champion the new style, and at No. 15 he evidently succeeded, for Stuart wrote to him at one stage that the house was 'a topic of much conversation among the connoisseurs in Architecture'.[23] Just as he had done at Holdernesse House, Stuart included one room – in this case, the front drawing-room on the first floor – with a ceiling based on that of the 'painted room' at Spencer House, though in this case it was, if anything, even more elaborate. This was probably completed towards the end of 1764, for in June of that year we find Stuart writing to his employer giving an account of the celebrations which attended the completion of the first floor. 'The grand function of wetting the first floor', he informed him 'was performed last Sa-turday when upward of 50 men had their bellies full of Beef pudding and Ale and your health was drunk with very cheerful huzzas, the Masters treated themselves and I had the honour of being president.'[24] Now that so much of St James's Square has been rebuilt, it is difficult to judge the original impact of the distinctive façade of No. 15, dressed as it was in Portland stone, while all the other houses were of brick. Certainly John Stewart, the author of *Critical Observations on the Buildings and Improvements of London*, published in 1771, considered it to be 'wonderfully beautiful'.[25]

Anson appears as a ratepayer for the house in 1766, and was certainly living in it by April 1768, for in that month Lady Shelburne noted in her diary that she had attended a 'breakfast and concert' in honour of Mrs Montagu at 'Mr Anson's, a very fine house built and ornamented by Mr Stuart'.[26] As it hap-pens this was none other than Mrs Elizabeth Montagu of Hill Street who in 1775 was to commission Stuart to build his last important London house.

The façade of Lichfield House, 15 St James's Square.

The drawing-room, Lichfield House.

Sir William Chambers, by Reynolds.

Below: The façade of Gower House, Whitehall.

Opposite: Basevi's drawing of the staircase hall at Gower House.

'Mr Stuart', wrote Robert Adam in the preface to his *Works*, 'with his usual elegance and taste has contributed greatly towards introducing the true style of antique decoration.'[27] He made no mention, however, of Stuart's closest rival, William Chambers. In 1755 Chambers had returned to England after spending five years living and working in Italy, and had almost immediately become successful. Introduced by the Earl of Bute to George, Prince of Wales, he had become his architectural tutor and, shortly afterwards, architect to the Prince's mother, who, in 1757, had commissioned him to design ornaments for her garden at Kew Palace, Surrey, including the Roman Arch, the Pagoda, and various classical temples and alcoves. The same year he also began work on the decoration of some rooms at Pembroke House, notable among which were a number of particularly fine ceilings, in the dining-room, the saloon, and the gallery. A proposal drawn up in 1759 (*see colour plate 10*) for the Duke of York in Pall Mall shows how well Chambers understood the requirements of a noble client, and sets the seal on what was to become his trademark – the grand staircase. It was a brilliant interpretation of the Norfolk House type of plan, but carried out with far greater panache, with its suites of rooms for entertaining opening off a large central circular staircase hall with a coffered dome, inspired by Kent's staircase at 44 Berkeley Square, and his hall at Holkham. Sadly, for it would have been magnificent, the scheme was never adopted by the Duke.

Chambers's great chance came in about 1765 when Lord Gower, a prominent courtier and politician, took the lease of a site in Whitehall and gave him the commission to design a house which old photographs and drawings show to have been one of the finest ever erected in London. From the outside Gower House was plain, in the Palladian style with a five-bay elevation and a central Venetian window, and was unusual in that the entrance, instead of being beneath this on the street front, was hidden from view round the back. From the entrance hall, guests went straight ahead into the staircase hall which filled the centre of the house, soaring up to a dome overhead. Basevi's drawing

The staircase, Gower House.

The ballroom, Gower House.

Elizabeth, Lady
Melbourne, by
(?) Joseph Sanders.

gives some idea of its splendour, with its double arcade, Doric below, Ionic above, and the staircase which divides, turns, and finally curves round to reach the level of the first floor – inspired, it is thought, by Baldassare Longhena's staircase in the monastery of San Giorgio Maggiore in Venice.[28] It was a brilliant stage for the fashionable world to parade upon as they climbed in all their finery up to the great drawing-room, 26 feet by 53 feet, which filled the back of the house.

The staircase was the main feature of the house in Piccadilly which Chambers designed for Peniston Lamb, first Lord Melbourne. Having inherited a fortune from his father and been created a peer, Melbourne had decided to demolish the house he had bought from Lord Holland in 1771, which stood to the east of Burlington House, and to build an establishment worthy of his new rank. It was a project in which he was encouraged by his nineteen-year-old wife Elizabeth, who was fast becoming one of the town's most popular hostesses. 'She is liked by everybody high and low and of all denominations', wrote Lady Sarah Lennox, 'which I don't wonder at, for she is pleasing, sensible, and desirous of pleasing, I hear, which must receive admiration.'[29] As well as being an admired beauty, she was extremely shrewd and intelligent, and was also known to be a woman of some means, since it was her husband's favourite boast that on their marriage he had given back to her her entire fortune in diamonds. She was single-minded in her ambition to be a leader of society, and for this she needed to be mistress of a house in which the fashionable world of London could be entertained in the utmost state.

Although Robert Adam had drawn up plans for a similar scheme for Lord Holland a few years previously, Melbourne chose to ignore these and, on the advice of his friend the second Baron Grantham, employed Chambers for the task. Work was begun in the summer of 1771, and by the following November Chambers was able to report that work was progressing 'very quickly and very well'.[30] Such a state of affairs seems to have continued, for the family were able to move in early in 1774, when Melbourne celebrated the opening with 'two public morning Concerts to show his house'.[31] The decoration was still to be completed, however, and Melbourne took the closest personal interest in it. We find him writing to Chambers in October, for example, forcefully expressing his views on the doing-up of the oval ante-room on the first floor:

Upon full consideration about furnishing the round room (in which you have exceeded my utmost wish) I am more and more averse to admit any gilding whatever even in the furniture, in my opinion the Elegance of that room is from the lightness of well disposed well executed Ornaments; vastly preferable to any load of gilding we Could have introduced. Therefore I am sure that carrying that Simplicity throughout, we shall succeed much better; and the novelty of a room of that sort finished without any gilding, cannot fail to Please. Therefore I wish you would Consider in what manner we can colour the glass frames and Chairs, so as to Correspond with that uniformity we have already so much attended to.

Chambers was firm in his reply. 'It is I think clear', he wrote,

that the Glasses and Soffas (*sic*) in the Niches should be gilt, for glasses without gilding are large black spots that kill the effect of everything about them, and the dead coloured silk with which the soffas are to be covered, must have gold to relieve it; when it will suit perfectly with the room; and I am under no apprehensions that the brilliancy of the gilding will hurt the effect of the rest, but rather set its plainness to advantage. The Chairs must of Course be gilt . . . [32]

Famous today as the Albany, and now little more than a façade – most of the original interior disappeared when it was adapted as bachelor chambers in the nineteenth century – Melbourne House was set back some hundred feet from Piccadilly, and protected from the street by a high screen wall which flanked that of Burlington House to the west. Two carriage gates, hung on rustic piers, with a tall, classical, pedimented arch between them, led into the great court, on the left of which were the stables and coach-houses, while the porter's lodge and the kitchens were on the right. As at Gower House, the Palladian exterior was simple and elegant, with the surprises kept for the inside. In this case visitors, having climbed a flight of ten steps at the front door, found themselves in a large oblong hall, with three archways in the north wall. These gave access to the 'great stair', which occupied a rectangular space

The façade of Melbourne House after its conversion into gentlemen's chambers (now the Albany).

The staircase
compartment of
Melbourne House. Sir
William Chambers,
architect.

in the centre of the main block and rose the full height of the building, adorned by classical statues standing in recesses. With its flying bridge between the half flights, the effect must have been very dramatic; but we can now only get an idea of what it was like from the somewhat similar but circular Navy Stair, designed by Chambers for Somerset House, and from flying stairs in country houses such as Glin Castle in County Limerick. The first-floor landing gave access to the private rooms in the south front, and a suite of four state rooms – the oval ante-chamber, the state dressing-room, the drawing-room, and the saloon.

No expense was spared in the painting and furnishing of the house, with artists such as Cipriani, Rebecca and Wheatley working on ceilings and other

The flying staircase at Glin Castle, Eire.

decorative work, James Paine designing chimney-pieces, and Chippendale making furniture, but the final cost evidently surprised even Melbourne, who was noted for his extravagance. 'His Lordship declared ... upon his honour,' recorded Mrs Steele, the companion of his mistress Mrs Baddeley, in an account of a conversation the latter had with her lover,

that when the house, in Piccadilly, which he was building, was finished, and the furniture in it complete, so as to sit down in it to dinner, from a just calculation, it would cost him one hundred thousand pounds. 'An astonishing sum!' exclaimed I. 'It is a much greater sum', continued his Lordship, 'than I intended, when I first began'; for Mr Chambers' the surveyor's estimate of the house and offices complete, did not exceed thirty thousand pounds; but, after they had gone on some way, and had made by his orders some few alterations, it came to twenty thousand more. So that the buildings of that house came to fifty thousand pounds, beside the sixteen thousand pounds paid for the old house and ground.[33]

Nevertheless Melbourne was delighted with the finished work, writing to Chambers in February 1774, 'I believe few people have had better reason than myself to be pleased with so large a sum laid out.'[34]

Lady Melbourne wasted no time in turning her new home into a centre for all that was gay and brilliant in society. 'The Melbournes are still in Town', wrote Lady Mary Coke in July 1777, 'and their House open to all the *bon-ton* who remain in Town: I hear of parties and suppers frequently.'[35] Here the leading Whig statesmen – Fox, Grenville, Lord Holland, Sheridan, the Duke of Bedford among others – flocked from the House of Commons to late-night suppers at which they ate and drank vast amounts, gossiped and flirted, played hard and deep, and vigorously debated politics and philosophy with wits like Sheridan, Selwyn and Walpole, and the cleverest and most beautiful women of the day. In becoming such a gathering place, Melbourne House established itself as part of a tradition of great Whig houses, which had its origins in the days of Southampton – later Bedford – House, where the party might be said to have been hatched, and which was to become the headquarters of a group known as the Bedford House Whigs or, more familiarly, as the 'Bloomsbury Gang'. Other Whig houses included Newcastle House, where George II's Secretary of State had reigned supreme, and, perhaps most famous of all, Devonshire House, in which the fourth Duke of Devonshire, known as 'the King of the Whigs', had laid the foundations of the political traditions which, during his successor's day, made his home the great centre of Whiggism. This was as much due to his wife as it was to the fifth Duke; a woman of infinite charm, she is most vividly remembered for the kiss with which she coaxed a vote for Charles James Fox from a reluctant butcher.

Georgiana, Duchess of Devonshire would have been the closest Lady Melbourne ever had to a rival, had she allowed such a situation to develop. Instead, from the moment Georgiana moved into Devonshire House, no more than a few hundred yards up the road, she deliberately cultivated her friendship, feigning indignation at the slightest suggestion that they were anything other than the best of companions. 'The Duke of Richmond has been here', she wrote to the Duchess on one occasion, 'and told me you and I were two rival queens, and I believe, if there had not been some people in the room, who might have thought it odd, that I should have slapped his face for such an idea ...'[36] They were an unlikely couple, the strong-willed and assertive Lady Melbourne, much happier in the society of men than women, and 'the pretty Duchess of Devonshire, who ... dines at 7, summer as well as winter, goes to bed at 3, & lies in bed till 4 ... has hysteric fits in a morning, & dances in the evening ... bathes, rides, dances for ten days, & lies in bed the next ten';[37] and for at least fifteen years they ruled over fashionable London.

George, Prince of Wales, by Richard Corbould. Engraving of 1791.

The peak of the careers of these remarkable women was probably reached in the 1780s, when the young Prince Regent became a constant guest in their houses. Newly come of age and bored by the narrow home life of his parents, who since their accession had remained almost completely out of touch with the glittering life around them, he could not wait to get away from the Court, and was once heard to say that he was 'glad the king's parties ended so soon as none of the agreeable entertainments began till after ten o'clock'.[38] Georgiana he called 'sister'. He was even more smitten by Lady Melbourne. 'I have no gossip to tell you', wrote Lady Sarah Napier to Lady Susan O'Brien, 'but that the P. of Wales is *desperately* in love with Ly Melbourne, & when she don't sit next to him at supper he is not commonly civil to his neighbours: she *dances* with him something in the cow style, but he is *en extase* with admiration at it.'[39] Lady Melbourne was evidently in a state of some ecstasy herself. When Frederick, Duke of York, the Prince's younger brother, told her while dining one evening at Melbourne House that he would much rather live there than in his own house in Whitehall, she replied that 'she would like the opportunity of looking on the park every morning when she rose and that were it possible, she would willingly exchange the chimes at night of St James's for those of the Abbey.'[40] For her, he said, anything was possible. The following year, 1791, 'His Royal Highness on or about the twenty-fifth day of December ... entered into and took possession of the ... premises in Piccadilly lately called Melbourne House and ... Lord Melbourne entered into and took possession of the ... premises at Whitehall lately called York House [Fetherstonhaugh House].'[41]

In many ways it is surprising that Lord Melbourne had chosen to ignore Robert Adam's plans, for they promised a far more exciting building than was subsequently erected. Adam's proposed house was to have been almost square and planned like a Roman villa, with single ranges of rooms round a central court, and approached by way of a large oval colonnaded forecourt, probably inspired by that at Burlington House. The design within was skilful. The house would have been entered through a circular lobby, intended for servants to wait in; this led into the entrance hall, at the north end of which was a

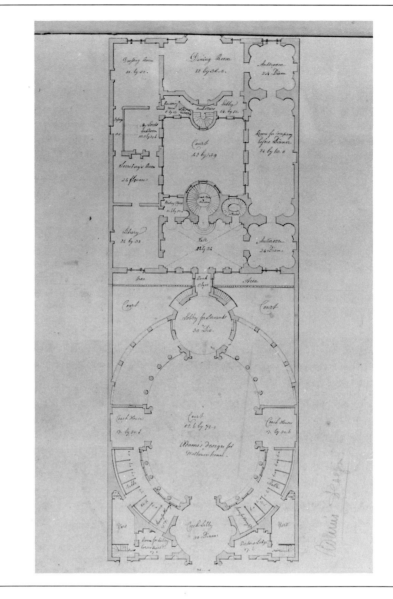

The unexecuted plan
drawn up by Adam
for Lord Holland in
1764.

circular staircase. To the left of the hall were the private apartments, a library,
a secretary's room, a bedroom, and a dressing-room, while to the right lay a
suite of reception rooms consisting of a circular ante-room, leading into 'a
Room for the Company before dinner', then another ante-room followed by a
dining-room in the middle of the garden front. Adam's style was more decorative than that of Chambers, and was therefore generally more popular, since
it was easier on the eye: it was also specifically aimed at the needs of the world
of smart society, whose inhabitants, as we have seen, led so much of their life
in public:

a life of continual entertaining in drawing-rooms and ante-rooms and eating-rooms
where conversation would not be wholly ephemeral, where a sentence might be delivered which would echo round political England, where an introduction might mean
the beginning of a career or a deft criticism the dethronement of a policy.[42]

7

The Clients of
Robert Adam

He has made me a ceiling and chimney-piece, and doors, which are pretty enough to
make me a thousand enemies; Envy turns livid at the first glimpse of them.

Elizabeth Montagu on Robert Adam, February 1767.

As soon as Robert Adam returned to England from Italy, in the winter of
1757–8, he determined to take London and Society by storm, and on his arrival
he began 'paying his respects to the great', 'putting on a face of brass' and
'trudging doggedly from one nobleman's ante-room to another'. It was also
necessary, he believed, 'to blind the world by dazzling their eyesight with vain
pomp', to which end he would need 'one of the handsomest chariots and
prettiest pair of horses that London affords, as I imagine there is no way to
get the better of these city fellows but by throwing them into despair at first
sight, and no way so good or proper to get a good price as to take all methods
to show you despise a bad one.'[1]

To begin with, things did not go quite the way he expected. On 20 January
1758, Lady Mary Wortley Montagu, whose acquaintance he had made on the
Grand Tour, mentioned his name to her daughter, Lady Bute, wife of the
third Earl: 'I saw, some months ago, a countryman of yours', she wrote, 'who
desires to be introduced to you. He seemed to me, in one short visit, to be a
man of genius, and I have heard his knowledge of architecture much ap-
plauded. He is now in England.'[2] His eventual presentation to the Earl ended,
however, in disaster, for the latter received him 'booted and spurred' as if he
were just going out, cut the interview short, and afterwards refused to help or
take any interest in him. This so infuriated Adam that he told a friend, 'I have
a great mind to go out to Kensington and when he and Madame la Princesse
are stewing together I'll have them put in a boat naked and brought down the
river like Adam and Eve and I'll fell him dead with Piranesi's four folio
volumes from Westminster Bridge.'[3] Although many people of rank and
fashion did flock to his door to admire his drawings, and some even asked for
designs, they were not very good at paying; 'and when they do', he wrote, 'give
nothing worth taking. So may the devil damn them altogether. I'll turn soap-
boiler and tallow chandler; they grow rich and eat turtle.'[4]

By the end of 1758 Adam's prospects had begun to improve. He was taken

Sir Lawrence Dundas
and his grandson at 19
Arlington Street, by
Zoffany.

up by men like Sir Nathaniel Curzon and Edwin Lascelles, who were to become important patrons, employing him at Kedleston and Harewood, and in 1761 he was reconciled with Lord Bute, then the King's first Minister, who got him the appointment of Architect of the Works, in company with Chambers. In the following year Adam began his first major London commission, designing a new staircase and a quantity of very grand furniture for Sir Lawrence Dundas at his house at 19 Arlington Street. Dundas – who, according to Walpole, had amassed a fortune of £800,000 in four years as a commissary during the war – also commissioned a 'great room', drawings of which show that it would have been of elegant simplicity, terminating in a huge masonry bay window twenty feet wide and three storeys high, but which was sadly abandoned. Judging from the following incident witnessed by Lady Mary Coke, who attended a ball there in 1769, Dundas and his wife appear to have been rather a brash couple.

At eight o'clock I went to Lady Dundas. She seemed afraid she should not have Gentlemen enough to dance, as the House of Commons was still sitting. The Ball, however, began, and the dancers complaining of the heat, Lady Dundas ordered one of the Servants to break a pane of glass in each window to let in the Air. I could not help saying I was sorry to see such fine glass broke for such a purpose. Everything was in the same magnificent style. I played at Loo with the Duchess of Bedford, Lady Waldegrave, Lord Weymouth, etc. and won fifty guineas. Sir Lawrence Dundas came from the House between ten and eleven o'clock. I told him I lamented his fine windows being broke: he smiled and said it did not signify. The Dowager Waldegrave was there and looked very cross. When the Company went to supper, I came home...[5]

In the same year that Adam began his work for Dundas, he also embarked upon a much larger project for Lord Bute, who had bought a site at the south end of Berkeley Square, and had been considering proposals, apparently by Matthew Brettingham, for the erection of a house there. Adam was called in to revise these. Hardly had the scheme got under way, however, than Bute was toppled from power. Among the accusations thrown at him by a populace dissatisfied at the concessions given to Britain in the Peace of Paris of 1763, was that he had betrayed his country for money, which he was using to finance his new house. So exaggerated were the stories surrounding him that there was even one in circulation to the effect that he planned to incarcerate twenty-seven fiddlers in a basement room at Bute House, from which a complicated system of pipes would convey their music to other rooms in the house, where it could be turned on and off at will. Bute therefore decided to sell. As it happened, the second Earl of Shelburne, of Bowood in Wiltshire, who had succeeded his father in June 1761, at the age of twenty-four, had for some time been considering building a London house, and had acquired a site at Hyde Park Corner, for which Adam had also prepared a plan. But all idea of building here was abandoned in the summer of 1765, after a visit to the Shelburnes from General Robert Clerk, a close friend of Robert Adam, and Lord Shelburne's architectural mentor. 'Col. Clarke came down from London', wrote Lady Shelburne in her journal of 16 September 1765. 'He told us Lord Bute was going to sell ye House he is building in Berkeley Square, upon which Lord Shelburne gave him a commission to buy it for him and it rests now in his hands.'[6] Shelburne paid £22,500 for Bute House, £3,000 less than it had already cost, and he bought it on the condition that Lord Bute should complete it to Adam's designs.

John Stuart, third Earl of Bute, by Reynolds, 1773.

The house stood at the south-west end of Berkeley Square, where Charles Street meets Bolton Row, and faced east, at right angles to its lodge and entrance gates which opened out onto the square itself. It was far advanced when sold to Lord Shelburne, and on 10 August 1768, his wife was able to write in her journal:

See colour plate 11

Arrived from Bowood. On the ground floor we have the Hall, Antichamber, & Dining Room, which are quite finished, except for the glasses, the window curtains & chairs, which makes it very doubtful if we can ask the King of Denmark to dinner. The attics are all complete, the middle floor we have the Library and three other rooms, all to the Square, which Royle is now busy in papering, but the masons who are cleaning down the staircase and the bell hangers make it as yet impossible for us to see any people but of business & very intimates.[7]

In spite of the chaos which evidently still ruled in the house, her husband was already living there, and ten days later Lady Shelburne herself moved in. 'I had the pleasure of coming to Shelburne House', she wrote on 20 August, 'from which I continue this diary. My Lord was going to Council as I arrived, with Lord Granby; we had some little conversation on the steps, and I had full time to walk over and examine the house. It is very noble, and I am very much pleased with it, tho' perhaps few people wou'd have come to live in it, in so unfinished a state.'[8] A further entry describes a shopping expedition:

... to Cipriani's, Zucchi's, and some other people employed for our house in town ... we first went to Zucchi's, where we saw some ornaments for our ceilings, and a large architecture painting for the antichamber, with which however my Lord is not particular pleased. From there to Mayhew and Inch where is some beautiful cabinet work, and two pretty glass cases for one of the rooms in my apartment, and which, though they are only deal, and to be painted white, he charges £50 for. From thence to Cipriani's where we saw some most beautiful drawings and where Lord Shelburne bespoke some to be copied for me, to complete my dressing room, which I should wish to be furnished with drawings and crayon pictures. From thence to Zuccarelli's where we also saw some pictures doing for us and from thence home it being half an hour past four.[9]

The new chatelaine was quick to put her stamp on Shelburne House. The entry in her journal for 22 August reads: 'Mr Townsend, Mr Porteen, Mr Sutton and Mr Adams dined here, with the latter I consulted on the furniture for our painted antichamber, and determined that it should be pea green and satin spotted with white and trimmed with a pink and white fringe, it was originally my own thought and met with his entire approbation.'[10] This ante-room was the first in what Adam referred to as 'the suite of Levee rooms', and guests were shown in there from the entrance hall, designated the 'porter's hall' on the plans. Adam was most meticulous in explaining to his client exactly how he thought the various rooms should be used. The ante-room, for example, was for receiving visitors, and would therefore be used partly by the family and partly by the upper servants. The far end of it was semi-circular to

prevent it from appearing near so large as either of the rooms to which it gives access, and tho' upper servants do wait there, we should imagine there could arise no inconvenience from hence, since the Room for Company before dinner will never probably be used by Your Lordship for private business, as there is the Bow window room, the room to the right of it and the Library for that purpose: and as one in the suite of Levee rooms it is infinitely better to go first into the anteroom and from thence directly into the room for Company before dinner, without any passages or backstairs intervening...[11]

From this latter room, distinguished by the delicate decorative pilasters and ceiling, painted by Cipriani, the company moved into the eating room, with its screen of columns, panels of enriched stucco by Joseph Rose, and a dramatic series of niches for statues. When dinner was over, they passed into the stair-case hall, which occupied the centre of the house, and across to the north-east drawing-room. The room adjoining this, which was by far the grandest in the house, was specified on Adam's plan as a music-room. It took the form of a central oblong connected at each end to a rotunda thirty feet in diameter and, though it remained uncompleted for many years, it was to become the most celebrated room in the house.

In January 1771 Lady Shelburne was taken suddenly ill and died. Her bereaved husband set out at once for Italy. Here, like so many others before him, he became entranced by the beauty of classical antiquities and conceived the idea of turning the music-room into a magnificent sculpture gallery. He already owned a number of busts, which he had bought from Robert Adam in 1765, and one of his first acts on reaching Rome was to buy a further fifty-five classical relics from the collector Thomas Jenkins. He also cultivated the friendship of a Scottish painter and antiquary, Gavin Hamilton, then resident in Rome, who agreed to supply him with marbles to the value of £1,500 a year for four years. Over the next two years Hamilton threw himself into this task with boundless enthusiasm, scouring all the neighbouring excavations to find suitable pieces that might fit in with a design for the new gallery which he had commissioned from the Roman architect Panini. He proposed a combination of antique sculpture and contemporary paintings, the whole to cost £6,050. At first there were to be sixteen statues, twelve busts, twelve bas-reliefs, eleven large historical pictures and four landscapes, but later, in January 1772, he advised increasing the number of statues to nineteen and concentrating the collection in this area. 'I don't mean a collection', he wrote, 'such as hitherto made by myself and others. I mean a collection that will make Shelburne House famous not only in England but all over Europe.'[12]

But Hamilton was to be disappointed, for a year later, after two shipments had been sent, Lord Shelburne abandoned the plan, deciding instead to devote his energies to the creation of a library, for which Adam had already made designs. This was in fact a natural progression, since he was a great collector not only of books, but also of historical manuscripts, maps, charts, tracts and pamphlets, as well as coins and medals. For some reason he now appears to have dispensed with the services of Adam, and employed instead one of his former assistants, Joseph Bonomi, to draw up a series of new designs. These were completed in 1789, for in March of that year Gavin Hamilton wrote to his old friend, 'I am glad to hear that the library is near finished and shall arrive in time to enjoy the finest room in England.'[13] A few years later, however, in 1805, Lord Shelburne died and his son replaced Bonomi with George Dance the younger, who had worked for his father at Bowood. He remodelled the library as a Roman Imperial Hall with a segmental coffered roof and a rotunda at either end, a design which was not finally carried out till 1819 when it was completed, with some revisions, by Sir Robert Smirke.

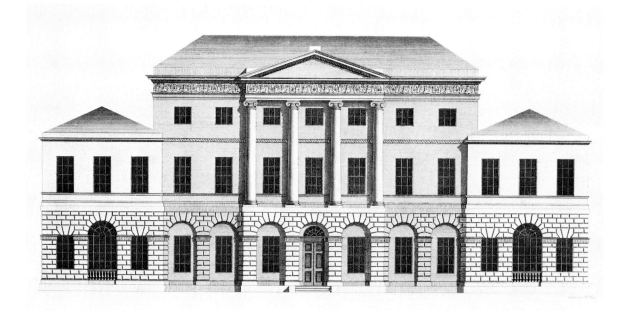

Opposite, top: The front elevation of Shelburne House.

Opposite, bottom: The ante-room of Shelburne House.

Above: The eating-room, Shelburne House.

Left: The first drawing-room, Shelburne House.

The gallery, Shelburne House, as completed by Sir Robert Smirke to a design by George Dance.

Some of the most fascinating and brilliant company in London gathered at Shelburne House, for Shelburne, who in the opinion of Wraxall 'in his person, manners, and address ... wanted no external quality to captivate or conciliate mankind',[14] was a man of great political ambition who had risen from being a Secretary of State to becoming, in July 1782, First Lord of the Treasury. He was a generous patron of the arts and literature, and made his house a meeting place, not only for politicians, but for all the cultivated and liberal society of the day. 'His house', wrote Wraxall,

or more properly to speak, his palace in Berkeley Square ... formed at once the centre of a considerable party, as well as the asylum of taste and science It is a fact, that during the latter years of Lord North's administration, he retained three or four clerks in constant pay and employment under his own roof, who were solely occupied in copying State papers or accounts. Every measure of finance adopted by the First Minister passed, if I may so express myself, through the alembic of Shelburne House, where it was examined and severely discussed. There, while Dunning and Barre met to settle their plan of action ... omniscient Jackson furnished every species of legal or general knowledge. Dr Price and Mr Baring produced financial plans, or made arithmetical calculations, meant to controvert and overturn, or to expose those of the First Lord of the Treasury: while Dr Priestley, who lived under the Earl of Shelburn's personal protection, prosecuted in the midst of London, his philosophical and chemical researches.[15]

Among those who were frequently entertained there were Dr Johnson, David Garrick, Jeremy Bentham, Benjamin Franklin, David Hume and Mirabeau. Its later history, during the time of Lord Shelburne's successors, when it was better known as Lansdowne House, was to be equally brilliant.

With a few exceptions, such as 44 Berkeley Square, the houses we have considered so far have all been the detached town houses of great families, and as such have been unaffected by the restrictions of space implied by a plot in a street or square. But three of Adam's finest works were erected on confined sites. Wynn House, Derby House and Home House, all completed in the 1770s, represent, in Sir John Summerson's view, 'the highest point of imagination and artistry in the handling of the London House. They are not mere repositories of delicious ornament; the basis of their splendour is their minutely considered arrangement.'[16] For example in the case of Wynn House, at 20 St James's Square – on which work began in 1772 – the site was no more than forty-six feet wide, yet Adam succeeded in constructing here for Sir Watkin Williams Wynn, a dilettante landowner from North Wales, what is generally acknowledged as one of the finest, and indeed grandest, town houses ever built.

He did this not only be designing the reception rooms *en suite*, so that vistas might be obtained in different directions, but by varying the form and height of the apartments to avoid monotony and produce a cumulative effect. Thus the entrance hall – almost disappointingly simple, since it was primarily used for servants to wait in – was merely a prologue to the grand design of the staircase hall, which rose the full height of the house. Since this was only one bay wide, however, width and breadth of space were obtained by cutting a deep apse in the south wall on both the ground and first floors. Oval rooms and domed rotundas were introduced, together with rooms containing semi-circular recesses, curve echoing curve in climax of decoration which culminated in the crescendo of the 'second withdrawing room', with its superb segmental barrel-vaulted ceiling, elaborately worked by Joseph Rose and painted by Zucchi. Looking out of the windows of this room, the illusion of grandeur was continued, for Adam had treated the courtyard below as a theatrical piece of scenery, the west wall being decorated with a Venetian window flanked by half columns, and the south wall built as an arcade to be occupied by statues.

Right: An elevation
of Wynn House,
20 St James's Square.

Below: A design for
one of the walls of the
courtyard of Wynn
House.

Opposite: Looking up
the staircase hall of
Wynn House.

He created a similar illusion at Derby House, 23 Grosvenor Square, where he designed a screen wall in the form of a triumphal arch to stand flush with the rear wall of the house and partially conceal the stable block behind. This long-vanished masterpiece, of which we have only Pastorini's engraving and a few of Adam's drawings to hint at its splendour, was a reconstruction of an existing house owned by Lord Edward Stanley, later twelfth Earl of Derby. It was perhaps the most skilful of all Adam's layouts, exemplifying his own statement that 'the parade, the convenience, and social pleasures of life, being better understood, are more strictly attended to in the arrangement and disposition of apartments.'[17] On the ground floor, the hall, ante-room, parlour, great eating-room, and library were all *en suite* and carefully contrasted in shape, character, and proportion, while on the first floor there were three drawing-rooms, described as 'noble, and well suited to every occasion of public parade'.[18] If the need arose, this floor also included a dressing-room and bedchamber which could be added to the suite – as they were for the great party Lord Stanley threw on the last day of March 1773 to celebrate his coming of age.

The second withdrawing-room, Wynn House.

Opposite: Lady Watkin Williams Wynn's room, Wynn House.

Pastorini's engraving of the third drawing-room at Derby House 1773.

'London has been extremely gay this Winter', wrote Elizabeth, Duchess of Northumberland, to her son, 'a vast number of private Balls. The French Ambassador has given four very fine ones and a fifth for Children.'[19] 'I was at the first and fourth which really were magnificent, but Lord Stanley gave one a fortnight ago which surpassed them all.'[20] Walpole's account of this is particularly valuable since it shows how these late eighteenth-century houses were actually used. 'That festival was very expensive', he wrote to Lady Ossory,

for it is the fashion now to make romances rather than balls. In the hall was a band of French horns and clarionets in laced uniforms and feathers. The dome of the staircase was beautifully illuminated with coloured glass lanthorns; in the ante-room [on the first floor] was a bevy of vestals in white habits making tea; in the next [the 'first drawing-room'] a drapery of sarcenet, that with a very funereal air crossed the chimney and descended in vast festoons over the sconces. The third chamber's doors [the 'second drawing-room'] were heightened with candles in gilt vases, and the ball-room [the 'third drawing-room'] was formed into an oval with benches above each other, not unlike pews, and covered with red serge, above which were arbours of flowers, red and green pilasters, more sarcenet, and Lord March's glasses, which he had lent, as an upholsterer asked Lord Stanley £300 for the loan of some. He had burst open the side of the wall to build an orchestra, with a pendent mirror to reflect the dancers ... and the musicians were in scarlet robes, like the candle-snuffers who represent the senates of Venice at Drury Lane. There were two more chambers [Lady Derby's dressing-room and bedchamber] at which I never arrived for the crowd. The seasons, danced by himself, the younger Storer, the Duc de Lausun and another, the youngest Miss Stanley, Miss Poole, the youngest Wrottesley, and another Miss, who is likewise anonymous in my memory, were in errant shepherdly dresses without invention, and Storer and Miss Wrottesley in banians with furs, for winter, cock and hen. In six rooms below were magnificent suppers.[21]

Since Adam only began his work on Derby House in 1773, very little of his decoration can have been in evidence when this ball was given, and one can only assume that the house had been temporarily fitted up by the upholsterers to conceal its unfinished state. The following June Lord Stanley married, providing an excuse for another costly extravaganza. 'This month', wrote Walpole to Mann, 'Lord Stanley marries Lady Betty Hamilton. He gives her a most splendid entertainment at his villa in Surrey, and calls it a 'fête champêtre'. It will cost five thousand pounds. Everybody is to go in masquerade, but not in mask. He has bought all the orange trees round London, and the hay-cocks, I suppose, are to be made of straw-coloured satin.'[22] Mrs Delany, who was among the guests, described it as being

a fairy scene that may equal any in Madame Danois ... The company were received on the lawn before the house, which is scattered with trees and opens to the downs. The company arriving, and parties of people of all ranks that came to admire, made the scene quite enchanting, which was greatly enlivened with a most beautiful setting sun breaking from a black cloud in its greatest glory.[23]

To provide a suitably whimsical stage for this spectacle, Adam was taken off his work in Grosvenor Square to design a special 'Fête Pavilion'.

Six months later, Derby House was evidently advanced enough for Lady Mary Coke to report in her journal that Lord Stanley's new wife, Lady Betty, 'is come to Town, & had a party the other night of three tables to shew her fine House'.[24] Perhaps Lady Mary would then have seen completed the splendid-looking 'third drawing-room', with its complex and elaborately decorated vaulted ceiling, and Lady Stanley's Etruscan dressing-room beyond, which Walpole described as being 'filigreed into puerility'.[25] Whatever Walpole may have thought, there is no doubt that the theatricality of these rooms perfectly reflected the rich and elegant lives of their inhabitants. One wonders what his impressions must have been of the 'glass drawing-room' which Adam was simultaneously creating at Northumberland House. In this unique room, *See colour plate 12* walls covered with mirrors reflected one another, thereby breaking down all architectural boundaries. It was by far his most extraordinary interior. Garishly

The glass
drawing-room,
Northumberland
House.

decorated throughout in red, gold, and blue, it might at first seem a trifle
vulgar, until one remembers that it was intended to be seen at night, at one of
the great assemblies for which the Northumberlands were famous, with the
light of hundreds of candles reflected in the glass.

Adam seems to have taken the illumination of the house at night into
particular consideration when designing his palatial residence at 20 Portman
Square for the Countess of Home. His drawings for the delicately beautiful
music room, for example, show candelabra and reflecting mirrors as forming
an integral part of the design. Elizabeth, Countess of Home, widow of the
eighth Earl of Home, was a rich and solitary old lady whose fortune came from
Jamaican sugar plantations and slaves. Since she was already living comfortably
in a large house on the south side of Portman Square, it has never been clear

why, at the age of seventy-one, she should suddenly employ Robert Adam to build and decorate an extremely grand house on an unusually large site on the north side, then newly under development. The likeliest reason appears to be that it was deliberately planned as a place in which to entertain the Duke of Cumberland, brother to George III, and his wife Anne, to whom Lady Home was related through her first marriage. Both had been rendered virtual outcasts from society by the King's fury at their union.

It was certainly worthy of royalty as the site was sixty-five feet wide, enabling Adam to work on a magnificent scale. Once again the deceptively simple exterior gave visitors no hint of the brilliance within, the first sign of which was the circular staircase hall, a unique Adam design which stretched up *See colour plate 13* through all three storeys to a dome and skylight above. The ground-floor circuit consisted of a front parlour, the most sober room in the house and notable for four porphyry scagliola columns in the corners. This opened into a back parlour, the inner end of which formed a complete semi-circle. A small ante-room then led into the library, where globes on circular pedestals stood in the niches and the chimney-piece was decorated with a scientific theme. Guests turned left at the head of the circular staircase, which divided at the first flight and returned in two curves to the first floor, the walls of which were embellished with paintings and reliefs. They then passed through a small ante-room into the music room, the ceiling of which was decorated with a complex pattern of circles, mirrored walls and a fine organ; from here they moved into the 'second drawing-room', the culmination of a spectacular progress. Beyond this, a tiny circular ante-room led into 'the Countess of Home's Etruscan Room', shown in Adam's drawings to have contained a canopied bed. No doubt, as in Lady Derby's bedroom in Grosvenor Square, this room could have been added to the suite when required; and indeed on another plan it is actually styled the 'third drawing-room'. When Home House was complete, with all its original decorations, furnishings, and fittings planned by Adam down to the last candlestick and lockplate, it must have been dazzling, for the success of his houses lay in the achievement of total unity.

The only description we have of a party at Home House in the time of the old Countess was written by William Beckford, himself a rich absentee Jamaican landlord, who was living in Portman Square in 1782. Since Beckford is known to be the author of a number of fakes, however, its accuracy must be open to question, and it may well be an amalgam of different stories. The Countess is represented as a flamboyant and foul-mouthed old eccentric – a view which is supported by her inclusion in *The Modern Characters from Shakespeare*, an eighteenth-century book of somewhat scurrilous content in which the following quotation from *The Merry Wives of Windsor* appears under 'The Countess of H--e': 'She's a witch, a quean, an old cozening quean:- Come down you witch; you hag you, come down I say; No doubt the devil will soon have her!'[26]

Top: A section of the music-room, Home House.   Bottom: Lady Home's Etruscan bedroom, Home House.

Top: The music-room, Home House.　　Bottom: The staircase, Home House.

Writing to Louise Beckford, the wife of his cousin Peter, Beckford relates how he had accepted an invitation from

no less a personage ... than the Countess of Home, known amongst all the Irish chairmen and riff-raff of the metropolis by the name, style, and title of Queen of Hell ... Aware of my musical propensities she determined to celebrate my accession to Portman Square by a sumptuous dinner and a concert of equal magnificence. Last evening it took place and you never beheld so splendidly heterogeneous a repast as the dinner nor ever heard such a confounded jumble of good and bad Music – such a charivari in fact – as the Concert. Poor old Giardini went fairly distracted.[27] Not without cause, as you shall hear, for during her morning round she happened to meet with a brace of tall athletic negroes in flaming laced jackets tooting away on the French horn, as loud as their lungs permitted. 'By God', exclaimed her majesty (she swears like a trooper), 'you play delightfully. You shall perform tonight at my Concert.' 'Here', said she to the hapless Maestro, who was waiting at the street door to hand her in, 'here, my fine fiddler, I have bought you a great acquisition. These glorious fellows have quite enchanted me. I never heard horns blow with so capital a gusto in all the days of my life.' 'My Lady', answered the Maestro, casting a very suspicious glance on the sable pair, 'I doubt whether they play in score; persons of their sort seldom do.' 'Never mind that', replied the despotic Countess, 'Put them into the orchestra; they shall chime in.' Happily for us all, having been made extremely welcome below stairs, they slept most of the time, nodding and bobbing their woolly pates about in so ludicrous a manner that I was convulsed with laughter. However, the moment her Ladyship approached, I was just able to assume a civilised expression of countenance and praised these charming examples of original talent as warmly as their patroness could possibly desire. 'There', said the Countess, turning round triumphantly to the rueful maestro, 'did I not tell you so? Mr Beckford is a real judge.'[28]

Beckford also tells how his company was sought after by another celebrated resident of Portman Square. 'Madame Montagu', he writes, 'who has just finished the palace, which goes slanting ... across a corner of the square, desires me to name a day for meeting at dinner certain Savii Grandi whom she promised to introduce to me...'

Elizabeth Montagu was a successful London hostess, whose house in Hill Street had for years been known as a meeting place for the wits and intellectuals of society. 'I never invite idiots to my house', she wrote to Garrick in 1770,[29] and a description by Hannah More of one of her gatherings certainly seems to bear this out. 'Just returned from spending one of the most agreeable days of my life, with the female Maecenas of Hill Street', she wrote to her sister in 1776:

She engaged me five or six days ago to dine with her, and had assembled half the wits of the age ... There were nineteen persons assembled at dinner, but after the repast, she has a method of dividing her guests, or rather letting them assort themselves into little groups of five or six each. I spent my time in going from one to the other of these little societies, as I happened more or less to like the subjects they were discussing. Mrs Scott, Mrs Montagu's sister, a very good writer, Mrs Carter, Mrs Barbauld, and a man of letters whose name I have forgotten, made up one of these little parties. When we had canvassed two or three subjects, I stole off and joined in with the next group, which was composed of Mrs Montagu, Dr Johnson, the Provost of Dublin, and two other ingenious men. In this party there was a diversity of opinions, which produced a great deal of good argument and reasoning. There were several other groups ... and it was amusing to see how the people of sentiment singled out each other, and how the fine ladies and pretty gentlemen naturally slid into each other's society.[30]

The intellectual ladies who attended these and other similar assemblies of rival hostesses became known as 'Blue Stockings', as they preferred blue woollen stockings to formal black silk. Elizabeth Montagu was soon dubbed the 'Queen of the Blue Stockings'.

Before too long the house in Hill Street was no longer grand enough for Mrs Montagu, whose ambitions dramatically increased with the great riches she had inherited on the death of her husband in 1775, so she bought the lease on a plot of land at the north-west corner of Portman Square, and built herself something more in keeping with her new station. Her first choice as architect for the new house had been Robert Adam, who had already done some beautiful work for her in Hill Street in 1766. 'He has made me a ceiling and chimney-piece, and doors, which are pretty enough to make me a thousand enemies', she wrote to Lord Kames, one of his potential employers, in February 1767: 'Envy turns livid at the first glimpse of them.' His involvement is shrouded in obscurity, however, although we do know that he was working for her in some capacity in the summer of 1779, for in July of that year she wrote to the Duchess of Portland an account of how she had been engaged in giving instructions to 'my architect ... Mr Adam':

Mrs Elizabeth Montagu, after a drawing by W. Evans, from an original painting by Reynolds.

He came at the head of a regiment of artificers an hour after the time he had promised: the bricklayer talked an hour about the alterations to be made in a wall; the stonemason was as eloquent about the coping of the said wall; the carpenter thought the internal fitting-up of the house not less important; then came the painter, who is painting my ceilings in various colours according to the present fashion. The morning and my spirits were quite exhausted before these important persons had the goodness to release me. I did not get back to my dinner till near five o'clock...[31]

Whether Mrs Montagu was mortally offended by his lateness on this occasion, or whether she was responding to the fickle dictates of a fashionable world that was, by the late 1770s, beginning to tire of what Walpole, once his greatest advocate, was to call 'Mr Adam's gingerbread and snippets of embroidery',[32] a short time after this Adam was dropped from the scheme. He was replaced almost immediately by James Stuart – a choice Mrs Montagu soon had cause to regret. 'I chose him for my architect', she wrote in 1780,

on account of his disinterestedness and contempt of money; I did not see how any mischief to my pocket could arise from these qualities ... but Satan is more cunning

Montagu House,
Portman Square.

than I am, and this sly enemy of human virtue found many assailable and weak places about him, and the said Mr Satan finding out some peephole into the human soul, or by observation in external action that what workmen did by bribes of guineas to many architects could be effected on him by pipes and tobacco and pots of porter in ale houses and night cellars. I speak it not on suspicion but certain information, that since he began my house he has been for a fortnight together in the most drunken condition with these fellows ... Tho he does not mean (I believe) to tell fibs, it is impossible to rely on anything he says. It would be tedious to tell you how often I have been obliged to confront him with the workmen whom he blamed for not having executed his orders, and he was then obliged to confess he had forgotten to deliver the designs.[33]

Her problems with Stuart, however, in no way curbed Elizabeth Montagu's overall enthusiasm for the project. 'I am more and more in love with my new House', she wrote to William Pepys in October 1780.

When a fog obscures Hill Street there is a blue sky and a clean atmosphere in Portman Square, and then for my dwelling it is so convenient and cheerful as a place of retirement, so ample for the devoirs of Society, and so calculated for Assemblies that it will suit all one's humours, and adapt itself to all ones purposes. I congratulate myself every hour on having taken the trouble to build for myself...[34]

It was an enthusiasm which she evidently communicated far and wide, for the curiosity of the fashionable world was soon aroused to such an extent that she was obliged to issue tickets to all those who wished to take a look. 'It appears to be very necessary', she instructed her agent, 'that no one should be admitted to see our House without tickets, & you will be so good as to give them to whomsoever you please ... It mortifies me to be obliged to exclude anyone who wishes to see the House, as such exclusions disoblige, but one cannot allow the painting etc to be damaged.'[35]

She finally moved from Hill Street some time in the summer of 1781, though not without inviting some friends 'to take leave of the Hill Street house'.[36] Among them was Hannah More. 'You never saw such an air of ruin and bankruptcy as everything around us wore', she wrote in her memoirs. 'We had about three square feet of carpet, and that we might all put our feet upon it, we were obliged to sit in a circle in the middle of the room, just as if we were playing Hunt the slipper.'[37] The move itself was accompanied by a considerable upheaval in her domestic ménage. 'Tomorrow I go into the city', she wrote,

to choose some lamps for my hall. I hope by the end of the week the wishes of my housekeeper, the caprices of my laundry-maid, the fancies of my housemaids, the demands of my cook, and the accommodations of my butler, will all be fulfilled, completed and answered, and I assure you they make a total of no small significance ... tho' I have not denied requests I have endeavoured to stop complaints, for I find that if I did not discourage them I should be plagued to death, for servants love to give significance to trifles.[38]

Once settled, Elizabeth Montagu was ecstatic, and as Christmas approached, she reflected happily:

At this time of ye year, the great city is solitary, silent, and quiet. Its present state makes a good preface to the succeeding months of crowd, noise, and bustle ... One always finds some friends in town; a few agreeable people may at any time be gathered together; and, for my own part, I think one seldom passes the whole of one's time more agreeably than before the meeting of Parliament in January; and this never appeared more strongly to me than this year, when so excellent a house was ready to receive me...[39]

She called it her 'palais de la veillesse'.

One of her earliest visitors was Horace Walpole. 'I dined on Monday with the Harcourts at Mrs Montagu's new palace', he wrote to Mann on 14 February 1782,

and was much surprised. Instead of vagaries it is a noble simple edifice. When I came home, I recollected that though I had thought it so magnificent a house, there was not a morsel of gilding, it is grand not tawdry, nor larded and embroidered and pompommed with shreds and remnants and clinquant like all the harlequinades of Adam, which never let the eye repose for a moment.[40]

But what Walpole saw was by no means the completed house, work upon which was to go on for a further ten years. In her old age Mrs Montagu appears to have been just as obsessive a decorator as she had been in her Hill

Street days, when she had created her famous Chinese room and her 'Room of Cupidons'; and over the next decade the house was rarely free from 'Carvers, Gilders, Carpenters, etc, which', she commented in a letter to her brother, 'is certainly no very agreeable experience.'[41] Much of her time, for example, was spent collecting feathers for a room which was to be hung with them from top to bottom. 'My great piece of feather work is not yet completed', she wrote to a friend in February 1784, 'so if you have an opportunity of getting me any feathers, they will be very acceptable. The brown tails of partridges are very useful, though not so brilliant as some others'; while two years later she was writing, 'The neck and breast feathers of the stubble goose are very useful, and I wish your cook would save those of the Michaelmas goose for us.'[42] The poet William Cowper immortalised the room in verse:

The birds put off their every hue
To dress a room for Montagu;
The peacock sends his heavenly dyes,
His rainbows and his starry eyes;
The pheasant, plumes which round enfold
His mantling neck with downy gold,
The cock his arch'd tail's azure shows,
And, river blanched, the swan his snow;
All tribes besides of Indian name,
That glossy shine, or vivid flame,
Where rises and where sets the day,
Whate'er they boast of rich and gay,
Contribute to the gorgeous plan,
Proud to advance it all they can.[43]

While all this was in progress, an endless stream of guests, quite oblivious to the smell of paint, the noise of the builders, and the dust which must have settled everywhere, passed through the house in a succession of fashionable pursuits. 'Another day, I went to Richmond with Mrs Boscawen', wrote Hannah More on 22 May 1788,

and came home in the evening to a Thé at Mrs Montagu's. Perhaps you do not know that a Thé is among the stupid new follies of the winter. You are to invite fifty or a hundred people to come at eight o'clock: there is to be a long table, or little parties at small ones; the cloth is to be laid as at breakfast; everyone has a napkin; tea and coffee are made by the company, as at a public breakfast; the table is covered with rolls, wafers, bread and butter; and what constitutes the very essence of a Thé, an immense load of hot buttered rolls, and muffins, all admirably contrived to create a nausea in persons fresh from the dinner table...[44]

Mrs Montagu's final project was a 'great room', which was to fill the whole of the north-east end of the house, and was intended to rival any other such room in London. 'I hope you will consider me rather as a busy than an ungrateful Woman', she wrote to her sister in June 1790, when I tell you Messrs Bonomi, Bartoli, Prichard, Evans and Black have all been with me this morning. No Minister has a greater Levee than a builder of Houses; but he can satisfy them all with sweet words and fine promises, and on this they will obey his orders. When they have executed mine I must pay in pounds sterling. However as I stand well in Mr Hoare's good books, I have been bespeaking Pillars of Scagliola in vert antique, and pressing forward the completing of my great Room.[45]

The house was completed in the summer of the following year, and its opening was suitably grand. 'Mrs Montagu was more splendid yesterday morning', wrote Walpole to Mary Berry, 'and breakfasted seven hundred persons on opening her great room, and the room with the hangings of feathers.'[46] On this visit Walpole would still have found 'a noble simple edifice' of seven bays with Venetian windows at either end of the first floor, standing at an angle to the north-west corner of the square; but the interior was by now much richer than when he had first set eyes upon it. The most elaborately decorated ground-floor room was the morning-room – the white and gold coved and coffered ceiling of which was reminiscent of the boudoir at Holdernesse House, except that the flat of the ceiling was filled with a familiar Adam pattern of intersecting circles. The route to the staircase took the guests through two halls separated by screens of Ionic columns. Upstairs they found a suite of five main rooms consisting of a reception room, with apsed ends and an Adamesque ceiling painted by Angelica Kauffman; a small drawing-room with a segmentally vaulted ceiling painted in the Pompeian style; a large drawing-room, at one end of which was a fine Ionic screen of free-standing scagliola columns supporting a round-headed, coffered arch; an ante-room, which could possibly have been the 'room of feathers' (described in the St James's Chronicle as being 'wholly covered with feathers, artfully sewed together, and forming beautiful festoons of flowers and other fanciful decorations. The most brilliant colours, the produce of all climates, have wonderful effects on a feather ground of a dazzling whiteness'); and finally Mrs Montagu's pride and joy, the new 'great room', designed by Bonomi, with a superb barrel-vaulted ceiling decorated with inset paintings and elaborate stucco ornament, door and window surrounds of white marble, and the whole space defined by green scagliola columns and piers with gilded Corinthian capitals. 'The room is hung with white figured damask', reported the correspondent of the St James's Chronicle, in a state of considerable excitement: 'the curtains are of white satin fringed with gold; the chandeliers and large looking-glasses are superb; and the whole is an assemblage of art and magnificence which we have never witnessed in a private room.'[47]

'Breakfasts', such as that given to celebrate its opening, became a regular feature at Montagu House. Beginning at around noon, they seem to have involved vast crowds of people eager to satisfy both their greed and their curiosity. Judging from this description of one by Madame d'Arblay, they must have been a complete nightmare: 'This morning', she wrote in May 1792,

The staircase hall, Montagu House.

I went to a very fine public breakfast given by Mrs Montagu ... I made for the dining-room which was filled for a breakfast ... The table was not a matter of indifference to the guests at large; and it was so completely occupied by company seated round it, that it was long before one vacant chair could be seized, and this fell to the lot of Miss Ord. The crowd of company was such that we could only slowly make way in any part. There could not be fewer than four or five hundred people. It was like a full Ranelagh by daylight ... We then went round the rooms, which were well worth examination and admiration; and we met friends and acquaintances every other step ... Dr Russell was in high spirits, and laughed heartily at seeing the prodigious meal most of the company made of cold chicken, ham, fish, etc, and said he should like to see Mrs Montagu make the experiment of inviting all the same party to dinner at three o'clock. 'Oh!', they would cry, 'Three o'clock! What does she mean? – who can dine at three o'clock? – one has no appetite – one can't swallow a morsel – it's altogether impossible!' Yet let her invite the same people, and give them a dinner, while she calls it a breakfast, and see but how prettily they can find appetites...[48]

Bonomi's original design for the great room, Montagu House, 1782.

Opposite: The drawing-room, Montagu House.

An elevation of
Buckingham House,
91 Pall Mall.

Opposite: The first-
floor landing,
Buckingham House.

Walpole had his own explanations for what he saw as the increased follies of society in the latter years of the century. 'One effect the American War has not had', he wrote to Sir Horace Mann,

it has not brought us to our senses. Silly dissipation rather increases, and without an object. The present folly is late hours. Everybody tries to be particular by being too late; and, as everybody tries it, no one is so. It is the fashion now to go to Ranelagh two hours after it is over. You may not believe this but it is literal. The music ends at ten, the company go at twelve. Lord Derby's cook lately gave him warning. The man owned he liked his place, but he should be killed by dressing suppers at three in the morning. The Earl asked him coolly at how much he valued his life; that is he would have paid him for killing him.[49]

The years of war, from 1775 to 1783, and from 1793 onwards, had another effect. As money became scarcer and more expensive, there was a definite decline in domestic building on a grand scale. In the country, out of twenty-nine great houses built between 1760 and 1800, only three – Attingham, Courteenhall and Ickworth – were begun after 1780. And apart from Mrs Montagu's schemes, some important alterations and additions carried out by Henry Holland at Carlton House in 1783 for the Prince of Wales, and at Fetherstonhaugh House in 1787 for the Duke of York, and the remodelling of two houses in Pall Mall by Sir John Soane in the early 1790s in order to create Buckingham House for George Temple, first Marquess of Buckingham, there was very little work of note carried out in London in these last two decades of the century. It was in the euphoric period following the Battle of Waterloo that the next great bout of building took place, the extravagance of which came close to eclipsing all that had gone before it.

Chiswick House and
garden from the
south-east by Jacques
Rigaud.

8

Gilded Magnificence

I have come from my house to your palace.

Queen Victoria to the Duchess of Sutherland

The late hours and general dissipation complained of by Walpole in his letter to Sir Horace Mann reached their peak in the first few years of the nineteenth century. One reason for this was a change in parliamentary procedure. In the first half of the eighteenth century, Parliament had risen before four o'clock in the afternoon, but by the early nineteenth century it did not begin sitting until then, and speeches were longer. 'Long speeches', lamented Lady Susan O'Brien,

are in daily practice on every topic, & by everybody. All are orators. This mania has occasion'd the lateness of every amusement & every topic & family transaction – dinner 7 or 8 o'clock, partys beginning at ten, balls at eleven or twelve. Thus everything is done by candle-light, which adds greatly to the expense in large families, is hurtful to the health of young persons, & the morals of the lower classes.[1]

Equally important, however, was the influence of the Prince of Wales, who, having successfully cut his teeth in the drawing-rooms of Devonshire House and Melbourne House, was by then the undisputed leader of society. His apparently endless capacity for enjoying himself was contagious. London became the most fashionable city in Europe, and its high life gayer and more opulent than ever. Elegant carriages crowded the streets, outrageously dressed dandies jostled for attention on the pavements, fortunes circulated in the gambling clubs, and in the great rooms of its private palaces hostesses competed with one another to entertain the Prince. 'The Duchess of Devonshire', announced the correspondent of one of the numerous society chronicles in 1805,

long conspicuous in the gay world for the superior merit of her entertainments, intends, immediately after the Birthday, assembling all the fashionables in town for the representation of a Comedy, written by her Grace ... The particulars are not yet ascertained; but it is said that the Marchioness of Abercorn, Countess of Bessborough, and the Honourable Mr Hill, have had each a part assigned them. The Great Saloon at Devonshire House is to be fitted up most conveniently and sumptuously, for the reception of the company. His Royal Highness, the Prince of Wales, has promised to honour the scene with his presence. Immediately after the play is concluded, a grand ball will take place, in which the younger branches of the family will take the lead...[2]

The very lucky were honoured with an invitation to one of the Duchess's breakfasts, which she held each Saturday of the season at her villa in Chiswick:

On Saturday, at Chiswick, the Duchess of Devonshire's Public Breakfast was attended by a small circle of her Grace's family and friends. The day being beautiful rendered the delightful villa and grounds another Paradise. Around the house pots of the finest flowers were placed, and similar attentions were paid to the internal decoration. Two tables, forming a triangle, were laid out for forty, in an elegant saloon adjoining the library. The breakfast consisted of lamb, veal, hams, fowls, chickens, with prawns etc, the dessert pines, strawberries, cherries etc. Much taste and elegance appeared in the arrangement of the tables, and her Grace's good spirits and affability greatly enlivened the repast. It was three o'clock before the company began to assemble, and four before the principal part arrived in different carriages, principally drawn with four horses. A few minutes after four, the Duke of York came in a post-chariot and four, with three outriders ... The company sat down to table, the Duke of York's Band, in full uniform, playing several favourite pieces of music. Soon after five the company returned to the lawn, and several little parties went on the serpentine lake, where they were rowed by Gentlemen adept in that healthful exercise. After perambulating through the walks till seven o'clock, the illustrious and distinguished visitors departed.[3]

They would have arrived back in town at a time when the fashionable day was almost at its peak. 'From six to eight the noise of wheels increases', wrote Louis Simond, a French visitor to London, in 1810.

A multitude of carriages, with two eyes of flame staring in the dark before each of them, shake the pavement and the very houses, following and crossing each other at full speed. Stopping suddenly, a footman jumps down, runs to the door, and lifts the heavy knocker – gives a great knock – then several smaller ones in succession – then with all his might – flourishing as on a drum, with an art, and an air, and a delicacy of touch, which denote the quality, the rank, and the fortune of his master. For two hours, or nearly. There is a pause; at ten a *redoublement* comes on. This is the great crisis, of dress, of noise, and of rapidity – a universal hubbub; a sort of uniform grinding and shaking, like that experienced in a great mill with fifty pair of stones; and, if I was not afraid of appearing to exaggerate, I should say that it came upon the ear like the fall of Niagara, heard at two miles distance! This crisis continues undiminished till twelve or one o'clock; then less and less during the rest of the night – till, at the approach of day, a single carriage is heard now and then at a great distance.

Great assemblies are called routs or parties; but the people who give them, in their invitations only say, that they will be *at home* such a day, and this some weeks beforehand. The house in which this takes place is frequently stripped from top to bottom; beds, drawers, and all but ornamental furniture is carried out of sight to make room for a crowd of well-dressed people, received at the door of the principal apartment by the mistress of the house standing, who smiles at every newcomer with a look of acquaintance. Nobody sits; there is no conversation, no cards, no music; only

elbowing, turning, and winding from room to room; then, at the end of a quarter of
an hour, escaping to the hall-door to wait for the carriage, spending more time upon
the threshold among footmen than you had done above stairs with their masters. From
this rout you drive to another, where, after waiting your turn to arrive at the door,
perhaps half an hour, the street being full of carriages, you alight, begin the same
round, and end it in the same manner. The public knows there is a party in a house
by two signs; first an immense crowd of carriage before the house – then every curtain,
and every shutter of every window wide open, shewing apartments all in a blaze of
light, with heads innumerable, black and white (powdered or not) in continual motion
... Such may be, it will be said, the life of the rich, the well-born, and the idle...[4]

Guests Arriving at a Reception, by Eugène Lami.

The influence of the Prince of Wales went far beyond establishing a climate
in which Society flourished more than ever before. He was a man of great flair
and taste, a lover of architecture, with a strong visual sense. This had first
manifested itself in 1783, when he commissioned Henry Holland to carry out
various alterations at his own residence, Carlton House, which stood in Pall
Mall to the east of Marlborough House and was noted for its magnificent

gardens, which had been laid out in 1734 by William Kent. 'There is an august simplicity that astonished me', wrote Horace Walpole to Lady Upper Ossory after he had first viewed the new work.

You cannot call it magnificent; it is the taste and propriety that strike. Every ornament is at a proper distance, and not one too large, but all delicate and new, with more freedom and variety than Greek ornaments, and though probably borrowed from the Hotel de Condé and other new palaces, not one that is not rather classic than French ... How sick one shall be after this chaste palace of Mr Adam's gingerbread and snippets of embroidery.[5]

Although the Prince, an enthusiastic francophile, was at first delighted with his new home, inspired as it was by the recently completed Hôtel de Salm in Paris, its simplicity soon began to bore him. He was fascinated by the Bourbons and the settings they had created for themselves, and it was probably their contributions to Paris and Versailles which finally determined him not only to improve the royal residences in England, but eventually to try to transform London from a collection of villages and private speculations into a capital city. He began by calling in the interior decorator Walsh Porter, who embel-

See colour plate 14
lished Carlton House out of all recognition in an effort to match the splendours of the Palace of Versailles.

In the same year – the year in which, incidentally, Henry Holland died – the architect William Porden began an equally extravagant scheme of decoration for the second Earl Grosvenor, who had bought the lease of Gloucester House at the corner of Upper Grosvenor Street and Park Lane, which for forty years had been the home of the Duke of Gloucester, one of George III's brothers. According to a survey carried out for Lord Grosvenor in 1805, it was a compact block, built in the 1780s, arranged round a central staircase compartment and set back at the end of a forecourt with curved screen walls. It was evidently in a very shabby state, the interior being, according to Porden, 'very dirty', and 'not so cheerful as the situation would lead one to expect', while *The Times* described it as being 'so gloomy, that it appeared to defy all endeavours to render it light'.[6] Since it was unfit for immediate occupation, Porden, who was in the middle of remodelling Eaton Hall, the Earl's home in Cheshire, into a fantastic Gothic palace, was brought in to effect a lavish transformation. He was told that his decorations must match the Earl's ever-increasing collection of pictures, to which he had recently added a celebrated group bought from Agar Ellis for £30,000. His unsparing use in all the main rooms of crimson velvet and damask, generously trimmed with gold lace and tassel fringe, echoed the kind of work which Walsh Porter was doing at Carlton House, its heavy grandeur reflecting the wealth and importance of his employer. But, as he explained to Lord Grosvenor, he never forgot that the purpose of the rooms was also for 'the living pictures which will frequently adorn them', and he reminded his employer of 'the difference that will be

Old Grosvenor House, Park Lane.

made in the appearance of the finest forms and faces when moving on a background of feeble and unharmonious colours; and one that by its contrast and harmony will define the form and give brilliancy to the face.'[7]

The house was ready for occupation in April 1808; two months later it was thrown open to the fashionable world, among whom its rich effects caused quite a stir. 'Grosvenor House,' wrote Lady Sarah Spencer,

is to be thrown open to the world for the first time. It is said to be a mass of damask, velvet, gilding, statues and pictures and magnificence of all sorts, beyond all powers of description or imagination, and has had already, while only in prospect, the advantage of furnishing conversation in plenty to all the insipid misses and empty beaux I have seen for a long while.

The following day, after attending the opening, she was able to confirm that 'the vast quantities of beauties of Grosvenor House really surpassed all my expectations. I derived besides great amusement from hearing every person in town, who had more than three rooms on a floor in their house, abuse and criticise that one, as if every one of their audience did not immediately guess at the nasty envy which dictated their observation.'[8] The correspondent of *The Times* echoed her views, reporting that it was

now transformed into a residence, which combines, in a superior degree, the several

qualities of magnificence, elegance, and convenience ... Indeed, it has undergone a metamorphosis, which, under the influence of a pure and solid taste, has produced a splendour, that possesses the happy medium between the cumbersome finery of a former period, and the fillagreen frippery, or motley vagaries of the present day.[9]

Not all its visitors were quite so unstinting in their praise. Lord Lonsdale, who went there with the architect Robert Smirke, commented rather dismissively that he found it 'expensively furnished, but in a bad taste'.[10]

Whatever Lonsdale may have thought, there is no doubt that such taste was beginning to catch on. When the rich and restless young sixth Duke of Devonshire, 'the Bachelor Duke', inherited in 1811, one of his first undertakings was a fervent bout of refurbishment at Devonshire House, the effects of which can be seen by comparing the 1811 drawing (p. 102) of the simple Kent entrance hall with the William Hunt watercolour of c. 1822, showing how it looked after its transformation into a saloon. In October 1819, Samuel Ware wrote of 'the liberal expense which has been lately incurred in gilding the ornaments of the principal rooms',[11] while on 1 June the following year Mrs Arbuthnot recorded: 'Went to a party at Devonshire House, the first time I had been there since the house was new done up. I never saw anything so magnificent as the profusion of gilding and the chandeliers, one of which was silver.'[12] But the Duke's preference for the new flashy style was merely an expression of the mood of the age, the seal on which had been set by the coronation of Prince George in the summer of 1821; for which no less than £243,000 had been voted by Parliament. It was, as a result, unparalleled in its splendour.

See colour plate 15

'Of the splendour of the whole spectacle it is impossible for me to give you the *slightest* idea', wrote the Earl of Denbigh to his mother, in describing the last coronation banquet to be held in England.

It exceeded all imagination and conception. Picture to yourself Westminster Hall lined beneath with the peers in their robes and coronets, the Privy Councillors, Knights of the Bath and a multitude of different attendants and chief officers of state in most magnificent dresses, and with a double row of galleries on each side above, filled with all the beauty of London, the ladies vying with each other in the magnificence of their apparel and the splendour of their head-dresses, some of them being literally a blaze of diamonds. Prince Esterhazy is said to have had jewels on his person estimated at *eighty thousand* pounds and the rest of the foreign ministers and their ladies were as splendid as jewels and fine clothes could make them.[13]

William Cavendish, sixth Duke of Devonshire, by Reynolds.

Opposite: A corner of the gallery, Grosvenor House.

The new king understood only too well the importance of Court ceremonial and the trappings of monarchy, and in establishing them in such a brilliant manner he gave the country a visual leadership which perfectly matched the spirit of the great houses which were to dominate the social scene during and after his reign. With the exception of the Duke of Wellington's Apsley House, these were the creation of large landowners whose ways of life had grown more prodigal along with their ever-increasing fortunes, to support which they either enlarged existing buildings or built new ones.

Among the first to embark upon a massive programme of improvements to his already considerable London house was the third Duke of Northumberland – who, like the sixth Duke of Devonshire, had only recently succeeded to the title. He employed Thomas Cundy to rebuild the entire south front of Northumberland House, to create a new staircase, and to undertake the complete redecoration of the drawing-rooms on the upper floor of the south wing, as well as the general restoration of the rest of the house. The Duke is thought to have spent £160,000 on the work – which seems quite credible, since the bills from Morell and Hughes, the upholsterers, alone came to £34,000 for the years 1821-3.[14] To ensure that his future guests should not miss a detail of the new work, he spared no expense on the lighting, as is shown by the following selection of bills from William Collins of the Strand, 'Glass Enameller and Glass manufacturer to the King':

December 12, 1822:
Enriching a 12 Light Chandelier for the Glass Drawing, with 1,056 additional large drops.　　　　　£60.0.0
March 18, 1823:
A very rich Chandelier put up in the Blue Room, with 6 lamps, the work richly chased and burnished.　　　　　£150.0.0
May 23:
4 Superb Chandeliers executed in Grecian Metal in the Drawing Room, Saloon, Anti Room and Grand Staircase.　　　　　£2700.0.0
May 31:
4 Large Candelabra for the Dining-Room very highly chased and finished in Grecian Metal bearing three lamps each.　　　　　£800.0.0
December 4:
Making 2 Large Candelabra 9 feet high with 5 Branches on each bearing lamps highly enriched, chased and finished and fixing the same upon Marble Bases at foot of staircase.　　　　　£2000.0.0
February 12, 1824:
A very superb 18 Light Chandelier put up in the Glass Drawing Room. A group of Dolphins in centre, the whole enriched with Large Shells etc. in cut glass and ornamented with very brilliant cut drops.　　　　　£400.0.0
March 29:
5 Altar Pedestals with 5 Bronze Lamps for Grand Staircase.　　　　　£52.10.0
May 3:
6 very rich Candelabra for the Saloon and Drawing Room highly chased and finished to bear 7 branches each.　　　　　£660.0.0
Altering and enriching 4 Large Chandeliers for the Gallery to bear 24 Lights each including 16,000 brilliant spangles etc.　　　　　£720.0.0[15]

This last item was completed just in time for the opening on 14 May. Mrs Arbuthnot, who attended, was suitably impressed, though she had reservations about the by now old-fashioned layout of the house. 'I went last night to Northumberland House', she wrote in her journal, 'which is opened this year

The grand staircase, Northumberland House.

to the world for the first time these fifty years ... It is very fine, the staircase of white marble & brass balustrades, the walls of yellow marble with black columns having bronze capitals. This last had a heavy effect. Sir Charles Long thought they ought to have been *gilt*; but, tho' he is supposed to have such fine taste, I am sure *gilt* capitals in a marble hall could never be right. The rooms are fine & magnificently decorated; but they are few in number &, from not going all round, have not so good an effect as many of the great houses in London.'[16]

Northumberland House was opened to the public during the Great Exhibition in 1851. It had changed little since Mrs Arbuthnot first saw it, and the rather lurid descriptions printed in the guide book seem particularly well suited to its lavish decor. The visitor looking at the staircase, for example,

at the base, on each side of him, sees two splendid columns of highly variegated marble, with a rich ormolu candelabrum, and a magnificently elaborate gilt scroll pattern railing staircase which, after ascending halfway by graceful and stately steps, branches off right and left, leading to the upper part of the mansion ... The floor, the steps, and the vestibule of this splendid staircase, consist wholly of marble, white and black, elegantly variegated. The carpet is of rich crimson, and at each extremity above is a statue of Cupid and Cerberus, or Child and attendant to match; while in the

The ballroom,
Northumberland
House.

Below:
Northumberland
House.

The picture gallery, Northumberland House.

centre of all descends a superbly massive ormolu candelabrum, suspended by a rich gilt chain from the lofty, carved, and elegantly lighted floor. The walls, where not of dark variegated marble, consist of yellow and variously tinted Scaglioli of the richest description.

Suitably transfixed by such beauty

the enraptured stranger will stand gazing for some moments on this splendid production before entering the Ante Room ... leading to the gorgeous suite of apartments on the drawing room floor of the edifice ... The walls are lined with figured, cream-coloured satin damask. The curtains are of a similar texture, and from the windows is commanded a fine view of the Thames, and the busy, though somewhat vulgar and common-place life here perpetually characteristic of its course. The next chamber is the Crimson Drawing Room. On entering the visitor will be struck by the rich splendour of the chamber, which is a mass of crimson, of the most brilliant description, walls, couches, ottomans, and chairs being all equally covered with richly damasked red satin ... A magnificent gilt candelabrum descends from the summit, which is splendidly arched ... The Second Drawing Room which the visitor now enters, is a continuation of the suite, and decorated in the same rich crimson style ... The next chamber of the suite, the Duchess's Drawing Room is a perfect bijou of an apartment ... decorated in the richest style of blue and gold satin furniture, after the fashion of Louis XIV.[17]

Here the tour ended, and the public had to double back to the grand staircase.

The third Marquess of Londonderry, a vain and conceited man whose love of dressing up in splendid uniforms while he was ambassador in Vienna had earned him the nickname of the 'Golden Peacock', spent over £200,000 on converting Holdernesse House and the adjoining property to the east into a residence suitably grand enough for himself and his equally ostentatious young wife. They could well afford it. Formerly Lady Frances Anne Vane-Tempest, and an only child, the Marchioness was perhaps the greatest heiress of her generation, with a fortune of £60,000 a year: this combined with her husband's £20,000 a year made them one of the richest couples in England. Such a combination of wealth and public position went straight to Frances Anne's head, and her pretentious displays of affluence created a poor impression both in Vienna, where she spent three years, and subsequently in London. Princess Lieven provides an amusing description of her bedroom in a house which the Londonderrys had leased in St James's Square in 1821: 'How you would have laughed yesterday', she wrote to Prince Metternich on 11 April 1822,

if you had gone with me to call on Lady Stewart [her husband did not succeed to the title till the following year]. She showed me her bedroom, which is the most important room in the house. Above the bed is a baron's coronet the size of the crown of the King of Wurtemburg on the palace at Stuttgart – red velvet, ermine, everything that goes with it. From it hang heavy draperies, held up at the four corners to the bed by

Right: Charles, third Marquess of Londonderry, by Lawrence.

Far right: Frances Anne, Marchioness of Londonderry, in the costume of Queen Elizabeth which she wore for the opening of Londonderry House.

four large gilt figures of Hercules, nude and fashioned like real men. The bed is as big as a room and almost on a level with the ground. While she was showing it to me, she laughed at least forty times, with that noisy laugh of hers, stopping and starting all over again every few seconds. What an extraordinary family! I should lose my taste for luxury in that house: it is displayed in such a vulgar way.[18]

She even made a public spectacle of the christening of her first child: 'Lord Stewart's child was christened yesterday with a great deal of vulgar ostentation. I was there; it took nearly the whole day. The famous bed ... with back-cloth and lamp hanging from the canopy, was transformed into an altar before dinner and a sideboard after, and back into a bed at the end of the festivities. The whole town came to see the farce...'[19] Her passion for display was also noted by the diarist Thomas Creevey: 'Lady Londonderry is the great shew of the balls here in her jewels', he wrote from Doncaster races in September 1824, 'which are out of all question the finest I ever beheld – such immense ame-thusts and emeralds, etc. Poor Mrs Carnac, who had a regular *haystack* of diamonds last night, was really nothing by the side of the other...'[20]

The Londonderrys bought Holdernesse House in 1822 soon after the un-fortunate suicide of Lord Londonderry's brother, the second Marquess – better known as Viscount Castlereagh, the then Foreign Secretary. They almost im-mediately brought in Benjamin Dean Wyatt, the son of James Wyatt, to remodel it. His main tasks were to build a new wing to house a banqueting hall and a ballroom gallery, to join together Stuart's eighteenth-century drawing-rooms, and to create a new staircase. Because the staircase had to be fitted into an existing house in which space was limited, it was less grand than Wyatt would probably have liked: even so, with its ascent framed by pairs of columns, its double returned flights, and its gallery running round all four sides at first-floor level, with columned features opening into the sculpture gallery and the ante-room on the south and north sides, there was an even greater emphasis on spectacle than in the staircases of the big eighteenth-century houses. It was designed not only to parade upon, but to be watched doing so from above by those guests who had completed the circuit of ante-room, drawing-rooms and gallery. Said to have been inspired by the room in which the Congress of Vienna met, the gallery was intended both to display Lord Londonderry's collection of marbles and paintings, and for entertaining. With its sumptuous decoration and almost baroque treatment, it was Wyatt's earliest contribution to the style of gilded magnificence, and was perfectly suited to the post-Waterloo period, when aristocratic life was at its most extravagant and, as Lady Susan O'Brien recalled, 'assemblies are become so numerous that it is common to go to two or three a night ... the crowd must be equal everywhere.'[21] How Frances Anne must have delighted in it all.

The Londonderrys' new house was not quite completed when they first moved in. 'It is dirty', wrote the Marchioness to her mother, 'but the luxury of having a home of one's own and five large windows looking onto the Park

Londonderry House,
Park Lane.

Opposite: The grand
staircase, Londonderry
House.

and a garden of our own covers many defects.'[22] When the house-warming
finally took place in the summer of 1828, it did so, needless to say,

in a style of extraordinary magnificence and taste ... Every apartment was illuminated
with girandolles or sidelights, except the first which contained an ormolu chandelier
of great dimensions. All the interior was illuminated with wax candles. At eleven
o'clock the company began to arrive: the dancing commenced half an hour after with
quadrilles and ended with waltzes. A regular supper was set out in the banqueting hall
at two o'clock. Covers were laid for fifty and the tables were replenished six times; on
the whole three hundred supped, which was the extent of the party. The dancing was
afterwards resumed and kept up till five o'clock.[23]

A few weeks later found Frances Anne presiding over a fancy-dress ball,
attended by the whole of the diplomatic corps – 'a scene', commented a
newspaper, 'unexampled in the annals of the Fashionable World since the
fifteenth century'. She took the part of Queen Elizabeth and held a mock
court, seated on a throne 'gorgeously decorated with crimson velvet and
gold'.[24]

Above: The gallery,
Londonderry House.

Right: Looking across
the first-floor landing,
Londonderry House.

The drawing-room,
Londonderry House.

For those who attended, this party was a foretaste of what was to come, for over the next forty years Frances Anne was to establish a kind of court at Holdernesse House. The Tory Party regularly came there to pay their respects; she ruled over the house like a queen, even to the extent of having a throne-like gilded chair, with a gold brocade canopy above it, placed between the sculpture gallery and the drawing-rooms, in which she sat in state to receive the salutations of her departing guests. 'At receptions in her own house', wrote Sir Archibald Alison,

her manner was polite and high-bred, but stately and frigid, such as invariably inspired awe in those who were introduced to or had occasion to pass her. To such a length did this go, that I recollect once, in one of her great assemblies at Holdernesse House, as the Marchioness had taken her seat near one of the doors by which the company were intended to go out, to bow to them in passing, the whole people, the moment they saw her seated in her grandeur, turned about, and went back the way they came, rather than pass through the perilous straits.[25]

Her behaviour, however, did not prevent people from clamouring for invitations. Disraeli, for one, was always thrilled to be asked, and immortalised the house as Deloraine House in *Sybil*. 'The saloons of Deloraine House', he wrote, 'blazed with a thousand lights to welcome the world of power and fashion to a festival of almost unprecedented magnificence.'[26] On this occasion he probably had in mind a banquet he attended there in Queen Victoria's coronation year, which almost certainly served as a pattern for many similar parties during Frances Anne's reign, and of which he wrote at the time:

Nothing could be more *recherché*. There were only 150 asked, and all sat down. Fanny was faithful and asked me, and I figure in the Morning Post accordingly. It was the finest thing of the season. Londonderry's regiment being reviewed, we had the band of the tenth playing on the staircase: the whole of the said staircase (a double one) being crowded with the most splendid orange trees and Cape Jessamines; the Duke of Nemours, Soult, all the 'illustrious strangers', the Duke of Wellington, and the very flower of fashion being assembled. The banquet was in the gallery of sculpture; it was so magnificent that everybody lost their presence of mind. Sir James Graham said to me that he had never in his life seen anything so gorgeous. This is the *grand seigneur* indeed, he added.[27]

One man who was not to be outdone by the Londonderrys was Lord Grosvenor. As each year the returns increased on his large estate in Mayfair and Belgravia, originally inherited from Mary Davies, who died in 1730, he was growing ever richer and more powerful, and in 1827 he was toying with the idea of carrying out a whole new series of improvements to Grosvenor House based on designs by Thomas Cundy and his son, and by Robert Smirke. These proposed the extending of the existing building both eastwards and westwards and involved, in effect, its almost total rebuilding. A central feature was to be a new picture gallery to house his remarkable collection of paintings, on which Richard Rush, the American Ambassador, had commented after attending an assembly there in 1819. 'Four rooms were open', he wrote,

the walls of each covered with paintings ... In the principal room, a large one, and very lofty, and which from abundant light had a sun-like brightness, were four large paintings by Rubens – scripture pieces, besides other productions of the masters. These four I was informed had been recently purchased by Lord Grosvenor, for five thousand pounds sterling. In another of the rooms, my attention was called by one of the guests, to a landscape by Paul Potter ... There were historical pieces, fancy pieces, landscapes, portraits – making the walls on all sides glow with this rich and beautiful collection of works of art.[28]

Robert, second Earl Grosvenor and first Marquess of Westminster. British School.

It was a scheme which held little appeal for Lady Grosvenor, however, who loved the old house with its sunlit, bow-fronted rooms on the south, and could not face the idea of the upheaval involved. Her daughter-in-law, Lady Elizabeth Belgrave, who was in favour of the project, spoke of these misgivings in a letter to her mother.

I am quite of the opinion that it will be a very good thing to do, as I have no particular regrets about the present rooms and the more because B. [her husband, Lord Belgrave] tells me that the new place is beautiful. But for Lady Grosvenor, you see, the case is different, because in the first place no earthly power could persuade her of the necessity of the measure, as she says it would very well last her time. Then she thinks it (which I do not) the most perfect house that ever existed and that she can never again have such another room and such a balcony and then all the trouble of moving everything. Then she says that all that was done last year in the way of painting and papering these rooms will now go for nothing. She even wishes the Rubenses back with their seller as the first cause of such a disturbance. But there is no fear of her dissuading Lord Grosvenor.[29]

Had these proposals been carried out in full, they would undoubtedly have made Grosvenor House the most imposing private house in London. The young Cundy's most ambitious scheme was for a pillared and porticoed façade of nineteen bays, providing a state suite of five rooms made up of a dining-room, music room, drawing-room, picture gallery, and a Rubens room, while another had a huge circular, domed statue gallery in the centre of the garden front. Robert Smirke's ideas were no less grandiose, and included a central drawing-room 160 feet long, opening into flanking rooms 40 and 34 feet long respectively. In the end, however, the alterations were restricted to general decoration and repairs to the old house, and the extension and remodelling of the existing picture gallery, which had been completed by William Porden in 1819. The work was carried out by the younger Thomas Cundy, who gave the gallery a new coved ceiling, similar to that which his father had recently designed for the great staircase at Northumberland House, and added onto it a new apartment to house the Rubenses. The only view of these rooms as they were at the date is in the charming conversation piece painted by Leslie in 1831. Entitled *The Family of the first Marquess of Westminster*, it was painted

See colour plate 17

to commemorate the marquessate conferred on Lord Grosvenor in William IV's coronation honours, and provided an informal picture of him and his family in the new gallery. Lord Westminster is seated in the middle, supporting his grandson, the future first Duke of Westminster; behind stands his heir, the new Lord Grosvenor, while Lady Westminster sits at the piano, and Lady Grosvenor is seated on the left. The Rubenses can be seen in the background behind the screen of 'large fluted scagliola yellow antique columns'.[30]

The fascination of the Leslie picture, the only nineteenth-century portrait group of its kind painted in a London house, lies not only in its architectural and decorative details, but in its symbolisation of one of the main reasons why they, together with families like the Northumberlands, the Devonshires, and the Londonderrys, spent such fortunes on their London homes: to express their own importance. This was not true, however, of the equally extravagant alterations carried out at Apsley House in Piccadilly by the first Duke of Wellington, the hero of Waterloo. For the Duke, Apsley House was more than just his town residence; it commemorated the victories of his armies. Here were displayed the relics and prizes of his campaigns, as well as the tributes of the kings and princes of Europe; and here, on the anniversary of his greatest victory, he used to entertain his officers. Solely for this reason he enlarged the house twice, and it is interesting to note that throughout its glorification the great Duke's own apartments remained simple to the point of austerity – in stark contrast to the crimson and gold and martial splendour of its state rooms.

When the British Government bought Apsley House for Wellington from his brother, Lord Wellesley, in 1816, it was a brick building five bays wide, which had been designed by Robert Adam in about 1771 for Henry Lord Apsley, later second Earl Bathurst. He made no major changes until 1819, when he decided to build on a new dining-room in order to give a banquet for his twenty generals on the anniversary of Waterloo. For this he employed Benjamin Wyatt, who had a long-standing connection with the family, having served as a secretary to Lord Wellesley when he was Governor-General of India, and as a private secretary to the Duke in Ireland in 1807. Compared with his later interiors, the room was restrained in its decoration, the only hint of what was to come being in the scagliola pilasters with heavy gilded capitals which framed the window and the sideboard. Nevertheless, it greatly impressed the Duke's friend Mrs Arbuthnot when she dined there in April 1820. 'I dined yesterday at the Duke of Wellington's,' she confided to her journal, 'the first day of his dining in his new dining room; it is a magnificent room & the greatest improvement to the house.'[31]

The main phase of building followed seven years later when the Duke was Prime Minister. With the passing of the years, the number of generals to be entertained at the anniversary dinner had increased rather than decreased as those who had held junior commands in 1815 were promoted, and soon the

Opposite, top: Grosvenor House, Park Lane, with the new picture gallery.

Opposite, bottom: Sir Robert Smirke's unexecuted design for a new Grosvenor House.

Apsley House as
designed for Lord
Bathurst

Below: Wyatt's
dining-room at Apsley
House.

1820 room was no longer large enough to contain them. This shortage of space prompted the Duke to undertake a major rearrangement of the interior of the old house, including the building of a new west wing, which contained a picture gallery that ran along its entire length. At the same time the exterior was to be faced with Bath stone, which was considered more appropriate to the importance of the site. Wyatt told the Duke he estimated the cost would be approximately £22,000, and work was begun in the summer of 1828.

Unfortunately things did not go with quite the military precision that Wellington might have liked. He almost immediately quarrelled with Wyatt over escalating costs, and in desperation he turned to Harriet Arbuthnot to look after the job for him. 'The truth is', she wrote in her diary in November,

he is too busy to pay proper attention to such a work, & no architect goes on well who has a careless employer. I dare say Mr Wyatt and I shall go on very well together, & the plan is, I think, as good as it can be. I am amused with the Duke, when he got out of humour with the alteration, laying it upon me ... I have given him fair notice that, when his house is the admiration of all London ... I shall consider the merit all due to me.[32]

But Mrs Arbuthnot appears to have been no more successful in keeping a close watch on the financial side of the operation than the Duke, and additional works were ordered at random without the cost being checked up on. For

Apsley House after the alterations carried out in 1828. A lithograph of 1853.

The Duke of
Wellington and Mrs
Arbuthnot sketched
walking in the park.

example, one particularly extravagant and theatrical idea, which annoyed Wellington, was the design of the window-shutters in the gallery – they were covered with huge sheets of mirror glass, so that at night they could be pulled down to match the pier glasses. 'I consider all the expense upon the window shutters thrown away', he wrote to Wyatt in September 1829. 'I might have had my room broader and much cheaper shutters even with looking Glasses.'[33] Consequently when the accounts were made up, early in 1830, Wyatt's original estimate had leapt to the enormous and unexpected sum of £66,000. The Duke was beside himself with anger.

'I never saw him so vexed and annoyed', wrote Mrs Arbuthnot.

He said the shame & ridicule of being so cheated & imposed upon, & the having been led on to an expenditure which must ruin his family, made him quite miserable, that he could not bear the sight of the house & really did not know what to do. It was with some difficulty I got him to tell me what it had cost, & only under a promise I would not tell it to anyone. I told him I thought it the most preposterous cheat I ever heard of, & I asked him what Mr Wyatt said for himself. He told me he had abused him furiously & told him it should be the last conversation he would ever have with him, that he had known him for forty years, knew all his circumstances &, with his eyes open, had ruined him ... I tried to comfort him as well as I could & said that, if the work was fairly measured & valued, he would know at least that he had his money's worth; and that, tho' it was certainly most provoking, still the house is beautiful &, as it will hold all his pictures & all his fine things, he must consider it as his Waterloo House...[34]

But Wellington was in no mood to be reassured, and instead went stomping through the house in search of more to complain about. He appears to have found it, for in October 1830, he wrote crossly to Wyatt begging him 'to have all the new work of this house reviewed, and put to rights, if only for the sake of his own reputation. Windows, Doors, Curtains, Window Shutters etc should be made so as to open and shut with ease, to keep out the weather; and the chimneys not to smoke ... It is not too much to expect this state of comfort in a house new built or repaired in the year 1829-30.'[35]

Though Wyatt was known to be extravagant, and probably did go beyond his original brief at times, it also seems that the house was in a much poorer state than anyone had realised in 1828. 'In the old building,' he explained in a letter to his employer,

there was five times as much work done as was originally thought of; and when your Grace considers that whole floors, on account of their decayed state, were renewed which had not been intended to be touched; that a general substantial repair, throughout the whole house, was unavoidably gone into, for the purpose of getting rid of the rotten timbers ... and the dangerous state of which could not possibly have been forseen by anyone; that almost every wall in the building was underpinned, because they were baseless, having been originally built upon timber which had so far perished, that little more than the hard knots belonging to it remained ... you will, I have no

The Waterloo Gallery,
Apsley House.

doubt, feel that the ultimate total of the expenditure had its origin in causes which are in no way attributable to me as a fault.[36]

By the time Wyatt wrote this letter, the decorations in the house were almost certainly finished, but though the Duke had asked Mrs Arbuthnot to supervise them, his ideas had not always met with her approval. About one in particular, she had felt strongly. 'We dined the day before yesterday at the Duke's', she wrote in her diary of 11 February 1830.

I had not dined upstairs in his house since the alterations & nothing can be finer & better done. I am rather discontented, however, for I think he is going to spoil his gallery & as I took infinite trouble about it, it vexes me. I made the drawings for the doors & windows, which I thought Mr Wyatt had proposed in a shape & design that was frightful. I made the drawings for the skirting board & altered the ceiling &, '*tho*' *I say it as should not*', it is really beautiful. He is going to hang it with *yellow* damask, which is just the very worst colour he can have for pictures & will kill the effect of the gilding. However, he *will* have it.[37]

See colour plate 16

In spite of her misgivings, and those of Wyatt, who bravely told the Duke that in his opinion 'yellow hangings will entirely destroy the effect of the gilding in the room',[38] the Waterloo Gallery was a great success. In 1830, William IV and Queen Adelaide attended the first of the Waterloo Banquets to be held in it. They entered the house by way of a simple entrance hall and vestibule, and from there proceeded into the staircase hall, which occupied the centre of the building, and was dominated by a cantilevered stone staircase which swept up round a colossal marble statue of Napoleon. On the *piano nobile* their stately progression continued through a series of Adam drawing-rooms, culminating in the great ninety-foot gallery which filled the whole of the new west wing, and is generally regarded as having been one of the masterpieces of Wyatt's 'Louis Quatorze' style. Fortunately an engraving was made of the banquet held there in 1836, so one can see exactly how it must have looked when the King first set eyes on it. The mirrored shutters, about which the Duke had complained, would have been pulled down, helping to reflect the light that blazed from the central ormolu chandelier and from the great porphyry *torchères*, a gift from Tsar Nicholas I, which are shown rising through the long table. On the walls hung part of the Duke's collection of pictures, almost a hundred of which were crammed in a formal pattern into every available space, including the window piers and over the doors and windows. Those which he had neither bought nor been given had been captured at the battle of Vitoria in 1813, when Joseph Bonaparte abandoned his carriage. This was found to contain more than 165 paintings from the Spanish royal collection, and when Wellington tried to return them to the restored Bourbon monarch, the latter insisted on his keeping them.

There can have been few spectacles to rival the magnificence of the Waterloo Banquets, which seem to epitomise the extravagance and ostentation of the age; yet they were taking place during the Indian summer of the Whig oligarchy that had virtually ruled England since the accession of George I. The death of his great-great-grandson, George IV, went unlamented except in so far as it forced Society to curtail some of its pleasures that season. In the years that followed political uncertainty was to have a dampening effect, some people going so far as to fear the kind of social upheavals that had become familiar in France since 1789. Agitation for reform, particularly of the franchise, was not only confined to the lobbies at Westminster: it spread into the streets, where mobs roamed, much to the alarm of those in prominent positions. In November 1830, after several days of unrest, Lady Gower, wife of the future second Duke of Sutherland, wrote: 'I think we are going on much better here, and rain and

9 Above: Design for the painted room at Spencer House, by James Stuart, 1758.

10 Left: York House, Pall Mall. A sectional design by Sir William Chambers, *c*.1759.

11 Above: A view of
the east front of
Shelburne House.
Published by
Ackerman in 1811.

12 Right: The glass
drawing-room at
Northumberland
House, from a
watercolour.

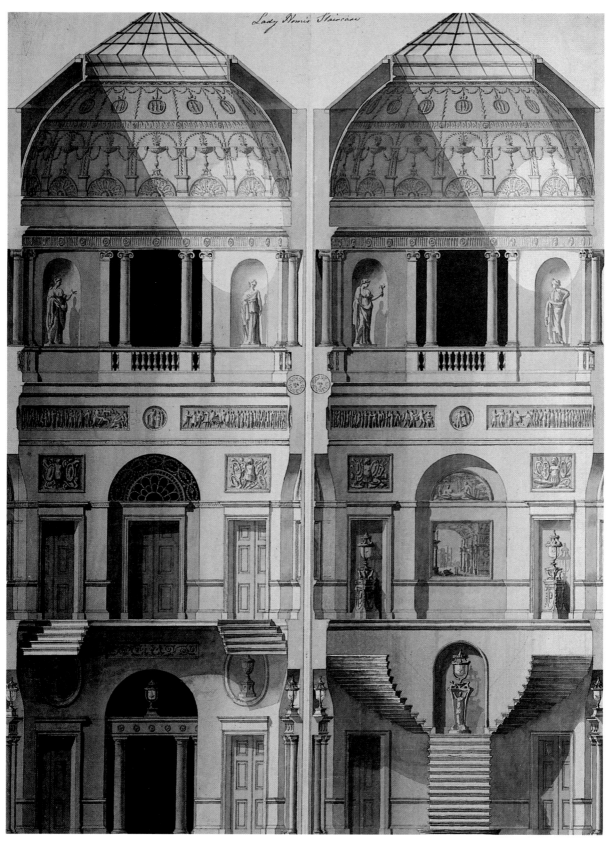

13 Sectional drawing by Robert Adam for the staircase at Home House, Portman Square, *c.*1759.

14 The crimson drawing-room at Carlton House from a painting by C. Wild, engraved by Sutherland, 1816. Part of Walsh Porter's extravagant schemes for the Prince Regent.

15 The saloon at Devonshire House, *c.*1822, by William Hunt.

16 The gallery at Apsley House prepared for the Waterloo Banquet. The banquets were held here from 1830 to 1852.

17 *The Family of the First Marquess of Westminster*, by C. R. Leslie, 1832.

18 Opposite: *A Reception at Stafford House*, by Eugène Lami, 1849.

19 *Chamber music in the ballroom at Wimborne House,* by Sir John Lavery. One of a series of concerts in the 1930s.

police have done much good. G. found a stone in his carriage the other day and Mama was groaned at, which made one feel we would all go about in omnibuses soon, without livery servants and one's coronet in one's heart.'[39] The following month Charles Greville noted in his diary that 'London is like the capital of a country desolated by cruel war or foreign invasion, and we are always looking for reports of battles, burnings, and other disorders. Whenever there has been anything like fighting, the mob has always been beaten, and has shown the greatest cowardice.'[40]

The worst trouble flared up in the autumn of 1831, when the Reform Bill was defeated in the Lords. Four days afterwards, on 12 October, the Duke of Wellington wrote to Mrs Arbuthnot, 'I understand that the Streets and Parks are full of mobs; and I don't propose therefore to go out till the evening.'[41] Later in the day, he wrote again to say that just as he had been about to send his previous note,

a Mob surrounded my House, upon which they commenced an attack with Stones which lasted 50 Minutes in broad daylight before any assistance came. They broke all the Windows on the lower floor looking towards Rotten Row, a great Number in my Room in which I was sitting, some in the Secretary's Room, and some in the Drawing Room above Stairs. All the blank windows fronting towards the Park & Piccadilly are likewise broken. They did not attempt to break into the Garden. We had men with fire Arms ready to receive them. They are quiet now; but there is a considerable body in the Park about the Statue, and another attack is threatened for this evening ... My Garden and the Area between my Room & the garden are filled with Stones. The Principal fire was directed upon my Room, which they reached easily from the Road.[42]

Given the rather strained atmosphere, it is hardly surprising that the season of 1832 was a failure, with 'so little gaiety, so few dinners, balls and fêtes'. Thomas Raikes, London merchant and Governor of the Bank of England, continued the lament in his diary: 'The political dissensions have undermined society, and produced coolnesses between so many of the highest families, and between even near relatives, who have taken opposite views of the question.'[43] But despite such fears, the Reform Act of 1832 did not destroy Society. Seats in the House of Commons had been redistributed and some of the worst abuses checked, but the extension of the franchise was not revolutionary. A property qualification remained the basis of the voting lists, and members of Parliament had to be men of independent substance. It was to be the second Reform Act of 1867 that really wrested political control from the landed interest. Thus for the time being, Society remained as impregnable as ever, and was quick to recover its composure.

Symbolic of this was the rise of Stafford House, the grandest private house ever built in London. 'In the extent, grandeur of proportions, solidity of materials, and beauty of situation,' wrote Dr Waagen, after a visit there in the early 1850s, 'it excels every other mansion in London.'[44] Standing at the extreme south-west corner of St James's, and bounded on two sides by the

Top: George, first
Duke of Sutherland,
by William Owen.

Above: Elizabeth,
Duchess of
Sutherland, by
Reynolds.

Opposite, top: The
west front of Stafford
House.

Mall and Green Park, it was originally designed by Wyatt for George IV's brother, the Duke of York. That it was always intended to be palatial is clear from a letter written by Wyatt in 1833 in which he describes his idea for the Duke as having been 'that of the best parts of the Palace of Versailles, and of the date of Louis XIV. The whole was intended to be finished with white and gold; and I am certain that a more splendid suite of Rooms than these would never have existed in France.'[45] The foundation stone was laid on 17 June 1825, and by the time the Duke died in January 1827, the shell of the house had been completed, and the interior was well under way. The vestibule, entrance hall and corridors were

in a very forward state, as to the plastering of the walls. The doors, windows, architraves for those parts are nearly ready to fix, and the scagliola columns and Pillasters, for the Entrance Hall; and for the opening between the Hall and the Staircase are completed ... The great Staircase is in fact more forward in its preparation for the finishing than would appear from the mere appearance of it on the spot...[46]

In its thus unfinished state, the house passed into the hands of the government in part settlement of large debts left behind by the Duke of York, and it was to their great relief that, a few months later, they were approached with a request to purchase the lease by George Granville Leveson-Gower, second Marquess of Stafford. 'Lord Stafford', wrote Lady Holland to her son, in July 1827,

has attained the great object of being possessor of York House, a most magnificent residence. It is not settled how it is to be called, whether Godolphin House, the name it bears on the lease, or Stafford House; not being a freehold the latter might be considered improper. Lord Stafford intends coming at the end of the summer to establish in London, in order to superintend the preparations, furnishing, etc so as to be ready for their reception at Easter.[47]

'It is a palace', she wrote the following year, 'and fit for them.'[48] In that they had the money to spend on it, she was right, for not only was the Marquess an extremely rich man in his own right, but his wife, Elizabeth, Countess of Sutherland, had brought a fortune into the family, along with an estate of over a million acres. They were, said Greville, 'leviathans of wealth'.[49] Being by then quite an elderly man, however, Lord Stafford decided against trying to finish the whole house, but instead to concentrate on the completion of the ground-floor rooms, and of the great staircase. He retained Wyatt and his brother Philip, who was also involved in the project, and in February 1830, after two years work and considerable expenditure, he and his wife were able to move in. The following June, the poet Tom Moore attended a reception there. 'In the evening to Stafford House', he noted in his diary of 18 June,

which was opened for the second time in compliment to Prince Frederick of Prussia. Nothing can be more magnificent than the staircase; its size and grandeur made the whole company look both pigmy and dingy. Seemed to remind everybody of the

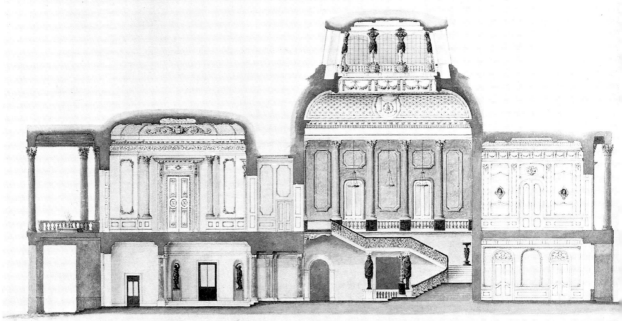

A section through the centre of Stafford House.

Caserta at Naples. Lady Stafford ... received the company in a manner worthy the staircase.[50]

Within three years of his moving into his new home, Lord Stafford, now created Duke of Sutherland, was dead. He was succeeded by his son George, the second Duke, whose wife, Harriet Howard, eldest daughter of the sixth Earl of Carlisle, was a remarkable woman. 'Built, mind and body, on a large scale and overflowing with joie de vivre',[51] she was to play an important rôle in the history of Stafford House. The Sutherlands were immediately faced not only with the problem of the unfinished state rooms, but with the lack of adequate accommodation for their fast-expanding family, which made it necessary to add an extra floor. It was a challenge they were well equipped to deal with, not just financially, but because they shared a keen interest in building and decorating; too much so, in fact, for Wyatt's comfort, since they travelled a great deal, and all drawings, however elaborate, had to be submitted to them for approval. They were inveterate shoppers on their travels, and frequently wrote to Wyatt either to ask whether some new find could be incorporated in the decoration, or to tell him to make use of some unexpected purchase, such as mounts for the chimney-pieces in the drawing-room and the dining-room. On one occasion Wyatt had great trouble steering the Duke away from the idea of having casts made of the bronze doors to the Baptistery in Florence, which the Duke wanted for the dining-room, despite the fact they were nineteen feet high. Such arguments eventually led to an irreversible breakdown of relations between the two men, and a subsequent court case in which Wyatt sued his employer for non-payment of certain fees, claiming that he had

ample evidence of an extreme degree of pretension to taste on the part of both the Duke and Duchess with very little sound knowledge, taste or judgment on such subjects and he clearly foresaw that he should have no sinecure in attending to all their notions and at the same time protecting the Designs against great absurdities.[52]

After this Wyatt was replaced by Charles Barry, whose palatial Travellers' Club, built between 1829 and 1832, had so impressed the Duke that he had commissioned him in 1838 to reconstruct his country house, Trentham Hall, Staffordshire, and it was Barry who completed the house in about 1843. But in the end Wyatt was responsible for the glorious interiors at Stafford House which, to quote Sir John Summerson, 'established Louis XV as the decorative rule in London society for seventy years and more – from Buckingham Palace to the Ritz'.[53] The entrance was pure theatre. A simple hall, low and rather dark, with a screen of columns suggesting a cool Greek Revival interior, gave guests not a hint of what was to come. Nothing on the scale of the great staircase had ever been seen in London before, and because it was so unexpected, its effect was that much greater.

'The great hall and staircase', wrote Lady Eastlake in her memoirs, recalling a reception and concert she attended there in 1854, are masterpieces of architecture, fulfilling every condition of beauty, in proportion, design, size, and decoration; and, as all places of entertainment should, it attains its fullest beauty when crowded with figures. Not that there could be any crowd: the size is such, that the stairs alone would accommodate hundreds, the galleries the same, the hall below thousands. All was marble, bronze, gilding pictures, gorgeous hangings and carpets, with flowers without end. No picture by Paul Veronese of a marriage feast can exceed in gorgeousness what was presented to our eyes. The dresses added by their gay and tender colours, seen through marble balustrades: figures looking up by hundreds, and looking down in the same proportion; and that which is always wanting abroad, even where the architecture is as fine, perfect *keeping up*. On the great wide stream of stair, where the two flights pour into one, stood the eighty Cologne singers, their voices more heavenly than ever in that vast domed space. We had two acts, and, between and after them, the guests circulated in the immense space. The *élite* were there...[54]

The Duke's son, Lord Ronald Gower, was another who waxed lyrical when remembering this quite extraordinary room. 'Viewed when lighted *a giorno*, full of festivity and flowers, of perfumes and music', he wrote in his memoirs,

or with only the cold moonlight streaking one of the tall grey columns or lending a ghostly brightness to a figure in one of the copies of the great Caliari's paintings, this hall has to me something almost sublime in its size and its proportions – like some grand poem turned into solid masonry, imperishable and immutable to time, and age, and human changes.[55]

He also recalled that on occasions 'the great hall can, if needed, be converted into a most commodious sitting-room.'

The entrance hall, Stafford House.

The grand staircase,
Stafford House.

Opposite, top:
The gallery, Stafford
House.

Opposite, bottom:
The great drawing-
room, Stafford House.

Opposite: The music-room, Stafford House.

Left: Harriet, Duchess of Sutherland, by Franz Winterhalter.

When the company reached the top of the stairs, which could well have been a laborious process, since it was not uncommon for a thousand guests to attend these assemblies, they passed through an ante-room into the 'green drawing-room', which appears to have been the first of the state rooms to be finished, in the autumn of 1836. Painted white and gold, it owed its name to the velvet hangings which covered most of the walls. From the east door a glittering enfilade opened through the adjoining four rooms – the first ante-room, the 'great drawing-room', a second ante-room, and the gallery, all decorated in white and gold. Like that at Londonderry House, the gallery was intended for receptions as well as for works of art, and it was considered a great success by contemporaries. 'It is not only the most magnificent room in London', wrote Mrs Jameson, 'but is also excellently adapted to its purpose, in the management of light, and the style of decoration. There is no colour but the dark rich crimson of the furniture, the walls being of a creamy white, the ornaments of dead and burnished gold.'[56] Beyond it lay the two most richly decorated rooms in the suite, the ante-room and the music room – one of the rooms known to have been completed by Barry. Though it was very splendid, it was almost over-ornamented, no doubt because the Duke and Duchess had become bogged down in details in their anxiety to create variety.

It is essential to bear in mind the colossal scale on which the Sutherlands lived in order to make sense of those huge rooms overlooking the Mall and St James's Park, remembered by the fifth Duke as being 'gay with sunshine and flowers through the spring and summer, and draped and gloomy in the winter months'. A household list of 1845, for example, shows that forty-eight servants were employed at Stafford House, and ten in the stables, together with a further thirty-one in their three other houses, Cliveden, Trentham, and Dunrobin. Such a household was necessary, especially since the Duchess, as Mistress of the Robes to Queen Victoria, was frequently required to entertain the Queen and Prince Albert, and may have inspired the famous remark that the Queen is said to have made on her first visit to Stafford House – 'I have come from my house to your palace.'[57]

See colour plate 18

Fortunately for posterity, one of these visits, in 1840, was recorded in a watercolour by Eugene Lami, while on another occasion Chopin described in a letter to his family a recital he had given before her Majesty in May 1848.

I wrote and told you that the Duchess of Sutherland had the Queen to dinner ... and in the evening gave a party consisting of only eighty members of London High Society. In addition to the Prince of Prussia ... and the Royal family, there were only such people as old Wellington, and others like him – although it is difficult to be like him. The Duchess presented me to the Queen. Her Majesty was gracious, and spoke with me twice. Prince Albert moved closer to the piano. Everyone said that these are rare favours ... you should have seen the Queen standing on the stairs in the most dazzling light, covered with all her diamonds and orders – and the noblemen wearing the Garter, descending the stairs with the greatest elegance, conversing in groups, halting in the various landings, from every point of which there is something fresh to be admired.[58]

Life at Stafford House did not only consist of grand receptions, however. Aware, perhaps, of the shocking extravagance of their way of life amid dreadful poverty and growing social unrest, Duchess Harriet was a keen supporter of good causes. Prison reform, workhouses, the conditions of miners, and slavery all received her attention. She was a close friend and supporter of the social reformer Lord Shaftesbury, and on numerous occasions lent him her house to hold meetings. 'She has been to me in heart, in temper, in demeanour,' he said on her death, 'the most uniformly kind, considerate and zealous ally and co-operator that ever lived ... She was ever ready to give her palaces, her presence, and her ardent efforts for the promotion of anything that was generous and compassionate and good.'[59]

This association with liberal causes was to be continued by the third Duke and Duchess, in whose day 'Poerio and his fellow-sufferers, still weak from their confinement in the prisons of Naples; Garibaldi the Deliverer, clad in his famous red garb; Livingstone and Charles Sumner, besides a host of princes and magnates, potentates and plenipotentiaries ... ascended these storeyed stairs'.[60] Among those who attended the reception for Garibaldi in 1864 was John Bright, who afterwards wrote in his diary: 'It was a singular spectacle to see the most renowned soldier of Democracy cared for as by a loving daughter by a Lady who is Countess and Duchess, at the head of the aristocracy of England. Lord Stanley said to me a day or so ago, I wonder if it ever occurs to the Duke that if Garibaldi had his way there would be no Dukes of Sutherland.'[61] Incongruous though it may have seemed to John Bright, it was on just such occasions, at the huge political receptions in which people of all persuasions mixed, that the private palaces played their important role. And their extravagance generated wealth which contributed to the development of London.

A view across
Piccadilly to
Devonshire House.

9

Echoes of Italy
and France

The house is now settled as to design and is what Father calls Anglo-Italian.

Diary of E. M. Barry, January 1846.

'All the people who have been at the Royal progress say there never was anything so grand as Chatsworth', wrote Charles Greville in his diary of 13 December 1843:

and the Duke, albeit he would have willingly dispensed with this visit, treated the Queen right royally. He met her at the station, and brought her in his own coach and six, with a coach and four following, and eight outriders. The finest sight was the illumination of the garden and the fountains; and after seeing the whole place covered with innumerable lamps and all the material of the illuminations, the guests were astonished and delighted when they got up the following morning not to find a vestige of them left, and the whole garden as trim and neat as if nothing had occurred. This was accomplished by Paxton, who got two hundred men, set them to work, and worked with them the whole night till they had cleared away everything belonging to the exhibition of the previous night. This was a great exploit in its way and produced a great effect. [1]

The sixth Duke of Devonshire had become increasingly disenchanted with London life during the 1820s, and had spent most of the next twenty years absorbed in the great works which he and Paxton were carrying out at Chatsworth, and which the Queen saw in such style in 1843. As a result, Stafford House rose to prominence without the rivalry of Devonshire House, which fell into a sad state of neglect. In the middle of the 1840s, however, the Duke suddenly decided that he'd had enough of being buried away in the country. 'After years of torpidity', he wrote on 12 August 1846, 'I became again amused and pleased with society, and re-occupied my place in the world. My materials of reception had however become so very dingy and out of repair that I have resolved to brush up and repair poor old Devonshire House.' [2]

This 'brushing-up' took the form of various architectural alterations carried out by Decimus Burton, and the rich embellishment of the decoration by John Crace and Company, Upholsterers. A portico was added to the front, leading into the entrance hall. This was lengthened to run the full depth of the house

The crystal staircase, Devonshire House.

Opposite: The ballroom, Devonshire House.

See colour plate 15

providing a way through to what was the most celebrated of the new additions, the 'crystal staircase', so-called on account of its glass handrail and the glass newel at its foot. It was circular, and rose up in a generous curve to the first floor where it led to the former 'great drawing-room', now joined to the west drawing-room to form the ballroom, and much enriched with added ornament. Here the Duke hung some of the finest pictures from his collection: among those that can be dimly discerned in old photographs are the Jordaens double portrait of the Prince and Princess of Orange, now in the National Gallery, and Rubens's *Holy Family with St Elizabeth*, now in the Walker Gallery, Liverpool. But even the grandeur of the new ballroom was eclipsed by that of the saloon, which the Duke had always intended to be the climax of the house. In the drawing (see page 102), showing the saloon without a trace of elaborate painting or stucco decoration, one gets a sense of the sober nobility of Kent's idea. The watercolour, painted by Hunt in 1822, shows the saloon after the Duke's first set of changes, with the ornate curtaining and pelmets that went so well with the splendid furniture, now to be found in the library at Chatsworth. Finally the photograph (on p. 272) indicates the grandiose Italianate style of decoration given to the room in the 1840s, with its great coved ceiling painted in the palazzo manner and the walls broken up with silk panels and mirrors in highly ornamented frames.

The saloon,
Devonshire house.

So Devonshire House was brought back to life, and once again the stage was set for the kind of glittering assembly attended by Lady Eastlake in May 1850:

... to Devonshire House. There was an immense concourse of carriages in Picadilly – a party at Miss Coutts' and Lord Lansdowne's besides ... We drew up under a large portico, where, as it was raining, hundreds of servants were clustered. Then we entered a very large hall, with pillars in couples, looking like the crypt of the whole building. This hall led to the grand staircase, which encompasses a space big enough for billiard table, statues, etc. Nothing could be more grand and princely than the *coup d'oeil* – groups sitting and lounging about the billiard table, where the Duke of Argyll and others were playing – crowds leaning over the stairs and looking down from the landing above: the stairs themselves splendid, shallow, broad slabs of the purest white

marble, which sprang unsupported, with their weight of gorgeous crystal balustrade, from the wall; and such a blaze of intense yet soft light, diffused round everything and everybody by a number of gas jets on the walls. The apartments were perfect fairyland, marble, gilding, mirrors, pictures and flowers; couches ranged round beds of geraniums and roses, every rare and sweet oddity lying about in saucers, bouquets without end, tiers of red and white camellias in gorgeous pyramids, two refreshment rooms spread with every delicacy in and out of season, music swelling from some masterly instrumental performers, and the buzz of voices from the gay crowd, which were moving to and fro without any crush upon the smooth *parquet*. The Duke looks just fit for the lord of such a mansion; he is tall and princely-looking, with a face like a Velasquez Spanish monarch. He walked about starred and gartered, and was very attentive ... The dresses were beautiful, and so fantastic they would have passed for fancy dress a few years ago ... There was so much to look at that the hours fled...[3]

A reception in the saloon at Devonshire House.

Dudley House, Park Lane.

Opposite: The ballroom, Dudley House.

Devonshire House was by no means alone in the 'brushing-up' which it received in the nineteenth century. Other houses which also underwent this treatment included Dudley House, Hamilton House, and, once again, Grosvenor House. Dudley House, situated at 100 Park Lane, had been built by William Atkinson in 1826 for the first Earl of Dudley, 'the Lorenzo of the Black Country',[4] who had died insane in 1833 after a lifetime of conversing with himself in two voices, one squeaky, one bass, 'like Lord Dudley conversing with Lord Ward', wrote Tom Moore in his diary.[5] In 1847 it was taken over by his descendant, the eleventh Lord Ward, who eight years later put in hand a spectacular campaign of improvements. Carried out by the architect Samuel Whitfield Daukes, who had been working for him at his country seat of Witley Court, Worcestershire, they included the creation, on the first floor, of a Louis XVI-style ballroom, heavily gilded and ornamented with a coved ceiling bearing emblems of music; a magnificent eighty-foot picture gallery, divided into three toplit sections by pairs of marble columns; and a suite of rooms called respectively the 'blue drawing-room', the 'red drawing-room', and the 'yellow drawing-room'. The entrance hall and the main staircase were also given a French flavour, and a conservatory was built out over Park Lane.

The picture gallery,
Dudley House.

Opposite, top:
The red drawing-
room, Dudley House.

Opposite, bottom:
The yellow drawing-
room, Dudley House.

The blue drawing-
room, Dudley House.

Opposite: The
conservatory, Dudley House.

Hamilton House, No. 22 Arlington Street, had been built by William Kent in about 1743 for the then prime minister, Henry Pelham; since then it had been owned successively by the second Duke of Newcastle, who was Pelham's son-in-law, the second Earl Gower, the Earl of Lincoln, the fourth Duke of Rutland, Lord Eardly, the first Marquess of Camden, the seventh Duke of Beaufort, and the eleventh and twelfth Dukes of Hamilton. In 1870, however, it was bought as a town residence for his new wife, Lady Cornelia Spencer-Churchill, daughter of the seventh duke of Marlborough, by Sir Ivor Bertie Guest, whose fortune came not from the ownership of great acres, but from a vast iron works in Wales. Although it already contained a splendid suite of reception rooms round an inner court – of which the most notable was the 'great drawing-room', based on the first-floor saloon at 44 Berkeley Square, with its coffered ceiling embellished with paintings *en grisaille* of gods and goddesses – Sir Ivor was unable to resist making his own additions. These included roofing over the inner court and turning it into a fashionable winter garden, and building on a ballroom of extraordinary grandeur, with great coupled Corinthian pilasters, and elaborate moulding and decoration, all of which were gilded. An unusual feature was a musicians' gallery, hidden when not in use behind heavy gold curtains. In addition to highly embellishing Kent's beautiful 'great room', he also bowed to fashion and added a 'French room', the 'white drawing-room'. In 1880, Sir Ivor was created Lord Wimborne, and the house was known thereafter as Wimborne House.

The great drawing-room, Wimborne, formerly Hamilton, House.

Above: The ballroom
Wimborne, formerly
Hamilton, House.

Left: The white
drawing-room,
Wimborne House,
formerly Hamilton
House.

At Grosvenor House, the first Duke of Westminster employed Henry Clutton, fresh from working for his father-in-law, the Duke of Sutherland, at Cliveden, to remodel the suite of state rooms in the Italian Renaissance manner. Work was begun in 1870, and by 1872 the dining-room, saloon, drawing-room, ante-room, corridor and gallery were finished, while the Rubens room was completed the next year. These were recorded in a sequence of photographs taken by Bedford Lemere in 1900, and were also described in a memoir by Lady Helen Seymour, a daughter of the first Duke. The main entrance to Grosvenor House, on Upper Grosvenor Street, was through large wrought-iron gates set in a 110-foot long Roman Doric screen, from where a paved drive, 'sprinkled with golden-yellow sand to prevent the horses from slipping', led up to a *porte-cochère*. 'The hall was of rather modest proportions', remembered Lady Helen: '... a sedan chair always stood there, and huge bowls of oriental pottery filled with pot-pourri. Inseparable from the hall was that dignified man, the hall porter, in livery, who, I thought, lived there. He was tall and slim and wore side-whiskers; his name was Martin and we were very fond of him.'[6]

Apart from the library, all the state rooms at Grosvenor House were on the ground floor, a feature which was strengthened by Clutton's alterations. Guests entered first an ante-room, originally the drawing-room, in which hung two of the most famous paintings in the Grosvenor collection, Gainsborough's *Blue Boy* and Reynolds's *Mrs Siddons as the Tragic Muse*. 'Below The Blue Boy', wrote Lady Helen,

stood a magnificent bureau, of exquisite workmanship, said to have belonged to Louis XVI. And there was one piece of furniture there I particularly admired. It was a sofa, hideous, shaped not unlike an elephant, and it had pride of place in the middle of the room. From the ante-room you passed through to the picture gallery. To the left of the door, on a table, stood a small clock which I find hard to describe. It was a fairy-tale dream clock, a gem, and its crowning splendour and joy was a tiny crystal waterfall falling into a tiny crystal river upon which swans floated. Our great treat was when my father could be persuaded to wind it up; then the waterfall moved and the swans sailed by.

Clutton made his greatest changes in the picture gallery and the Rubens room. Whereas Cundy had linked them by a screen, he separated them more distinctly, so that they became in effect two large reception rooms. Now

large double doors led into the once famous Rubens room where hung three immense pictures by Rubens, completely covering the walls on each side of the doors, and filling the huge wall-space facing the windows. I was, I think, conscious of the glorious depth of colouring of these wonderful pictures, but I was also somewhat overawed by the huge bare feet of the figures appearing almost on a level with my astonished eyes.

Lady Helen also mentions a stage set up at one end of the Rubens room so that it could be used for charity concerts and meetings, for which it was much in demand. To give access to the public on such occasions, Clutton made a corridor on the north side, connecting it with the entrance hall.

An extraordinary feature of both of these rooms was that their ceilings were designed so as to be entirely independent of the main structure. They were suspended from iron girders, and a network of wheels and pulleys ensured that they could 'be lifted bodily when required without trouble or expense'. Moreover, 'every portion of the joiner's work and fittings has also been prepared so as to be moveable'.[7] The supposed purpose of this elaborate system was to enable the rooms to be heightened in the event of future rebuilding. At first the rooms were illuminated by a number of brass candlestands and chandeliers, and in particular a massive candelabrum in the Rubens room which is said to have held 190 candles and to have weighed two and a half tons. Then, in January 1882, the Duke went to a demonstration of electricity at the office of the Edison Company, after which, he enthused, 'Edison's Electric Lighting is the best thing out, and apparently perfect for house lighting everywhere I mean for rooms, passages, everywhere, no more lamps nor candles nor steam nor nothing! And all perfectly safe – you may lay hold of the wires with perfect impunity – delightful'.[8] The candelabrum was sold and electricity installed – and not just in the two galleries, but throughout the house. In the early days of electricity, those who had installed it were so proud of the new addition to their homes that they made no attempt to disguise it: as the photographs show, bulbs were left unshaded, and were not only clustered in candelabra but were dotted along the lines of the cornices and ceiling compartments as well.

The drawing-room, Grosvenor House.

The gallery,
Grosvenor House.

Opposite, top:
The Rubens room,
Grosvenor House.

Opposite, bottom:
The dining-room,
Grosvenor House.

A reception in the picture gallery, Grosvenor House.

From the other end of the ante-room one stepped into a room of particular charm and grace, called the saloon. From the French windows steps led directly down into the garden, which was spacious for London, with grassy lawns and huge shady plane trees. In the saloon hung my father's favourite picture, a small landscape with cows by Paul Potter ... From the saloon you passed into the huge dining-room. . .

The walls of this room were hung with stamped leather; it glittered with gold leaf, and contained thirty-five paintings, including five Rembrandts.

We had great fun seeing the preparations and arrangements for the huge dinner parties ... The dinner table for these events stretched the whole length of the dining-room and was a lovely sight. The snowy table-cloth was lit by candelabra and ornamented by my father's racing trophies, and some of earlier days. Those that specially delighted us were the groups of silver horses plunging artistically on their ebony stands. The flowers were usually pale pink Malmaison carnations grown at Eaton. The fruit, also from Eaton, was delicious: grapes, peaches and nectarines.

In choosing to base his refurbishment of Grosvenor House on the Italian Renaissance, the Duke may well have been influenced by Bridgewater House, an impressive palazzo built in 1847 by Sir Charles Barry for Lord Francis Egerton, first Earl of Ellesmere, and the younger brother of the second Duke of Sutherland. Formerly the home of that voluptuous figure Barbara Villiers, Duchess of Cleveland, under whom it was known as Cleveland House, it stood on Cleveland Row, with Spencer House to the north, and Stafford House to the south. It had passed into the hands of the Dukes of Bridgewater and then, on the death of the third Duke in 1803, to his nephew Lord Stafford, along with a remarkable collection of over three hundred pictures acquired by the first Duke in 1798 as part of the break-up of the famous Orleans collection. To house these he built onto the house a special gallery, designed by Charles

Tatham, which he opened to the public, a revolutionary step at a time when there were no public picture galleries in London; and town houses, unlike those in the country, were virtually never open to visitors. Joseph Farington attended its opening on 21 May 1806, and recorded that it was open from twelve to five.

The collection was increased by Lord Stafford until it filled every inch of space on the walls. Among the admiring visitors was Richard Rush, the then American Ambassador to London, who dined there in 1818.

Last night we were at the Marchioness of Staffords. The rooms were full. The Prince Regent, Royal family, many of the nobility, and others thronged them. It was past eleven when we arrived; yet fresh names were every moment announced . . . The rooms abounded in ornamental articles. The paintings commanded admiration. Under light judiciously disposed, they made a magnificent appearance. There is said to be no such private collection in Europe.[9]

There were in fact other serious collectors in London, among whom the most important were Thomas Hope, and J. J. Angerstein, whose pictures were to form the nucleus of the National Gallery, Samuel Rogers, Lord Grosvenor, the Duke of Wellington, whose collection can still be seen at Apsley House, and Sir Robert Peel, many of whose pictures were bought for the National Gallery after his death. It is impossible in a brief space to give a true idea of the riches of these collections, but detailed accounts of these and others are given by Mrs Jameson in her *Companion to the most celebrated Private Galleries of Art in London*, published in 1844, and by Dr Gustav Friedrich Waagen in his *Works of Art and Artists* (1838), *Treasures of Art in Great Britain* (1854), and *Galleries and Cabinets of Art in Great Britain* (1857).

As we have already seen, Lord Stafford moved to Stafford House towards the end of his life, leaving Bridgewater House to his second son Francis, the future Lord Ellesmere, who soon found himself having to remove the roof of the old part of the house because it was in danger of falling in. This led to the discovery that the supporting walls were too decayed to sustain a new roof; in 1840 it was decided to demolish the entire structure and build a new house to the designs of Charles Barry, a natural choice since he had been working for his brother at Stafford House since 1838. Exhibited at the Royal Academy in 1841, Barry's first plan was for a monumental edifice, with a front of 195 feet onto Cleveland Row, containing no less than five picture galleries of different sizes and five smaller rooms *en suite*, each eighteen feet six inches square, for cabinet pictures. The cost of this would, however, have been enormous, and the plan was abandoned. His next proposal was for an Elizabethan-style mansion, rather similar to the work he had done a few years previously for the Earl of Carnarvon at Highclere, but this also proved unacceptable. Finally, in July 1845, he came up with a scheme that was approved, and the following January his son recorded in his diary,

Francis, first Earl of Ellesmere, by H. Cousins.

Barry's unexecuted plan for Bridgewater House.

All in the office engaged in preparing drawings of the new Bridgewater House ... the House is now settled as to design and is what Father calls Anglo-Italian or with Gothic principles of design, perpendicular lines prevailing, with pure Italian profiles and interior decoration. It will I think be very handsome and imposing from its size – the ground plan being 165 ft by 122 and the height from ground line 64 ft.

A few days later he wrote, 'This will I think be a very grand mansion but one that will excite much animadversion on account of its style as being far from a pure one.'[10]

'Grand' is something of an understatement for this massive exercise in the Renaissance manner, work on which was not actually completed until the spring of 1854, though the picture gallery was finished in time for the Great Exhibition of 1851. Its most impressive feature was undoubtedly the great central hall, or saloon, which rose the full height of the house and was reminiscent of a roofed-over Italian *cortile*, surrounded as it was by domed and vaulted arcades opening to the ground- and first-floor corridors. Its decoration was not in fact carried out for a further four years, by which time Lord Ellesmere had been succeeded by his son who, without consulting Barry, employed a rather vulgar German decorator by the name of Francis Gotzenberg to undertake the work. Though some of this was reasonably faithful to its sources – the decorations of the Villa Madama and Raphael's loggia in the Vatican – much of it was tainted with Victorian sentimentality, including the dome in the upper corridor, the surface of which was painted as a representation of an Italian Renaissance arcade with cupids on swings in the garlanded openings, and roses and hollyhocks rising against the sky. It horrified Barry so much that he 'retired with deep regret'.[11]

The first flight of the 'Italian staircase' rose from the central bay of the east arcade in the saloon; its walls were panelled in coloured marbles, while the barrel vault over it was richly painted and gilt. At a half-landing a second

The saloon,
Bridgewater House.

flight led off at right angles, with a third flight culminating in the south gallery. Here, at the south-east corner of the house, were the Ellesmeres' private apartments; the remainder of the south front was occupied by the 'state dining-room', the walls of which were hung with brown and gold stamped leather. On the west front, in the centre, lay the 'state drawing-room', and beyond it an ante-room leading into the picture gallery, which filled most of the north range of the house. This was a tall, oblong room, with a Corinthian screen at each end opening into a shallow bay; although it was a fine enough setting for the paintings it was designed to house, it lacked the magnificence of its counterpart at Stafford House. In a photograph taken in about 1900,

The picture gallery,
Bridgewater House.

looking from east to west, it is just possible to recognise some of the pictures
that made the collection so famous, including Titian's *Diana and Actaeon* and
his *Three Ages of Man*, both now in the National Gallery of Scotland. In
building this huge gallery and giving it a separate staircase and entrance specifically for the public, Lord Ellesmere continued the tradition of his father,
and in so doing gave the house a purpose that many of the other great houses
in London were to lack once they had ceased to serve a political function.

Hardly was the shell of Bridgewater House complete, before an obscure
Gloucestershire squire, R. S. Holford, who had made a fortune from his
holdings in the successful New River Company, decided to outshine Lord
Ellesmere with a 'palazzo' of his own. And whereas Bridgewater House was
tucked away in St James's, his occupied the site of the former Dorchester
House, the town house of the Earls of Dorchester, with space enough for two
imposing façades, one facing south down Park Lane towards Decimus Burton's
Ionic screen at Hyde Park Corner, and the other looking west across the Park.
It was the ideal setting in which to make a grand impression. Holford was a
dilettante with a keen interest in building and a wide knowledge of the arts,
and he knew exactly what he wanted. He chose as his architect Lewis Vulliamy,
a former pupil of Smirke's, upon whose versatility and practicality he knew he
could rely to carry out his ideas. Like Lord Ellesmere, he drew his inspiration from Italy; but whereas Barry had looked towards Venice, Holford and
Vulliamy turned to Rome, to Peruzzi's Villa Farnesina across the Tiber from
the Palazzo Farnese, from which were derived the block-like shape seen in
views from the south and west, the use of the superimposed orders of the
façades, the long, level, low-pitched roof and the design of the richly carved
frieze.

The precise dating of the scheme is not entirely clear, but the design was apparently worked out in 1848–9, at the end of which building was begun. By August 1852 work was evidently far enough advanced for *The Builder* to comment,

This mansion is a very good specimen of masonry, and is built for long endurance ... If the New Zealander, who is to gaze on the deserted site of fallen London in some distant time to come, sees nothing else standing in this neighbourhood, he will certainly find the weather-tinted walls of Dorchester House erect and faithful, and will, perhaps, strive to discover the meaning on the shield beneath the balconies, 'R.S.H.', that he may communicate his speculations to some Tasmanian Society of Antiquaries.[12]

R. S. Holford Esq, from a photograph copied by Emery Walker, 1862.

But another four years were to pass before the Holfords were able to move in, and it was not until 1860 that the first of the principal rooms were completed, and Mr Holford was able to congratulate himself on the success of a venture which, in the view of Beresford Chancellor, was 'without hyperbole ... the finest private dwelling in London'.[13]

On the south front a bold, triple-arched portico led into a dark entrance hall, even more sober than those in many of the great eighteenth-century houses. A single-storeyed and marble-paved ante-hall led off it, beyond the dark columns of which could be caught an enticing glimpse of the glories to come. To the right, in the east wing, lay the porter's room, the steward's room and all the other offices and servants' quarters, served by a back staircase in a tower at the north-east angle. To the left a door led into a vestibule serving Mr Holford's own room and a waiting-room. Apart from these two rooms, the west front was devoted to two libraries. On the north side of the staircase hall lay the family dining-room, and beside this was a secondary staircase leading to the private apartments above.

The entire centre of the house was given over to the grand staircase hall which, in terms of pure spectacle, outshone both Wyatt's hall at Stafford House and Barry's saloon at Bridgewater House. It was inspired by the Palazzo Braschi in Rome, which Holford had visited in 1855, and was designed by Vulliamy so as to make the most of the views through the screens of columns on both floors which, particularly in the gradual revelation of the vaulted upper galleries, offered ever-changing perspectives to visitors as they climbed the stairs. The galleries on the upper floor overlooked this hall on only three sides, the space on the fourth, the west side, being thrown into the saloon, so giving it extra width. Originally Vulliamy intended the wall between the saloon and the staircase to be solid until, according to tradition, Sir Edwin Landseer suggested that two great arches be cut through so that the saloon should appear as an extension of the staircase hall. The effect was dramatic, 'bringing to mind', wrote Christopher Hussey,

Paul Veronese's interiors and the Bibienas' settings for masques and operas. For ball purposes no more enchanting contrivance could be imagined. From the farther gallery

Dorchester House,
Park Lane.

Opposite: The grand
staircase hall,
Dorchester House.

the dance would be visible through the arches across the well of the hall, and from the ballroom could be watched the gay throng crowding the staircase, while ringletted and crinolined nymphs and whiskered Guardsmen conversed in the gallery arcades.[14]

Work on the saloon, which had ceiling paintings designed by Holford's brother-in-law, Sir Coutts Lindsay, went on through the 1860s, much of it taken up by the chimney-piece of Carrara marble which Holford had commissioned from Alfred Stevens in 1859. The completion of this took ten years, and it was probably frustration at the delay, rather than the cost, which prompted Holford to write to Stevens in May 1870, 'had I known that the saloon chimney piece would have cost so large a sum as £1,800 I should, while admiring its beauty, have been content with a good form and less ornament.'[15]

One of the galleries
round the first-floor
landing, Dorchester
House.

Opposite, top: The
saloon, Dorchester
House.

Opposite, bottom:
The dining-room,
Dorchester House.

Opposite, top: An
elevation of Montagu
House, Whitehall.

Opposite, bottom:
The saloon, Montagu
House, Whitehall.

Alfred Stevens was a sculptor, architect, designer, and painter, who took his inspiration from the Italian Renaissance, and whose talents have been likened to those of Michelangelo. Yet apart from the Wellington Memorial in St Paul's, the only commission of any importance he carried out was for R. S. Holford, and even that was never completed. Stevens was introduced to Holford in 1859 by John Morris Moore, who had studied with him in Italy, and he was immediately commissioned to design not only the saloon chimney-piece, but the eight doors on the *piano nobile* and, most important of all, the entire state dining-room. He was a painfully slow worker, however, not producing the models for the chimney-pieces until December 1864, nor all the designs for the woodcarving until June 1866. Over the next four years he supplied nothing, while Holford continued to support him – by May 1870, he had been paid £5,400, of which only half could be accounted for in work completed. 'My house has been rendered partly useless to me by the delay', Holford complained in a letter to Stevens.

When I first consulted you on the decoration of the dining room, I felt that it was so complicated an affair that reliable estimates were impossible and I therefore asked for none ... You must be able to tell me with tolerable accuracy what the ceiling and the completion of the dining room will cost; and as my outlay has been large and I am anxious to know how I stand, I must request you will give me some information on this point. It has always been my wish to deal liberally with you, and to give you as little trouble as possible in matters of account; but it is absolutely necessary that business should be done in a business-like way in order that a satisfactory result may be arrived at.[16]

Unfortunately, three years later, Stevens suffered a stroke, and he died in the early summer of 1875. It is a tragedy that the state dining-room, on the east side of the house, remained unfinished, for it would undoubtedly have been one of the finest rooms of its kind ever created. Palladian in style, it was intended to be full of colour; the ceiling was to have been painted with the *Judgment of Paris* and the *Flight of Aeneas*, the coves with designs from Geoffrey of Monmouth's Chronicle, and the areas round the doors and over the mirrors with arabesques. None of this was carried out, however, with the result that the work which was completed – the architectural treatment of the walls, the painted doors, and the marble chimney-piece, with its massive Michelangelesque supporting figures – had little unity. The two other state rooms, the 'green' and the 'red' drawing-rooms, both had fine painted ceilings by an Italian called Anguinetti, whom Holford had brought back from Italy in 1861, and the latter also had a frieze by his brother-in-law, Sir Coutts Lindsay. But, as much as anything, they were notable for the wonderful pictures which hung in them, including works by Velasquez, Domenichino, Murillo, Van Dyck, Tintoretto, Hobbema and Cuyp.

While Holford and Lord Ellesmere looked to Italy for their inspiration, the fifth Duke of Buccleuch looked to France. In 1853 he commissioned William

Burn, a former pupil of Robert Smirke, to build him a French Renaissance château on a superb site between Whitehall and the Thames. Complete with a high-pitched and turreted slate roof, Montagu House was constructed of Portland stone, and had gardens which ran down to the river. The interior contained some fine rooms, in particular the saloon which had an arcaded treatment to the walls, open on the staircase side. 'The Montagu House I knew', wrote Lady Constance Cairns, one of the daughters of the sixth Duke, in a charming memoir,

was a perfect family home, containing two floors of bedrooms, and on the first floor pleasant sitting rooms, apart from the big room used for entertainment. There was no sunk basement, as usually found in London houses; kitchens and all domestic offices were on the ground floor; also no attics. A broad white marble staircase led from the front door to a big room called the 'saloon', out of which opened all the reception rooms. At the top of the marble staircase were the secretary's room, and my father's most delightful sitting room, which faced south, and beyond these rooms was the staircase to the bedroom floors, which could be shut off by glass doors. The big rooms, including the dining-room, faced east, opened on to a broad stone terrace overlooking the Thames. My mother's sitting-room was at the southern end of the terrace. The comfortable family room which we all used faced west. Beyond the terrace was the garden, which was bounded by a wall, and then came the Embankment. The garden was big enough for a full-sized tennis court, and many flower beds, filled in Victorian fashion with geraniums and lobelia; also two Catalpa trees which did not bloom till August, therefore the flowers were seldom seen in that month by the usual inmates of the house. There were also two fine old hawthorn trees.

From the bedroom window there was a really wonderful view of the Thames, right down to the dome of St Paul's Cathedral. Barges and rivercraft were always picturesque. In an east wind one could have a faint smell of the sea. My parents' bedroom and dressing-rooms faced the river, and beyond on the same passage were the bedrooms and sitting-room used by my sister and myself, and a bathroom ... the only one in the whole house. On the west side there were many rather smaller bedrooms. When my eldest brother married and had children, these were used as nurseries. On the floor above there were more nurseries, gradually filled by the increasing families of my brothers. I have been told that the average number of human beings sleeping under the roof was sixty-five to sixty-eight, but only during the months of the London season. During the rest of the year the big rooms containing the pictures and beautiful furniture were shut up ... If my parents were in London in the winter, they used a small dining-room with the west drawing-room.

... Montagu House was a perfect setting for my mother as hostess. In the season balls were held there, and parties of different kinds, the garden being large enough for a garden party. There was a strange custom handed down from my grandparents, that anyone who knew the family could arrive for luncheon ... Owing to the situation in Whitehall ... there was an influx from Foreign Office, Admiralty, War Office, and often a Prime Minister or some very high-up official. Sometimes by arrangement their wives met them, but usually there was a great majority of men. There is still alive a member of the household at that time, and I recently asked her how the catering was

managed. She was then one of the kitchen maids under the French cook. Her reply
was that twenty guests were anticipated, but there were in reserve a ham, tongue, and
cooked chicken! My sister and I sat at a small table quite apart from the guests, and
our governess placed us with our backs to the rest of the company; we retreated
directly we had finished our meal.[17]

The palaces of Lord Ellesmere, R. S. Holford, and the Duke of Buccleuch
reflected the heady atmosphere of a time when Society was even more brilliant,
and certainly more cosmopolitan, than it had been in previous centuries. The
Queen was still young, and in the 1840s and 1850s she not only held her levees
and drawing-rooms regularly but, since she greatly enjoyed dancing, gave many
balls as well. Lady Dorothy Nevill, who 'came out' in the 1840s, remembers
going to 'a great many gaieties. That season I think I went to fifty balls, sixty
parties, about thirty dinners, and twenty-five breakfasts.'[18] 'I took a long range
among people of rank and fashion of both sexes', wrote the American historian,
William Prescott, in 1850,

whom I chased round in a succession of lunches, dinners, afternoon breakfasts, balls
and routs, with a perseverance and power of endurance quite astonishing to myself. I
had a dozen invitations for a single day, and was booked up in the way of dinners for
more than a month in advance. I had the satisfaction of dining with Sir Robert Peel,
though only a week before his death. Five times I was obliged to decline the invitation
of the premier, Lord John Russell, and was invited to dine with five of the mitred
nobles, including the Archbishop of Canterbury, I was at court several times, and had
three invitations to the palace. . .[19]

It was, however, an Indian summer.

A reception at Stafford House, by Eugène Lami.

The grand staircase, 148 Piccadilly.

10

The Palaces of the Plutocrats

Why, his house would go into my hall!

Barney Barnato on Alfred de Rothschild's house in Seamore Place.

In the 1850s two events took place which severely undermined the self-confidence of the nation and its leaders: the first of these was the outbreak of the Crimean War in 1854, lightly entered into and disastrously conducted, followed closely, in 1857, by the Indian Mutiny which sent shock waves through the Empire. Finally, the death of Prince Albert had a profound effect in that it led to Queen Victoria's complete withdrawal from society – which now looked for leadership to the Prince of Wales. It was a position he assumed with enthusiasm. He established his own court at Marlborough House, and within a few months his mother was already complaining that her son and daughter-in-law had become 'nothing but puppets, running about for show all day and all night'.[1] 'The Queen thinks', she wrote to Lord Granville, 'that with the exception of Lord Granville, Lord Palmerston, and possibly Lord Derby, and the three or four only great houses in London, Westminster House [Grosvenor], Spencer House and Apsley House, the Prince and Princess of Wales should not go out to dinners and parties, and not to *all* these in the *same* year.'[2] But during the years in which his mother remained in mourning, the Prince helped to adapt society to the changing spirit of the new age, and to break down its narrow structure. By the 1870s, at Marlborough House the great landed families, whose fortunes were beginning to come under pressure as a result of a severe agricultural depression, learned to mingle with a new moneyed class whose wealth came from industry and finance.

'I can recall no evening that could vie in sheer happiness with that of a Marlborough House Ball', wrote Frances, Countess of Warwick in her memoirs.

The Prince would have his army friends ... There would be the racing folk, represented by the big owners, and the financiers, the Sassoons, the Rothschilds, Baron Hirsch, and the rest. The Princess would be seen with her great friend, Lady de Grey, and the music lovers. Under the Marlborough House roof, and in the gardens, all these diverse types mixed quite happily and informally.[3]

The most celebrated of these occasions was a fancy-dress ball given on 22 July 1874, to which fourteen hundred people were invited. Sir Frederick Leighton superintended the decorations, and the Prince appeared as Charles I. It was, commented *The Times*, a display of 'well-ordered magnificence', while the Prime Minister, Mr Gladstone, who was permitted to appear in uniform instead of fancy-dress after dining and speaking at the Mansion House, described it as 'gorgeous, brilliant, fantastic'.[4]

As the guests danced that night, they might well have reflected on the irony of the fact that, in another part of London, an event was taking place which was in effect one of the first blows struck against the way of life which the great houses represented. For over two hundred and fifty years Northumberland House had stood at the corner of the Strand, the last of the Strand palaces, and a symbol of the old order. Now it was being demolished to give public access to the Embankment. The fifth Duke of Northumberland had fought compulsory purchase as far as he could, but in the end an act of Parliament was passed to force the scheme through. In the popular press this was hailed as a victory against privilege. 'The gloomy frontal', claimed one newspaper triumphantly, 'will presently make room for a magnificent road.'[5]

One of the reasons why the Prince of Wales was so keen to cultivate the plutocracy was that the landed classes, hit by the changing economy, were finding it harder to keep up with the spiralling costs of entertaining their future monarch. Indeed in his excessive demands he had come close to bankrupting a number of his old friends, including Lord Hardwicke and Christopher Sykes. Naturally, once they found the doors of society open to them, the industrialists and financiers became only too keen to own the kind of houses in which they were entertained. In 1872, for example, the banker Henri Louis Bischoffsheim, a notable connoisseur of French furniture and art, took over 75 South Audley Street, the former residence of the Earls of Bute, under whom it had been known as Bute House, and turned it into what one visitor called a 'Versailles in miniature'.[6] In its lavish interior he displayed his sumptuous collection of pictures and furniture, including Tiepolo's famous ceiling painting *The Allegory of Venus and Time*, which, along with its four accompanying roundels in grisaille, was installed in the 'blue drawing-room' – so-called because its walls were covered with a delicate, hand-painted blue satin. Situated on the ground floor at the back of the house, it adjoined a ballroom and boudoir; the latter was also hung with blue satin, and had a ceiling covered with pieces of tapestry set in gilded mouldings. On the first floor was a large dining-room, and a room called the 'black drawing-room', in which the furniture was upholstered in black satin.

The Rothschilds, with whom Edward had been friendly since his brief sojourn at Cambridge, were all equally grandly established. Nathaniel, the first Lord Rothschild, lived at 148 Piccadilly, which his father, Lionel, had created in the early 1860s by combining Nos. 147 and 148. It was a gloomy-looking

building with ugly plate-glass windows of the kind that were then all the rage; and, being four storeys high, it dwarfed its beautiful neighbour, Apsley House. Inside it boasted an impressive white marble staircase, and suites of large reception rooms decorated in what came to be known as 'Rothschild taste'. Summed up by Sir Algernon West as 'an exaggerated nightmare of gorgeousness and senseless and ill-applied magnificence',[7] this was best represented in Alfred Rothschild's house, round the corner at No. 1 Seamore Place, Mayfair, where elaborate French furniture and white gold panelling predominated.

Alfred was the most extravagant of the brothers, and his parties became famous not just for the wonderful food and wine that were served, but for the celebrities whom he entertained at them. 'Mr Alfred can best be described as a connoisseur in the fine art of living', wrote Lady Warwick. 'In the famous white drawing-room in Seamore Place, I have heard the greatest artists in the world, who were paid royal fees to entertain a handful of his friends.'[8] Here he also held what he called his 'adoration' dinners, to which he would invite a beautiful actress and a small number of his own men friends to worship at her feet. At the end of the evening he would draw the lady aside, and ask her, 'What shall I give you, beautiful lady?', before presenting her with some trinket. When Lillie Langtry was the chosen beauty, he got rather more than he bargained for, for when he asked her the question, she replied, 'Oh, this will do', her eyes having alighted on a particularly priceless Louis XVI ena-

Left: The blue drawing-room, 75 South Audley Street. The Fables of La Fontaine are depicted on the seats and backs of the chairs.

Above: The boudoir, 75 South Audley Street.

The ballroom, 148 Piccadilly.

Opposite: The conservatory, 5 Hamilton Place.

melled snuff-box, set with diamonds, and one of the jewels of his collection. 'He had a weak heart', she wrote later, 'and for a moment I thought I had stopped it. When he got his breath he promised me something much prettier and out came one of the well-known gift-boxes.'[9] Rothschild extravagance was not to everyone's taste. 'I have seldom seen anything more terribly vulgar', wrote Eustace Balfour, after a visit to Alfred's country home, Halton House, near Wendover. 'Oh, but the hideousness of everything, the showiness! The sense of lavish wealth thrust up your nose! The coarse mouldings, the heavy gildings always in the wrong place, the colour of the silk hangings! Eye had not seen nor pen can write the ghastly coarseness of the sight!'[10]

The third brother, Leopold, lived at 5 Hamilton Place, Park Lane, a tall house of grey stone, the design of which was based on an annexe to the palace of Chantilly. On the ground floor there was a library, richly carved in the Italian Renaissance manner, with tall French windows leading to a terraced

Derby House,
Stratford Place.

garden which bordered on the Park. This communicated with a dining-room, the walls of which were entirely covered with white marble, in stark contrast to the crimson of the upholstery and the curtains. On the first floor were two interconnecting Louis XV drawing-rooms; a conservatory ran parallel with them, and was filled with 'plants and palms standing about in richly coloured vases, and chairs and tables all in intimate disorder'.[11] The bedrooms on the floor above particularly impressed the correspondent of a magazine which reviewed the house.

In his own bedroom Mr Rothschild has, to use an Americanism, 'gone one better' than our neighbours across the Atlantic. He has provided himself with a perfectly fitted up bathroom actually at a stone's throw from his bed! What dreams of luxury could surpass this! The other bedrooms, in American fashion, have their bathroom adjoining.[12]

Such luxury was a far cry from the uncomfortable existence led by many of the aristocracy, however grand their houses may have been. 'I called on Mrs Leslie in her glorious old house in Stratford Place', wrote Augustus Hare, 'which is beautiful because all the colour is subdued, no new gilding or smartness. She herself sat in the window embroidering, with the bright sunlight just glinting on her rippled hair and sweet face at once a picture and a poem.'[13] Had he had to spend the night, however, he might have written a different account, for according to Sir Shane Leslie, whose grandparents occupied it, the house was

absurdly magnificent and uncomfortable within ... a great Y-shaped staircase branched to either side of the balconied landings which led into the drawing-rooms. The whole house was sacrificed to these enormous vistas. It was of them that Disraeli said, to please my grandmother, 'What perspective! What perspective!'. The ceilings in drawing- and dining-rooms were by Angelica Kauffman ... But within and apart from the stains of gas and fog it was filth and corruption like the whited sepulchre which gave Our Lord so memorable a metaphor. The 'New River' had been used to fill an open cesspool which fumed the house ... My grandfather rejoiced in the old sanitation and was offended when Murray Guthrie, who subsequently bought the house, asked permission to cover the cesspool at his own expense for fear his prospective bride should die of typhoid. The house contained only two garde-robes: one for the gentlemen, windowless, under the stairs, and one for the ladies which let into the servants' bedrooms. The footmen slept in the servants' hall. The kitchens were out of doors and contained the only hot-water tap in the establishment. A stream of house-maids supplied with unending cans every hot bath taken by the family. Upstairs there was a single sink from which proceeded a chilly bilge. Owing to the lack of a decent bedroom, two of my brothers had to be born in the drawing-room![14]

Aldford House,
26 Park Lane.

Towards the end of the century the Rothschilds' supremacy was being challenged by a number of new millionaires, men who had made vast fortunes from businesses connected with South Africa. Alfred Beit, the South African diamond magnate, was the first to build on any scale. Aldford House, at 26 Park Lane, was erected on a site bought from the Duke of Westminster, but only after Beit had agreed to certain stringent conditions. For example, on the very eve of his signing the contract, an urgent note arrived from the Duke insisting that Beit must spend at least £10,000 on the house; to which Beit replied that he intended to spend that on the stables alone. Nor was it allowed to stand more than two storeys high: which is why, when it was completed in 1896, it came to be described as a cross between a glorified bungalow and a dwarf Gothic country mansion. Inside it conformed to the *nouveau riche* taste for the French; its most striking rooms were the billiard room, which had a vaulted ceiling and walls covered in silk brocade, and the extensive winter garden. 'Here was a rockery and a fountain on one side', wrote a contemporary, 'and a palm grove on the other. Tesselated pavements, brown rocks, and green ferns were all intermingled. It was an abode of dim coolness and sheltered silence, and a silence made noticeable by the vague hum of the world outside.'[15] It goes without saying that the house was stuffed with priceless works of art.

Soon after Beit moved into Aldford House, another South African millionaire, J. B. Robinson, a mean and spiteful man whose ruthlessness had earned him the nickname 'the Buccaneer', took the lease of Dudley House. He too filled his house with treasures, with Rembrandts, Gainsboroughs and Romneys, Italian Old Masters, and seventeenth-century Dutch paintings – not, unlike Beit, out of any artistic discernment, but simply in a calculated attempt to establish his financial superiority. To one man this represented an open challenge. Barney Barnato was, without any doubt, the most bizarre figure ever to occupy a great London house. A cockney from the slums of Whitechapel, he built up a fortune in South Africa by trading in everything 'from diamonds and gold, right through wool, feathers and mealies, to garden vegetables'.[16] He had the golden touch, and his skill in predicting share prices led to a five-fold increase in his riches. In 1895, the year in which Robinson took Dudley House, he was at the very summit of his career, with the Lord Mayor of London giving a banquet in his honour at the Mansion House in recognition of the millions of pounds he had poured into what was, at the time, a falling market. Megalomania was beginning to set in. Passing Dudley House one day, Barnato turned to a companion and said, 'I'd half a mind once to buy that property. It's got such a splendid place for the baby's perambulator.'[17] He applied to the Duke of Westminster to buy a plot of land on the Grosvenor Estate, but was turned down on the grounds that 'he does not stand in a high position in South Africa, and he is a land speculator', and finally settled on a site further south in Park Lane, overlooking Stanhope Gate. He commissioned the architect T. H. Smith to build him a Renaissance mansion, with a staircase of marble, four flights high and top-lit by a glass dome, a conservatory and winter garden, and a ballroom of at least two thousand square feet. He also ordered two billiard rooms, and insisted that the whole house was to be heated by radiators. Soon after construction began, he and his wife were swung aloft in a crane to cement photographs of themselves under a corner-stone. Once the word got out that he was building himself a mansion, he was besieged by dealers eager to unload on him endless bric-à-brac and bad pictures at vastly inflated prices, for it was well known that he knew nothing about art. His son, Woolf, suggested that he might benefit from the great knowledge of his friend Alfred de Rothschild, to which he replied, 'I don't need his help. Why, his house would go into my hall!'[18]

Barney Barnato, by H. Furniss.

The house was to take two years to complete, during which time Barnato found it impossible to live anywhere less imposing than Beit and Robinson. He tried first to persuade the Duke of Wellington to rent him Apsley House, 'until my own place is ready', but to no avail. He was luckier, however, with the Spencer family, who agreed to rent him Spencer House. 'It's not a bad position,' he told a journalist. 'Exactly half way between the Prince of Wales in Marlborough House, and the Prime Minister in Arlington Street.'[19] Though Barnato was now superficially one up on his rivals, the reality was somewhat different, for while they were received by Society, and were friends of the Prince of Wales, he was never considered *persona grata*, and during the years he lived there Spencer House echoed, not to the genteel chatter of great lords and ladies, but to the rumbustious jollifications of actors, journalists, racing trainers, boxers, theatre managers and the like. One of the first parties he gave there was to celebrate the circumcision of his second son. To commemorate the occasion, he had ordered Cartiers to send over a magnificent diamond necklace for his wife. Over the dinner table he showed it to one of his friends, a low music-hall comedian, and invited his opinion. 'Don't you think something better, perhaps?' asked Barnato. 'Certainly,' agreed his friend, tossing it across the table. 'But wouldn't this do for the baby to play with?'[20]

In his book, *The Great Barnato*, Stanley Jackson relates an amusing story which took place while Barnato was living at Spencer House, on Christmas Eve, 1896. Barnato had promised to stand bail for a Hatton Garden friend who was being charged under the Bankruptcy Act, and went along to Marlborough Street magistrates' court.

The magistrate glanced sharply at the jaunty little man in the checked suit with the outsize rose in his lapel.
'Where do you live?' he snapped.
'Spencer House.'
'But that's Lord Spencer's house. Are you his major-domo?'
'I'm my own bloody domo,' he shouted back, quickly apologising as the Clerk flashed him a warning.
'Are you worth £500 a year after the payment of your just and lawful debts?' continued the magistrate. Barney laughed, and coughed into his bowler hat before emerging to nod agreement.
'What rent do you pay?'
'£2,000 a year.'
'What are you exactly, Mr Barnato?'

'A diamond merchant and a director of a couple of companies,' said Barney, with a broad wink at the public. 'And I've got a bit of freehold in Park Lane.'[21]

By the early summer of 1897 the Barnato house at 25 Park Lane was almost complete. As a final touch, a series of stone figures were placed on the roof – representing, so people said, the owner's creditors, petrified while awaiting settlement. No more suitable time could have been chosen for its completion, for this was the year of Queen Victoria's Diamond Jubilee, and London was overflowing with subjects who had come from all over the world to pay homage to their Queen and Empress. Lavish parties were planned by all the leading hostesses and, determined not to be outdone, Barnato arranged to throw a great housewarming on Jubilee night itself, 22 June. It was one party he was not to attend. On the journey home from South Africa, where he had been on business, he was lost overboard. The inquest heard that he had recently been suffering from deliriums, in which he saw banknotes crumbling into dust between his fingers as he counted them, and searched for diamonds in the wall; a verdict of 'Death by drowning while temporarily insane' was returned. The house, which he wanted so much, and never spent a night in, was subsequently bought by another celebrated plutocrat, Sir Edward Sassoon.

That summer, while the city was gripped by Jubilee fever, was the occasion of perhaps the greatest party ever given in a private house in London. The Devonshire House Ball was the inspiration of Louisa, Duchess of Devonshire, wife of the eighth Duke and the most influential of all Society hostesses. She planned the entire evening single-handed, for her husband had a general abhorrence of social life, preferring pigs to parties.[22] He would anyhow have been a liability, since he had a pronounced habit of cat-napping at every opportunity. 'One afternoon', reminisced the Duke of Portland, 'finding the ministerial bench in the House of Lords occupied, he sat on another bench next to me, and in two minutes he was asleep. When he woke with a start he looked at the clock and said "Good heavens, what a bore, I shan't be in bed for another seven hours."'[23]

The ball was in fancy dress. The Duchess had chosen as its theme 'allegorical or historical costume before 1815', and it was suggested that there should be a number of Royal Courts, and processions on different themes in which people could, if they so wished, join. Those lucky enough to be on the guest list were thrown into a frenzy of excitement. 'For weeks, not to say months, beforehand', wrote Lady Randolph Churchill,

it seemed the principal topic of conversation ... Great were the confabulations and mysteries. With bated breath and solemn mien a fair dame would whisper to some few dozen or more that she was going to represent the Queen of Cyprus or Aspasia, Fredegonde or Petrarch's Laura; but the secret *must* be kept. Historical books were ransacked for inspirations, old pictures and engravings were studied, and people became quite learned in respect to past celebrities of whom they had never before heard.

The less well known the character, the more eagerly were they sought after. 'Never heard of Simonetta? How curious! But surely you remember Botticelli's picture of her, one of the beauties of the Florentine Court? No? How strange! ...'[24]

As the day of the ball approached, the activity in and around Devonshire House became increasingly frantic. Hundreds of workmen laboured furiously to erect an enormous marquee in the garden and a special staircase to connect it to the house. Inside, the housekeeper marshalled a squadron of housemaids to sew and clean and sweep, while the steward organised battalions of footmen to rearrange the house. In addition, the Duchess had decided that all the servants were also to be in fancy dress. Those hired from outside were to wear Elizabethan or Egyptian costumes, hired from a theatrical outfitter, while the rest, many of whom were brought in from the other Devonshire households, were to have theirs specially made – the men in the blue and buff Devonshire livery of the eighteenth century, the women in Elizabethan sprigged frocks. It was an inspired idea, as it involved the entire household in the excitement. The comings and goings reached their climax on the great day itself, 2 July, beginning early in the morning with the arrival of waggon after waggon bearing vast quantities of plants and flowers and fruit from the gardens and the great orangery at Chatsworth.

'On the night of the ball,' wrote Lady Randolph Churchill, 'the excitement rose to fever pitch. Every coiffeur in London and Paris was requisitioned, and so busy were they that some of the poor victims actually had their locks tortured early in the morning, sitting all day in a rigid attitude, or, like Agag, walking delicately.'[25] The first guests began to arrive from their various dinner-parties at about half-past ten, to find a huge crowd assembled round Devonshire House, including many members of society who had been unlucky enough not to be invited, and were as eager as the populace to watch the spectacle. Inside, they gathered in the hall, where they were serenaded by the Blue Hungarian Band while awaiting their turn to climb the 'crystal staircase', at the top of which stood their host and hostess, dressed respectively as the Emperor Charles V and Zenobia, Queen of Palmyra. A particularly impressive entrance was made by Sir Henry Irving, as Cardinal Wolsey. 'As the Cardinal swept up the staircase', a guest told Ellen Terry, 'his long train held magnificently over his arm, a sudden wave of reality seemed to sweep upstairs with him and reduce to pettiest make-believe all the aristocratic masquerade that surrounded him.'[26] This was somewhat galling for Lord Dunraven, who was also dressed as a Cardinal. It was, he later wrote, 'a beastly shame and quite put my nose out of joint'.[27]

There was disappointment for others too.

Many ... were the heartburnings over failures or doubles. In one case a well-known baronet had been perfecting himself for weeks in the role of Napoleon, his face and figure lending themselves to the impersonation. But what was his dismay at finding in

The Devonshire House Ball

Below: Sir Henry Irving as Cardinal Wolsey.

Bottom: The Earl of Dunraven as Cardinal Mazarin.

the vestibule a second victor of Austerlitz, even more lifelike and correct than himself. It was indeed another Waterloo for both of them.[28]

There were three Queens of Sheba: the Princess of Pless, Lady Cynthia Graham, and the Dowager Lady Dudley; and two Cleopatras, of whom poor Lady de Grey was completely overshadowed by Mrs Arthur Paget, the rich American wife of a dashing Guards officer. Her costume was made by Worth in Paris, the leading dressmaker of the day, and was described in a New York newspaper, *The New York World*, as being

a marvellous story in white and gold, and ... literally covered in jewels. Nothing like such jewels on the American lady's dress were ever seen in London or elsewhere. The costume was simply ablaze with diamonds, rubies, and emeralds. When she entered, people accustomed to the greatest displays of jewels the world has ever known, gasped with wonder and astonishment. Lady de Grey's dress, though it cost 6,000 dollars, was quite eclipsed by Mrs Paget's costume ...[29]

After the arrival of the Prince and Princess of Wales, dressed as the Grand Prior of the Order of St John of Jerusalem and Marguerite de Valois, the guests assembled in the saloon to watch and take part in the processions. The first of these was the English Court, led by Lady Tweedmouth, 'a striking figure as Queen Elizabeth, with eight gigantic guardsmen surrounding her, all dressed as Yeomen of the Guard'.[30] Then came the Austrian Court, led by Theresa, Marchioness of Londonderry, as the Empress Maria Theresa, ablaze with jewels, the 'family fender', as she called the famous Londonderry tiara, crowning her powdered hair. They were followed by the Russian Court of the Empress Catherine the Great, represented by Lady Raincliffe, attached to whose dress was an ermine-lined train of yellow velvet with the Russian Imperial double-headed eagle embroidered upon it in black. The next to dazzle the spectators were the Orientals, headed by the Duchess herself, who was carried into the saloon in a palanquin borne by slaves holding huge fans, no mean feat considering her stoutness. Her procession included a number of the celebrated beauties of the day, among them the Princess of Pless as the Queen of Sheba, Lady Randolph Churchill as the Empress Theodora, Lady de Grey as Cleopatra, and Lady Dudley as Queen Esther. Then came the Italians, led by Lady Plymouth as Caterina Cornaro, followed by those in costumes of the reigns of Louis XV and XVI, notable among whom were Lady Warwick as Marie Antoinette, Mrs Keppel as Madame de Polignac, and the Duchess of Sutherland as Charlotte Corday. The last procession was that of the 'allegorical costumes', with representations of Night, Medusa, and various goddesses, the final curtsey to the Prince and Princess being made by Lady Wolverton as Britannia.

With the processions over, the royal party were led into supper, which took place in a special marquee, as lavishly decorated as the house, with a thick crimson carpet on the floor, three Louis XIV tapestries, lent by Duveen, large

mirrors on the blue and gold walls, and heavy crystal chandeliers hanging from the ceiling. Each table had a palm growing up through the middle of it, while all the flower arrangements were illuminated by tiny electric lights, a novelty for the time. 'Few people danced', wrote Lady Randolph Churchill,

as in a raree-show of that kind people are too much occupied in gazing at each other or in struggling to play up to their assumed parts. Sometimes this was carried farther than intended. Towards the close of the ball two young men disputed over a certain fair lady. Both losing their tempers, they decided to settle the matter in the garden, and pulling out their weapons, they began making some passes. But the combatants were unequally armed, one being a crusader with a double-handed sword, the other a Louis XV courtier armed with his rapier only. He, as might be expected, got the worst of it, receiving a nasty cut on his pink silk stocking.[31]

The gardens, where these keen young men fought, were as brilliantly illuminated as the house, with twelve thousand lamps of varying colours picking out the walks, and the trees hung with Japanese lanterns.

The ball ended at dawn. Consuelo, Duchess of Marlborough, who was seven months pregnant and miserably unhappy in a marriage into which she had been forced, has left a poignant account of her return home.

The ball lasted till the early hours of morning, and the sun was rising as I walked through Green Park to Spencer House, where we then lived. On the grass lay the dregs of humanity. Human beings too dispirited or sunk to find work or favour, they sprawled in sodden stupor, pitiful representatives of the submerged tenth. In my billowing period dress, I must have seemed to them a vision of wealth and youth, and I thought soberly that they must hate me. But they only looked, and some even had a compliment to enliven my progress.[32]

Such an entertainment was everything that the *nouveaux riches* would have liked to emulate, but they always somehow managed to over-gild the lily, however great their pretensions to taste. When Sir Ernest Cassel, for example, the friend and financial adviser to Edward VII, both as Prince of Wales and King, bought Brook House, on the corner of Park Lane and Upper Brook Street, it was already very splendid. Built of red brick, with a very French appearance to the façade, it had been completed in 1869 to the designs of Thomas Henry Wyatt for the banker and MP Sir Dudley Coutts Marjoribanks, subsequently Lord Tweedmouth. No expense had been spared. On the ground floor, off a broad hall, were a library, panelled in cherry wood, and a large dining-room, in which had been installed 'the entire carved work of one of the rooms at Drapers' Hall'.[33] A mahogany staircase, rising in double flights and lined with variegated marbles, led to a great suite of drawing-rooms in the French style, with elaborate gilded ceilings and French furniture, the walls of which were adorned with paintings by artists such as Boucher and Fragonard. 'There is not need for dwellers in Brook House to dream that they dwell in marble halls. They do dwell in them', wrote a contemporary observer.

They realise what the poet merely imagined. This is the first reflection that occurs to your mind as you enter the home of Lord Tweedmouth. You find yourself in a veritable *Salle de Marbres*. There are marble pillars; there is a marble floor; the very walls are of marble ... Let your eye wander up from this marble hall, taking in the vast paintings on the wall, the two galleries, and finally the immense and ornate dome and skylight. It looks best perhaps lit up at night from top to bottom, with all the gilt gleaming and the marble shining and the metalwork glistening, the whole justifying for once the use of that much-abused adjective, brilliant.[34]

For Cassel, however, who had already bought Lord Tweedmouth's Scottish estate at Guisachan, there was simply not enough marble. When he bought the house, he did so only on the condition that he could add to it 27 Upper Brook Street, which adjoined it and was part of the property. This was heightened and enlarged, and transformed into an entrance hall, with a grand,

Above: Brook House, Park Lane.

Sir Ernest Cassel, renowned for his likeness to King Edward VII, drawn by Max Beerbohm. The caption reads: '*H.M. the King*: "Do you know, Ernest, what they are saying? That I have Jewish blood!" *Sir Ernest Cassel*: "Dat is all von pig opfious lie, Zir."'

The reception room at Lord Tweedmouth's London home.

dome-topped staircase and upper hall beyond. The entrance hall was lined from top to bottom with a rare blue marble from a quarry in Ontario, while for the staircase and upper hall eight hundred tons of white marble were imported from Michelangelo's quarry at Sarravezza in Tuscany. It was not long before it acquired the nickname 'the Giant's Lavatory'.[35]

At Bath House, 82 Piccadilly, once the home of Sir Robert Walpole's most persistent opponent, William Pulteney, Earl of Bath, Sir Julius Wernher, another financial speculator who had made his millions in South Africa, presided over a household in which extravagance was taken to the limits of bad taste. 'Dined at the house of a millionaire - Sir J. Wernher, Bath House', wrote Beatrice Webb in her diary on 2 July 1906.

We went there ... partly from curiosity to see inside such an establishment ... Though our host was superior to his wealth, our hostess and her guests were dominated by it ... The company was composed, either of financial magnates, or of the able hangers-on of magnates. The setting in the way of rooms and flowers and fruit and food and

wine and music, and pictures and works of art, was hugely overdone – wealth-wealth-wealth – was screamed aloud wherever one turned. And all the company were living up to it. There might just as well have been a Goddess of Gold erected for overt worship – the impression of worship, in thought, feeling and action could hardly have been stronger.[36]

The drawing-room, Bath House.

Naturally Beatrice Webb, along with her husband Sidney, disapproved of such a way of life. The aristocracy, on the other hand, who, had they so wished, could have absorbed and dominated the *nouveaux riches* and imposed upon them their own standards of behaviour, were beginning to have a new respect for money. This was partly due to the influence of their pleasure- and money-loving king, but also to the decline in many of their fortunes as a result of the severe agricultural depression during the latter half of the century which, in many cases, had as much as halved their landed incomes. It was reflected in a rash of marriages to American heiresses, the most notable of which was that of the ninth Duke of Marlborough to Consuelo Vanderbilt, who brought with her a dowry of two and a half million dollars, which was subsequently used to renovate Blenheim Palace. Nor did Mr W. K. Vanderbilt's generosity stop there. When the ninth duke embarked upon a political career, the acquisition of a suitable London establishment seemed only natural. 'I only had to mention our wish', wrote the duchess, 'for my father to promise its fulfilment.' The result was Sunderland House, a large grey stone mansion, sixty feet wide and one hundred feet deep, which they built on the corner of Curzon Street and Shepherd Market, on the site of the present Lombard Bank. Designed 'in eighteenth-century style' by a French architect, Achille Duchêne, it consisted, on the ground floor, of an 'entrance hall with a white and red tiled floor, a small morning-room, Marlborough's sitting-room and a dining-room ... decorated in the Louis XVI manner', with a long gallery and two saloons on the first floor.[37]

Many of the landed families also began to take a much closer interest in the Stock Market, becoming increasingly familiar with the world of the Beits, Cassels and Wernhers. 'Disintegration set in', wrote the Earl of Dunraven. 'Society was hard-pressed and took to worshipping the Almighty Dollar unabashed ... Wealth and notoriety became the prime necessity of political and social life ... Society was dying. Luxury and extravagance became almost insane during the few years before the war. I wonder why? Was it perhaps some premonition that the end was near?'[38]

One man who saw a bleak future ahead of him, in spite of his still vast estates and riches, was the fourth Duke of Sutherland, whose wife, Millicent, had continued the tradition of her predecessors in making Stafford House a brilliant centre of political and social life. Her party to celebrate the coronation of George V and Queen Mary was attended by most of the crowned heads of Europe, and was acclaimed one of the most splendid ever held there. It was also, however, her last. For some years her husband had been growing increasingly worried about the general outlook for the landed families of England. The introduction of death duties in 1889, which were subsequently increased in 1894, was followed in 1909 by Lloyd George's proposed budget: with its planned increment value and undeveloped land duties, and its provision for a valuation of all the land in the kingdom, it threatened a frontal attack on the 'land monopoly'. Despite its defeat, it triggered off a flurry of land sales, and it has been calculated that in the five years before 1914 800,000 acres changed hands.[39] In 1911, the Duke of Sutherland sold his house in Staffordshire, Trentham, to contractors; soon after, part of the estate, and another at Sittenham in Yorkshire, were also auctioned. 'I'm just now in a state of bewilderment', wrote his wife to her friend the portrait painter, William Rothenstein, 'between the awakening of democracy ... and the suicidal despair of the ruined aristocracy.'[40] There was worse to come. In 1912, the Duke sold her beloved Stafford House to the soap manufacturer Sir William Lever. 'Strath has a mad lust for destruction on the plea of death duties', she wrote to Lord Esher.

Never is there another phrase in his mouth ... I shall have to leave Stafford House and I can't afford to bring a single real bit of furniture. I can't live without lovely things around me, associated historically with the past. Strath lives in rooms with nouveau art furniture bought on the hire system. I feel as if my heart were breaking at this last blow.[41]

The Great Gallery, Sunderland House.

In selling Stafford House on purely economic grounds, the Duke was to prove the first ripple of a wave which before long was to engulf every one of the grand private houses of London.

The demolition of
Devonshire House,
Piccadilly.

11

The Passing of
an Order

Archaeologists have gathered round me and say I'm a vandal ... but personally I
think the place is an eyesore.

The purchaser of Devonshire House, reported in The Times *19 May 1920*

'I do not believe I have seen or spoken to you', wrote the Duke of Wellington
to Millicent Sutherland, in June 1954, 'since the days before the first war when
you used to receive at the top of the stairs at Stafford House. I shall never
forget the beauty, charm and sparkle which I shall always associate with you
and Stafford House in your time. As Talleyrand said, Ceux qui n'ont pas
connu la vieille cour n'ont connu la douceur de vivre.'[1] The demise of those
days began in the aftermath of the First World War. When the Marquess of
Salisbury sold his town house in Arlington Street in January 1919, *The Times*
commented:

Lord Salisbury's severance of long associations with Arlington Street will not be lost
upon other owners of town houses, and further sales of this class of property may be
expected. The question may well be asked whether the transaction may not prove to
be in the matter of town houses what such sales as those effected some years ago by
the Duke of Bedford proved to be in the matter of landed estates. If other large town
houses should come into the market, it is probable that, while here and there one may
be bought by those who value associations, some of them will be demolished to make
room for hotels and blocks of flats...[2]

Within a few months, the same correspondent was writing, 'The break-up of
London estates, which has been foreshadowed for some time in these columns,
has now most unmistakably begun.'[3] This referred to the decision by Lord
Camden to sell off a large part of his Camden Town estate, which had been
in the family for nearly one hundred and thirty years. Others who joined the
rush to sell included the Duke of Bedford, who sold £2 million worth of his
Bloomsbury ground rents, Lord Portman, who disposed of seven acres of
Marylebone, and Lord Southampton, who sold part of Euston.

This movement by the landed aristocracy to unburden themselves of part of
or, in some cases, all of their town property reflected a post-war trend which
was beginning to revolutionise the holding of agricultural land. The war had

had a drastic effect on the fortunes of the great landlords, weakening their social and political influence, and severely reducing their incomes as a result of increased taxation and death duties, thereby forcing the sale of vast quantities of land. 'We all know it now', exclaimed *The Times* in May 1920.

England is changing hands ... Will a profiteer buy it? Will it be turned into a school or an institution? Has the mansion house electric light and modern drainage? ... For the most part the sacrifices are made in silence ... The sons are perhaps lying in far away graves; the daughters secretly mourning someone dearer than a brother, have taken up some definite work away from home, seeking thus to still their aching hearts, and the old people, knowing there is no son or near relative left to keep up the old traditions, or so crippled by necessary taxation that they know the boy will never be able to carry on when they are gone, take the irrevocable step.[4]

Though there was some truth in this rather romantic account, the vast majority of sales of both agricultural and urban land were prompted by a shrewd awareness among a growing number of the aristocracy that they needed to adjust the scale of their landed possessions to altered social and economic conditions, and to do so while the market was still land-hungry.

The first of the great private palaces to be affected by such thinking was Devonshire House, which was sold by the ninth Duke in 1920. To see it out in style, the Duchess of Albany held a charity fancy-dress ball there. 'Yesterday evening', reported *The Times* of 15 April 1920,

was the occasion of the Duchess of Albany's historical ball ... historical because those present would be the last invited guests to Devonshire House as a great town house, and historical because the house this week passes into other hands. Measured by all that has come and gone since Devonshire House was first built ... there were few present yesterday evening who did not share in the regret at the change of ownership; but Devonshire House as a princely home of hospitality maintained its reputation to the last...[5]

A month later, Devonshire House, for so long the resort of fashion, the centre of wit and talent, became, for the sum of one million guineas, the joint property of Mr Shurmer Sibthorpe, of Southampton Street, Holborn, and Mr Lawrence Harrison, a Liverpool shipowner. 'Mr Sibthorpe was enthusiastic about his purchase', commented *The Times*, 'and talked of a cinema with a magnificent façade, flanked by wonderful bank and office buildings, and with a huge vestibule in the centre. "Archaeologists have gathered round me and say I am a vandal", he added, "but personally I think the place is an eyesore."'[6]

The Duke and Duchess moved to a house in Carlton Gardens, not quite on the scale of their old home, but by most standards still palatial. 'It's interesting to see what the pictures look like in a small house,' the Duchess was heard to say.[7] Most of the pictures and furniture were removed to Chatsworth and were absorbed in the house, while many of its fittings, in plaster, marble, and wood, were deposited in a huge, mysterious store on the Derbyshire estate, where they have remained to this day, awaiting eventual reassembly with the help of a set of detailed photographs taken before their removal. The great gates, with piers surmounted by sphinxes, which once formed the entrance to the fore-court, can now be seen on the opposite side of the street, opening into Green Park. The porters' lodges were shipped brick by brick to America to form the approach to a private estate at Syasset, Long Island. Devonshire House never became the cinema visualised by Mr Sibthorpe. It was demolished in 1925, and on its site there arose an eight-storey block of flats which retained the name of the old palace, and which was regarded with a sense of wonder by many who saw it.

'Devonshire House has always been a romantic place', wrote one architectural pundit.

The romance that hung about the old house was that of mystery and gloom. Dark walls hid it from the outside world; there was no more than a glimpse of it to be seen through the gates. All of us who walked past it as children, or perhaps jingled past it in a hansom with the street lamps reflected in the wet street, can never quite forget our visions of a shrouded Marquis of Carabbas dwelling in silent splendour in that great silent house. Now the old house is gone; the gates are on the other side of Piccadilly, the stags' heads looking a little wistfully across the road at their ancient home; but the romance and excitement in a new form are still there. At the moment when I am writing there stands a wonderful tall forest of trees with criss-crossed, interlacing branches, and among the tree trunks, which, as a prosaic matter of fact are girders, are the beginnings of what will soon be a cloud-capped palace of white stone.[8]

As for the flats themselves, 'modelled upon the most up-to-date designs of London, America, and Paris', they were so modern and convenient and cheap to run as to banish from the memory the beautiful rooms which had once stood in their place. They came in many sizes, from four rooms to twenty. There were no stairs within, just 'an endless vista of rooms ... leading one into another'. They were full of the latest time-saving devices and conveniences, and could be run with a minimal number of servants. 'I find it most refreshing', continued our pundit,

to think how few I shall want ... and how very much less cross and tired they will be, because they have not got to run up and down stairs to answer my behests. As I wander through this airy kingdom, I find out various other alluring things. I discover that each of my bedrooms has got its own bathroom, and that lined with marble; that between my drawing-room and dining-room are folding doors, so that I can make them into one really big room in which, I suppose, I may give a dance if I want to. I find that I am ventilated by electricity and, most thrilling of all, that I am heated in a secret and mysterious manner from the ceiling ... At the same time, if I want to feel particularly snug and Christmassy and Dickens-like, I have got a fireplace and I can sit over a fire. Here, then, I shall live and move, and have my dinner, cooked in my own kitchen, but if I want to enjoy the sensations of dining out I shall not really have to go out at all, for the lift will take me downstairs, and there, in the middle of the

New Devonshire
House, 1926.

Opposite top: The
hall, 38 South Street.

Opposite bottom:
The drawing-room,
38 South Street.

building, is my restaurant waiting for me. There I can dine, either on the floor of the house or in one of the 'terraces', or indoor balconies looking down upon it. I feel that I shall want to do that now and then.[9]

The new Devonshire House was the shape of things to come.

The moment in which the heavy breakers' ball first smashed into the wall of Devonshire House, sending dismal echoes through the streets of Mayfair, marked the beginning of the end for the great London houses. Two years later, and even more ominously, Grosvenor House went the same way, in October 1927: if England's richest Duke thought his house a white elephant, what hope was there for others? On its site there arose yet another block of flats and an American-style hotel, the first in London to have a separate bathroom and a separate entrance lobby to each bedroom, and running iced water in every bathroom. Thus 'the Grosvenor House of the Dukes of Westminster' became 'the Grosvenor House of innumerable misters'.[10]

In the period between the wars only one private house of any significant size was built – 38 South Street, built between 1919–22 for the industrialist Henry MacLaren, the future second Baron Aberconway. Almost entirely designed by the young architect John Murray Easton in classic neo-Georgian style, it was remarkable for the large scale of its rooms. On the ground floor a great hall, strikingly decorated with a black marble floor and black marble pilasters, ran almost its whole length, culminating in a staircase which curved dramatically up to the first floor where a long gallery matched the size of the hall. There were only two other rooms on each of these floors – a dining-room and morning-room on the ground floor, and a music room and drawing-room above – thereby giving the house a feeling of spaciousness and simplicity.

But 38 South Street was an exception, for the age of the high-rise block had undoubtedly arrived. Within ten years of the demolition of Grosvenor House a further six important mansions were to go, namely Dorchester House, Aldford House, Brook House, Lansdowne House, Chesterfield House and Norfolk House; while by the outbreak of war in 1939 only four – Apsley House, Bridgewater House, Londonderry House and Portman House – were still occupied by their original owners. At least, however, those that faded into the sunset did so against a background of routs and revelry such as they might have enjoyed in their heyday.

Daphne Vivyan and her friends cavorted on the stairs of Dorchester House.[11] Loelia Ponsonby attended 'big scale balls in four or five houses', including Brook House, Dudley House, Grosvenor House, Dorchester House and Londonderry House.[12] Derby Week parties were a regular feature each season at Derby House, Stratford Place, which Lord Derby had bought before the war and claimed to keep up only because 'Lady Derby must have somewhere to change when she comes up from Coworth to go to the play'. At Barney Barnato's old house, 25 Park Lane, Sir Philip Sassoon, acknowledged as one of the greatest hosts of his day, gave elegant dinners and small dances, often attended by the Prince of Wales, at which guests wondered at the extraordinary blue and gold mirrored ballroom he had commissioned from Jose-Maria Sert, the Catalan painter who had decorated many of Diaghilev's ballets. Norfolk House was a frequent meeting-place of the so-called 'bright young people'. 'By this time', wrote a *Daily Mail* reporter of a 2 am treasure hunt,

slow cars had given place to high-powered ones, and slow wits to faster wits, so that the field, which had started some 50 cars strong, all closely packed, jostling and manoeuvering for position, was straggled out, though still travelling well ... Lovely coiffures and beautiful dresses deftly arranged were no longer in that form. Shingled heads scored heavily, for long hair was in many cases streaming in the breeze. Dressmakers should rejoice for the birth of the Bright Young People, for few of the frocks which went to Seven Dials yesterday morning will ever see the light of a ballroom again. A crawl on all fours in that none too clean neighbourhood ... in search of an elusive clue chalked on the pavement, had soiled the majority beyond repair. The hunters found their final clue in Norfolk House, St James's, and here a splendid breakfast had been prepared and a string band to cheer them after their strenuous adventures.[13]

The gaiety reached its climax in the season of 1928. Under the headline 'Europe's Baghdad', the *Daily Express*'s columnist, 'the Dragoman', better known as Tom Driberg, wrote that 'London these last few weeks has been a veritable fairyland by day, and by night a Baghdad of the West, crowded with youth and beauty. Pleasures have been pouring from an apparently inexhaustible cornucopia and seem to have been enjoyed almost as much by the old as by the young.'[14] In July, Lady Ellesmere gave a ball at Bridgewater House to which she invited fifteen hundred people. 'It is difficult to describe the scene there last night', wrote Driberg,

so great and so dazzling was the crowd which made its way from the enormous marble hall up the staircase to the ballroom. Lady Ellesmere received her guests half-way up the stairs, dressed in a white gown with a wonderful emerald and diamond tiara, and the guests were swept on upwards by the press of people behind them. Everybody of note in London, covered with scintillating jewels and ablaze with decorations, seemed to be present.[15]

To the annoyance of Lady Ellesmere a number of people who had not received invitations decided that they could slip into such a huge party unnoticed, an idea which would have been unthinkable in earlier days. Among these were Stephen Tennant, and Cecil Beaton's sister, Nancy, who, somewhat unfortunately, arrived just when their hostess 'had already seen 300 people whose faces were unintelligible to her, and her sense of hospitality had reached breaking-point'.[16] She threw them out, and announced in the papers the following day, 'I wish the fullest publicity to be given to the names of my uninvited guests ... The problem will have to be dealt with most severely, and I think that invitation cards to be given up to servants at the door, who will watch each guest as he arrives, are the only way to deal with the difficulty.' For over a week the newspapers were full of the 'Great Mayfair War', carrying interviews with Lady Ellesmere, Lord Ellesmere, Stephen Tennant and Nancy Beaton, other uninvited guests who were either thrown out or not thrown out, their friends and families, and anybody in the social world who had the slightest opinion on the matter. Whatever the rights and wrongs of the situation may have been, Lady Ellesmere, in her indignation, may be forgiven for failing to understand the true significance of the event – namely that the young were, once and for all, expressing their contempt for the whole principle of formal entertaining in the pre-war sense. It was the end of an era.

The following year Dorchester House made way for a new hotel. 'Yesterday the last grisly office was performed,' reported *The Times* of 16 July 1929.

Dorchester House for sale.

Limb by limb, bone by bone, tissue by tissue, the corpse was sold to Jeremiah Cruncher and his kind. Crawling under cranes and creeping round engines of destruction, men and women slunk through the once lordly doors, and in the dust and dirt traipsed and trailed through gaunt and empty rooms ... And upstairs, in a vast and dingy hall, once sumptuous and nobly apolaustic, men were grudgingly bidding in units for splendours designed in pride and bought for lavish hundreds. The bookshelves, where lurked, hidden from the knowledge of all but their owners, incredible treasures of manuscript and book, were knocked down for a few poor guineas; and the Grand Marble Staircase, trodden by feet of princes, lit by and lighting up of old the bright eyes of beauty, fell at £273. It had cost £30,000. Dorchester House is dead; and it is better so. The present age is not attuned to it. There is too much of XANADU and of KUBLA KHAN, too much even, perhaps, of the Palace of Art about it for modern hesitation and modern self-excuse ... It is not only the size and the nature of the Italianate fittings of this magnificence that make them unsuited for modern use; it is a change not only in artistic fashion which leaves nearly all of them disregarded. A deeper change has fallen. 'The Dorchester site is of nearly 80,000 square feet' – that is the important point today. On these square feet how many floors cannot be raised for how many feet to tread in swift and frequent change! The new building will be very luxurious of course; but populous, bustling, a common ground...[17]

The record of demolition which followed that of Dorchester House is a melancholy one. Aldford House and Brook House both went, in 1931 and 1933 respectively, the latter being replaced by a new Brook House, and the very embodiment of the luxurious inter-war Mayfair apartment block. With a single flat on each floor, its crowning glory was a duplex penthouse reached by a high-speed lift, of which its first tenants, Sir Ernest Cassel's grand-daughter, Lady Mountbatten, and her husband were particularly proud. It had altogether thirty rooms, and the five main reception rooms overlooking the park were ingeniously arranged with collapsible walls so that they could be converted into a single 'saloon' for parties, or into a cinema with seating for 150 people. The somewhat lurid decor was by Mrs Joshua Cosden, a famous New York decorator, while on the top floor, reached by a spacious curving staircase, both the walls and ceiling of Lady Mountbatten's boudoir were painted by Rex Whistler. With every modern convenience, it was grand, and yet at the same time cost a great deal less than the £20,000 a year that it had taken to run the mausoleum which it replaced.

The following year, Lansdowne House, which the Marquess had sold seven years previously, became the victim of a decision by Westminster City Council to drive a new street south from Berkeley Square to Curzon Street which necessitated the cutting off of the whole of the façade of the house to a depth of forty feet, and with it all the front rooms. One of these, the 'First Drawing Room', the painted room referred to by Lady Shelburne, was fortunately saved from destruction by the intervention of a rich American benefactor, who bought it and shipped it lock, stock and barrel across the Atlantic for reconstruction in the Pennsylvania Museum of Art. Though the new owners of

Above: The boudoir,
Brook House
penthouse.

Left: The hall, Brook
House penthouse.

A view of Lansdowne House from Berkeley Square.

Lansdowne House managed to retain a few of the original features, notably the sculpture gallery, which was turned into a ballroom, it was so extensively remodelled that it must count as a loss. The ghosts of the great men who had once gathered under Lord Shelburne's roof, of Benjamin Franklin, Garrick, Mirabeau, Dr Johnson and Priestley, now flitted aimlessly through the corridors of a social and athletic club. 'Where a single noble Lord entertained his brilliant circle (or dined in solitary state when there wasn't a party)', wrote an enthusiastic correspondent of *Country Life*, 'scores of country families can lodge in a great deal more comfort, young people can bathe and exercise their limbs, businessmen and their wives keep fit in the squash courts and gymnasium. The gain is enormous...'[18] As the Lansdowne Club, it serves the same purpose today.

Chesterfield House disappeared in 1937, and Norfolk House in 1938. The loss of Norfolk House was all the more tragic because the London County Council had an opportunity to save it under the newly passed Town and Country Planning Act. They rejected the scheme, however, because of the heavy compensation which would have been payable. Instead, in November 1937, it was sold to 'Rudolph Palumbo of Culross Street, Park Lane, engineer, and P. M. Rossdale, of South Audley Street, company director', who formed a private company, 'Norfolk House Limited of Newcastle-upon-Tyne', and pulled it down. 'The passing of Norfolk House', commented *The Times*,

is regretted for its own sake and also as a symptom of the wholesale destruction of these buildings which lend dignity and grace to the capital ... It is not an exaggeration to suggest that since the war the damage done by the housebreaker and flatmonger to the aesthetic value of London is comparable to the results that may be conceived from an air raid of the future.[19]

In Margot Asquith's opinion the decline of the great houses went hand in hand with the decline of great personalities. Writing in 1933, she observed that

London Society was just as frivolous, ignorant, callous, and inaccurate in the eighties as it is now, but where today are the distinguished leaders both in politics and in fashion who foregathered in Devonshire House, Grosvenor House, Dorchester House, Lansdowne House, and Stafford House? People will say: 'Oh! These houses are sold and their owners too poor to entertain.' But it is not the houses, but the *individuals* that you go to see. Where are the fine manners and originality of men like the old Dukes of Westminster, Beaufort, Devonshire and Sutherland, the Lords Granville, Ribblesdale, Spencer, Pembroke and Cowper, to mention only a few of those we met? There are several owners of beautiful houses who entertain us today but – with a few exceptions – they do not take a conspicuous part in public affairs, or exercise a dominating influence over society.[20]

The exceptions to whom she referred were undoubtedly Lord and Lady Wimborne and Lord and Lady Londonderry.

Anyone who came out in the 1920s or 1930s will tell you that by far the grandest and most elegant parties, for which invitations were fought over, were those given at Wimborne House. Here the best bands played, the most delicious suppers were served, and the ballroom was always candlelit. But Wimborne House was more than just a background for sumptuous entertainments. Its owners were a remarkable couple. Lord Wimborne, born the Honourable Ivor Guest, was head of the Guest Steel Works in South Wales, where he was known and respected as a benevolent employer who worked hard to improve the lot of the working man. A dedicated Liberal, he had served as Viceroy of Ireland from 1915 to 1918, and had fought hard to try and achieve a settlement there. 'He enjoyed too,' wrote Osbert Sitwell, 'the planning and creation of beauty, and himself had largely contrived the Capuan vistas of Wimborne House, which he had remodelled ... he contrived always to dominate the splendour in which he lived and to remain a person, a human being of great character.'[21] Naturally he had his eccentricities. Though his house adjoined the Ritz, he would never walk there, but was always driven the fifty or so yards by his chauffeur, who would then wait outside until his master returned from whatever business he was conducting and then, rather than turn the car round in the narrow street, reverse back into the forecourt of Wimborne House. He was also known for his quirky sense of humour. There is a celebrated story of how he was on one occasion asked by the Ritz whether he would be prepared to sell Wimborne House so that they could build an extension to the hotel. He wrote back saying that, as a matter of fact, he was planning to enlarge Wimborne House, and would they be interested in selling him the Ritz?

See colour Plate 19

Alice, Lady
Wimborne, by Cecil
Beaton.

His wife Alice, a great beauty and woman of razor-sharp intelligence, had 'continued the tradition of entertaining all kinds of men and women which she had inaugurated in Ireland', and together she and her husband had made Wimborne House into

a social institution, and in its hospitable rooms could be met many sorts of people, the heads of foreign states, many members of the cosmopolitan world of fashion, and the most prominent men of the three political parties in England, writers, editors, and trades union leaders. In addition, this mansion, in the middle of the old aristocratic quarter of London, possessed its own older political traditions, to help the conducting of negotiations...[22]

There was no better example of this than the rôle played by Wimborne House in the talks that led to the conclusion of the General Strike in 1926. At a time of stalemate between the trade unions and the coal-owners, Lady Wimborne, apparently on the suggestion of Osbert Sitwell, gave a lunch party to which she invited, amongst others, two of the most powerful coal-owners, Lord Londonderry and Lord Gainford – who was also the President of the Coal-Owners' Association – together with the Chairman of the Trade Union Council, J. H. Thomas, and the editor of the *Westminster Gazette*, a well-known Liberal paper, J. A. Spender. 'We went into luncheon to the minute,' recalled Osbert Sitwell,

passing through a vista of fine rooms on our way to the dining-room. Almost directly we had sat down, the conversation took the turn we had so ardently wished it might, and, guided by Lady Wimborne's superb tact – for she never in any way interposed herself between the talkers, or aired her own views, but adroitly, and with the utmost sympathy, drew everyone out – maintained it until the end. So important in its matter, so vehement in its manner, so frank was the talk, that the footmen, I recall, had to be told almost at once to leave the dining-room, and only return when summoned.[23]

This turned out to be the first in a series of meetings at Wimborne House which contributed directly to bringing the strike to an end.

In his novel *Brideshead Revisited*, Evelyn Waugh used Wimborne House as a model for Marchmain House, with its 'forecourt, the railings, the quiet cul-de-sac ... bays of windows opening into Green Park ... the light streaming in from the west in the afternoon', and 'the garden door, into the park' from which Charles and Cordelia 'walked in the twilight to the Ritz Grill'. Unlike Marchmain House, however, it was not pulled down to make way for flats, though that was the subsequent fate of four of its neighbours, Nos. 17 to 20 Arlington Street, on the site of which there now stands a modern block called Arlington House. The family managed to remain in occupation until the outbreak of war, when it became the centre of the 'Invalid Comforts Section of the Prisoners-of-War Department', which sent out Red Cross parcels. Fortunately, unlike Portman House, which was destroyed, and Dudley House, which suffered severe damage, Wimborne House also managed to escape bombing, though the Wimbornes never reoccupied it after the war. In 1946 it was sold

to the Eagle Star Insurance Company; they have since remodelled it as their headquarters, while keeping some of its best features, such as the famous 'great room'.

The great political hostess of the 1920s and 1930s was Edith, Lady Londonderry, who carried on the traditions of her predecessors with resounding success. During the First World War, when Londonderry House was taken over as a hospital, she and her friends established a kind of club there. The house was known as the Ark, and an order was created called the Order of the Rainbow, all of whose members 'had to bear the name of either bird, insect, beast, or reptile, or else a mythological creature. The name had to begin with the first letter of the Christian or Surname, or else it had to rhyme or be funny'.[24] Lady Londonderry herself, who had a snake tattooed on one of her legs, winding up from the ankle, was named Circe the Sorceress, who had the power to turn men into beasts. Lord Londonderry was Charley the Cheetah, Churchill was Winston the Warlock, Sir William Orpen was Orpen the Ortolan, Lord Balfour was Arthur the Albatross, and so on. Each animal received

The ballroom of Wimborne House in use as an office in the 1950s

The gallery of Londonderry House in use as a hospital during World War I. Painting by Sir John Lavery.

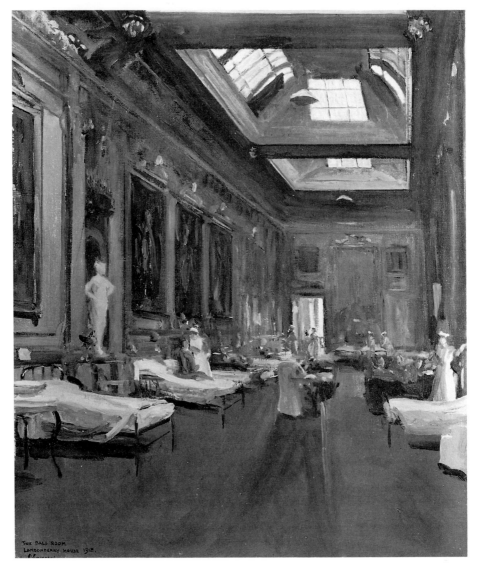

a separate invitation to Ark parties, and each was invited to bring its mate to Circe's den. It was not long before an invitation to join the Order became one of the most sought after in London.

Much worse than the Park
In the dark is the Ark
With its tandems of beauty and breeding
That swarm to Park Lane,
In sunshine or rain,
For Antediluvian feeding.

To that classical spot
(Whether married or not)
Flock couples of fashion and passion:
Each animal toys,
By gesture or noise,
With its chosen peculiar ration.[25]

Some idea of Lady Londonderry's forceful character can be gleaned from her conquest of the Labour Prime Minister, Ramsay MacDonald, who, in spite of the fact that the Londonderrys stood for everything against which he had fought all his life, became one of her most devoted admirers, and a frequent visitor at Londonderry House. It was not long before he too was invited to join her Ark Society. 'The invitation to enter your Ark delights me', he wrote to her from 10 Downing Street on 8 July 1929.

What ponderings it awakens! Am I to escape the flood which is sure to come upon this ungodly nation? What am I to be? – a bear? a serpent? a wolf (in sheep's clothing or not)? a lamb? What? I am sure that the doves are already chosen ... I am in the midst of a despatch to a friendly Power so I cannot pursue this speculation ... Life is really hard and I am trying to stave off the day when you and yours will enter the prison house where I am, and you will put your thumbs down and your stiletto in, and Chequers and Downing Street will see me no more.[26]

He became Hamish the Hart.

Edith Chaplin, Marchioness of Londonderry, by Philip de Laszlo.

Not surprisingly, their friendship was regarded with suspicion in all quarters. 'Lady Londonderry told me of a strange anonymous letter she had recently received', wrote Henry 'Chips' Channon in his diary of 17 March 1935:

It was dated AD 2035 and described the visit of a mother and daughter to Ulster House (Londonderry House) by that time, apparently, a museum. The child, pointing to a portrait of 'The Duchess of Ulster' (*ie* Circe Londonderry) asks, 'who is that pretty lady?' 'Don't look at it – she was an evil woman who tempted the Labour Prime Minister, Ramsay MacDonald, and turned him into a Tory. She ruined England and was very wicked.'

'Circe L. is enchanted with the ingenuity of the malice and is preserving the letter', Chips added – which shows just how little she cared what people thought.[27] She remained the leading Tory hostess of the day, and her annual receptions for the Conservative Party on the eve of each parliamentary session continued to be among the most glittering occasions of the year right up to and after the Second World War.

Given the role it played in social and political life, one last house is worth mentioning, even though its position puts it just outside the scope of this book. It has been included, however, because the life that was lived there, indeed its very concept, was becoming rarer and rarer by the end of the 1930s. Henry Channon III, known to one and all as 'Chips', was the son of a rich Chicago businessman; he had taken up residence in England soon after the First World War, and soon became a leading figure in society and a close friend of the Prince of Wales. In 1933 he married Lady Honor Guinness, the eldest daughter of the second Earl of Iveagh, and in 1935 took over her mother's seat in the House of Commons, as MP for Southend-on-Sea. The Channons' way of life soon became celebrated for its lavishness. Their first home was at Moir House, 21 St James's Place. 'This evening we had the second of our London festivals', he wrote in his diary of 25 February 1935,

Sir Henry 'Chips'
Channon, by Howard
Coster.

Opposite: The
Amalienberg dining-
room, 5 Belgrave
Square.

A riotous, outrageous success. Most of the afternoon, a grey London Sunday, I spent in fussing and telephoning. Eric Duncannon and Seymour Berry chucked at seven o'clock and so I rang up Douglas Fairbanks Jr who immediately accepted. Dinner was staggering, champagne flowed and the food was excellent. We began with blinis served with Swedish schnapps, to wash down the caviare. Then soup, followed by salmon, then an elaborate chicken. Then a sweet and savoury. The candlelight was reflected in my gold plate and the conversation was incessant ... Eventually Cole Porter was sufficiently intoxicated to play the piano. He played for hours, all the latest American airs. I got to bed at 4.30 absolutely exhausted ... but I suppose what we take from our nights we add to our days.[28]

A month later the Channons bought 5 Belgrave Square. 'It has a distinguished air', wrote Chips, 'and we will make it gay and comfortable.'[29] Its transformation was carried out with the help of the famous Paris decorator, Boudin, and included the creation of what was undoubtedly one of the most extraordinary rooms of the day, the Amalienberg dining-room, which was inspired by the Mirror Room in the Amalienberg, built for the Elector Karl Albert at Nymphenberg by François Cuvilliès in 1734-9. 'Monsieur Boudin of Jansen came to us this morning with his final drawings and estimates for our dining-room which is to imitate and, I hope, rival the Amalienberg. It will shimmer in blue and silver, and have an ochre and silver gallery leading to it. It will shock, and perhaps stagger London. And will cost us over £6,000...'[30] It was a masterpiece of theatricality. The entrance to the corridor leading to the dining-room was reached by way of a dark ante-room, and was guarded by a pair of torch bearers, one Chinese, the other Nubian, wearing splendid gold and coloured liveries. The corridor itself was based on the bedroom of the Amalienberg, with silver rococo scrollwork on a rich apricot ground, and was lit by candles set in brackets and in a porcelain and ormolu chandelier.

'The transition from the dark ante-room, through the golden glow of the passage, to the flickering silver radiance of the big dining-room is a remarkable experience', wrote Christopher Hussey.

On a ground of soft greyish blue like the sea, many mirrors reflect the brilliantly burnished silver decoration, as exquisitely modelled as in the Cuvilliès originals ... But it is true to say that every motif is to be found in Cuvilliès' executed or published work. The silvered sidetable in the middle of the west wall is an authentic Cuvilliès piece from the Palais Parr in Vienna, whence came also the parquet floor ... From the same source came the stone stove in the opposite recess. Above the mirrored doors, which have beautifully chased silver locks, are paintings in the manner of Oudry, and above the cornice, extending over the coved ceiling, the finest rococo decoration is seen. In the centre of each side a nymph, almost in the round, sits beneath a tree, accompanied by pairs of spouting dolphins, scallop shells, and exotic fowl. Here and there, on brackets, perch porcelain birds. The chairs ... are silvered, with the same sea-green silk upholstery as the curtains. All this eighteenth-century elegance is reflected, and concentrated, in the table-top made of squares of mirror, and garnished with delightful

pieces of Meissen porcelain ... The soft glow of the candles in the crystal chandelier and wall brackets gleams on mirrors and silvery forms and mingles on the table with gold glints from the corridor and the reflections of the porcelain figures ... It can be imagined how fine a sight must be a dinner-party here before a Court ball.[31]

Opposite: A corner of the Amalienberg dining-room, 5 Belgrave Square.

Considering his close friendship with them, it is hard to believe that Chips did not have entertaining the Royal family in mind when this room was planned. The first of many such occasions took place on 11 June 1936, when the new king, Edward VIII, came to dine.

We arranged the house until it was a bower of flowers: then there was a long pause, as we were both dressed at 8.30, Honor looking lovely and a little nervous, I quite calm. We both drank a brandy and soda and waited for the guests to arrive. The king had rung up and said it was to be white ties. The first to arrive were Leslie Hore-Belisha and Barbie Wallace, and then quickly the others followed, the men still in white ties and black waistcoats, the women in black dresses. The Kents were punctual at 9.05 and as we were introducing people to them ... the King drove up. I went to meet him and he did the circle charmingly ... He kissed Princess Marina who curtsied. Dinner was announced. Doors were flung open, and we suddenly realised Lady Cunard had not appeared, but we processed into dinner and there was a pause as everyone's breath was quite taken away by the beauty of the dining room ... Dinner was perfect, we began with Blinis and Caviar, then Sole Muscat followed by Boeuf Provençal. It was served so speedily that we had finished before eleven, and then the ladies left, curtseying as they got up. I then moved over to the King and we talked *à trois*, he, Duff and I about the Amalienberg dining room which he was in ecstasies over ... The room was full of glamour and candlelight, everybody was gay and a little elated ... After dinner we went up to the drawing room and library, and scattered ... At last the two musicians from the Ritz appeared and they began to play Austrian music and eventually jazz. The King asked Mrs Simpson to dance ... I was sad when it was over, it was the very peak, the summit, I suppose. The King of England dining with me.[32]

Seven years later, on 1 February 1943, Chips wrote,

On this date I spent my first night in this house, and remember it well: only my room was ready: the servants were still unpacking: there were crates and un-hung curtains and general confusion. What a seven years! 5 Belgrave Square has played a considerable role in politics and society, and since the war has been, if it was not already so before, the centre of London ... no true chronicler of the time could fail to record its glories and its influence. Today begins my eighth year in Schloss Chips.[33]

'The Lord of Hosts', as he described himself,[34] carried on until his death in 1958 – the same year in which the Queen of Hostesses, Lady Londonderry, gave her last reception, with Harold Macmillan as her guest of honour. She died the following April. In July 1962, Londonderry House, the only great private house still fully occupied by the family, but by then overshadowed by the Hilton Hotel to the north, and another lower tower to the south, was sold for redevelopment. The young ninth Marquess decided that the house should go out in style, and on 19 July he gave a final party there. The three hundred guests danced to the music of Benny Goodman, and in the latter half of the evening the stage was taken by an unknown young singer called Mick Jagger. 'We wanted to give the old house a wake,' said Lady Londonderry the following day. 'It was a wonderful, gay night, but for us sad too. I am sure that once the house is auctioned it will be pulled down.' Her premonition turned out to be only too accurate, for shortly afterwards the house was indeed demolished. If it was a sad day for the Londonderrys, it was a sad day for London too.

Postscript

Today a foreigner, or indeed an Englishman, could walk through Mayfair or St James's and be quite unaware that these districts provided the setting for a way of life which complemented that of the great country houses. That endless process of change, development and redevelopment, which has always been such an integral part of London's history, has left behind few of the private palaces whose history we have looked at. Of these, only Apsley House still has the family living in it, albeit in just a wing. The rest have been turned over to public or institutional use. Burlington House is the home of the Royal Academy; Bridgewater House now belongs to a Greek shipping company; the future of Spencer House, which until recently housed the Economist Intelligence Unit, is, at the time of going to press, uncertain; Marlborough House belongs to the Crown; Stafford House, better known today as Lancaster House, is used by the government to entertain foreign dignitaries; Lichfield House is the headquarters of the Clerical, Medical and General Life Assurance Society and Wynn House belongs to the Distillers' Company; Home House is the home of the Courtauld Institute, while 44 Berkeley Square is a smart gambling club and is still witness to nightly assemblies of the rich and powerful, though they are more likely to be made up of Arab and Japanese businessmen than the dukes and duchesses of former days.

The often senseless demolition or spoliation of so many beautiful and important houses, depriving London of such a valuable part of its heritage, inspired Herbert Farjeon, in 1938, to write a song, the lyrics of which serve as a suitable epitaph:

PULLING DOWN LONDON
A Tract for the Times

Oh, a fisherman's life is a life that's gay
As he sails on the open sea,
And a vagabond's life on the great highway
Is a life that is fine and free,
The steeplejack and the blacksmith black
Rejoice in their employment,
But a job I've got that tops the lot
For open-air enjoyment,
As here I stand, my pick-axe in my hand,
'Neath God's blue sky I make the plaster fly –

Pulling down London, smashing up the town,
That is the life for me,
A-breaking up of beauty and a-knocking of it down,
Under the sky so free,
So whack that roof and bang those walls,
And scatter the old brickbats,
And down with the Adelphi, and the Temple and St Paul's,
And up with the service flats, by gee,
Yes, up with the service flats.

Sir Christopher Wren was all right then,
But he ain't no great shakes now,
So drill that drill, my lads, until
You can't see the dust for row.
Oh, the face of the world is changing fast,
But only fossils want things to last,
So shiver the foundations and blast the past,
Pulling down London Town.

If aeroplanes with bombs on high
Destroyed what I destroy,
Oh, wouldn't there be a great outcry,
You bet there would, my boy.
If what them Adam brothers built
Was bashed by the foe's barrage,
Oh, wouldn't we shout about the guilt
Of doing it free of charge, by gee,
Foreign labour free of charge!

But who will grouse if Pembroke House
Is bust by an Englishman,
Or shake his fist if I assist,
At the death of the best Queen Anne.
There's not much money in the past that's gone,
But there's oodles in a brand new Odeon,
So civilisation marches on,
Pulling down London town![35]

Notes

16 Stone, *op. cit.* p. 361.
17 *A Treatise Concerning the Causes of the Magnificence and Greatness of Cities*, Giovanni Botero (London, 1606) p. 65.
18 *English Country Houses*, Christopher Hussey (London, 1955, 3 vols) vol. 1 *Early Georgian 1715–1760*, p. 197 (Rev. ed. 1965).
19 *The History of St James's Square*, A. Dasent (London and New York, 1895) pp. 5, 6.
20 A *Regency Visitor: The English Tour of Prince Pückler-Muskau* (London, 1957) p. 87.
21 *A Critical Review of the Public Buildings, Statues and Ornaments in and about London and Westminster*, James Ralph (London, 1734. New ed. 1971)

Prologue: **The Magnetism of London**

1 *Life in a Noble Household, 1641–1700*, Gladys Scott Thomson (London and New York, 1937) pp. 213, 214.
2 'In London many stately Palaces, built by Noblemen upon the river Thames, do make a very great show to them that pass by water.' See *Moryson's Itinerary*, 1617. Quoted in W. Harrison's *A Description of England . . .* (see note 4) (London, the New Shakespeare Society, 1908) vol. 4.
3 *The Travels of Cosmo III through England, 1669*, ed. L. Magalotti (London, 1821).
4 *A Description of England in Shakespeare's Youth*, William Harrison (London, 1877–1908, 4 vols, ed. by F. J. F. Furnivall from *Holinshed's Chronicle*) vol. 1, p. 35.
5 *Travels of Cosmo III, op. cit.*
6 *London Past and Present*, H. B. Wheatley (based on *The Handbook of London* by Peter Cunningham) (London and New York, 1891, 3 vols) vol. 3, p. 295.
7 *Life in the English Country House*, Mark Girouard (New Haven and London, 1978) p. 6.
8 *The Crisis of the Aristocracy, 1558–1641*, Lawrence Stone (Oxford and New York, 1965) pp. 391-2.
9 *Ibid.* p. 388.
10 *The Days of Duchess Anne: Life in the household of the Duchess of Hamilton*, Rosalind Marshall (London, 1973; New York, 1974) p. 156.
11 *Ibid.* p. 155.
12 *Ibid.* p. 162.
13 Stone, *op. cit.* pp. 386, 387.
14 *Hanoverian London, 1714–1808*, George Rude (London and San Francisco, 1971) pp. 39, 40.
15 *Sir Robert Walpole: the King's Minister*, J. H. Plumb (London, 1960 and Boston, Mass., 1961, 2 vols) vol. 1, p. 7.

1. The Rise of the Great Houses

1 Evelyn to Lord Cornbury, 20 June 1666.
2 *Architecture in Britain; 1530–1830*, Sir John Summerson (London and New York, 1977, 6th rev. ed.) Penguin ed. p. 57.
3 Evelyn's *Diary* (London and New York, 1818) 21 September 1674.
4 *The Architecture of Sir Roger Pratt*, ed. R. T. Gunther (Oxford, 1928) p. 140.
5 *Ibid.* p. 148.
6 Evelyn to Lord Cornbury, 20 June 1666.
7 'Clarendon's House Warming', quoted in *The Growth of Stuart London*, N. G. Brett-James (London, 1935) p. 382.
8 Pepys, 14 June 1667.
9 Evelyn, 9 December 1667.
10 *A History of His Own Time*, Bishop Gilbert Burnet (Oxford, 1833, 6 vols) 2nd ed., vol. 1, p. 431.
11 Evelyn, 20 December 1667.
12 *Travels of Cosmo III, op. cit.* pp. 293-4.
13 *Ellis Correspondence*, vol. 1, p. 64.
14 Evelyn, 19 June 1683.
15 *Ibid.* 18 September 1683.
16 *Ibid.* 25 September 1672.
17 *Ibid.* 12 June 1684.
18 *Calendar of State Papers* (Domestic, 1660-61) p. 76.
19 Evelyn, 18 October 1661.
20 *Survey of London*, vol. 32 (1963), p. 392.
21 *Ibid.* p. 393.
22 *Ibid.* p. 393.
23 *A Tour Through the Whole Island of Great Britain*, Daniel Defoe, with an introduction by G. D. H. Cole (London, 1927, 2 vols) vol. 1, p. 328. (Originally published in 1724-27 in 3 vols)
24 Dasent, *op. cit.* p. 4.
25 Brett-James, *op. cit.* p. 370.

26 *A Social and Economic History of England*, Asa Briggs (London, 1962) p. 152.
27 *Ibid.*
28 *Cosmo III, op. cit.* pp. 293-4.
29 Dasent, *op. cit.* p. 15.
30 *Ibid.* p. 71.
31 *Survey of London*, vol. 29 (1960), p. 119.
32 BM Add. MSS 22267, ff. 68-71.
33 HMC Ormonde MSS, New Series, vol. 6, p. 502.

2. Rival Dukes

1 *The Russells in Bloomsbury 1669-1771*, Gladys Scott Thomson (London, 1940) p. 34.
2 *Memoirs, Anecdotes . . .* Laetitia Hawkins (London, 1824, 2 vols) vol. 1, p. 52.
3 *Stow's Survey of London*, ed. J. Strype (1720) vol. 4, p. 84.
4 *Wynn Papers, 357.* Quoted *Restoration England*, Arthur Bryant (London, rev. ed. 1960) p. 17.
5 *The Great Fire of London in 1660*, W. G. Bell (London and New York, 1920) p. 8.
6 *Fumifugium: or The Smoake of London Dissipated*, John Evelyn (London, 1661) p. 22.
7 Strype, *op. cit.* p. 84.
8 *The Complete Peerage.*
9 *Country Life*, 14 September 1951.
10 *The Letters of Lady Rachel Russell* (London, 1773) vol. 1 of 1853 ed., pp. 179-80.
11 Evelyn, 19 January 1686.
12 *Country Life*, 14 September 1951, p. 813.
13 *A Microcosm of London*, Rudolph Ackermann (London, 1732) vol. 1, pp. 210, 211.
14 *Anecdotes of Painting*, Horace Walpole (Strawberry Hill, London, 1762-71, 4 vols).
15 *The Journeys of Celia Fiennes*, ed. Christopher Morris with a foreword by G. M. Trevelyan (London, 1947) pp. 235, 291.
16 *The Letters of Saint-Evremond*, ed. John Hayward (London, 1930) p. 357.
17 *The Dictionary of National Biography.*
18 *The Lyme Letters 1660-1760*, ed. Lady Newton (London, 1925) p. 281.
19 *The Private Palaces of London Past and Present*, E. Beresford Chancellor (London, 1908; Philadelphia, 1909) pp. 132-3.
20 *Ibid.*
21 *Country Life*, vol. 112, pp. 1651, 1652.
22 Chancellor, *op. cit.* p. 77.
23 *Works*, Duke of Buckingham, 1729.
24 Information from John Cornforth.
25 Walpole to Mann, 24 December 1741.
26 *Ibid.* 14 March 1743.
27 *London Past and Present*, H. B. Wheatley, vol. 1, p. 293.

28 *Ibid*. See Powis House.

29 *Sarah, Duchess of Marlborough*, David B. Green (London and New York, 1967) p. 104.

30 *Marlborough House*, John Charlton (Her Majesty's Stationery Office Pamphlet, 1962) p. 9.

31 *Blenheim Palace*, David B. Green (London, 1951) p. 106.

32 *The Private Correspondence of Sarah, Duchess of Marlborough* (London, 1838) p. 189.

33 Wheatley, *op. cit.* vol. 2, p. 473.

34 Charlton, *op. cit.* p. 10.

35 *Ibid*. p. 13.

3. The Palladian Influence

1 *Works*, Shaftesbury (London, 1732, 5th ed., 3 vols), vol. 3, p. 398.

2 *Ibid*. pp. 404.

3 *Survey of London*, vol. 13 (1930), p. 167.

4 *The Letters of Horace Walpole*, ed. Mrs Paget Toynbee (Oxford, 1903–25, 19 vols) vol. 2, p. 445.

5 *Anecdotes of Painting*, Walpole, *op. cit.* vol. 4, p. 109.

6 Chancellor, *op. cit.* p. 63.

7 *Ibid*. pp. 64, 65.

8 *Ibid*. p. 60.

9 *A Journey through England*, John Macky (London, 1714, 2 vols) vol. 1, p. 191.

10 *Survey of London*, vol. 32, p. 458.

11 *Country Life*, 20 February 1958, p. 352.

12 Walpole to Mason, 7 May 1775.

13 Defoe, *op. cit.* vol. 2, p. 195.

14 *Complete Peerage*, vol. 3, p. 130.

15 *Georgian London*, Sir John, Summerson (London and New York, 1978) Penguin rev. ed., p. 110.

16 *A Tour thro' London about the year 1725*, Daniel Defoe, ed. Sir Mayson M. Beeton and E. Beresford Chancellor (London, 1929) p. 21.

17 *Ibid*. pp. 97–8.

18 *Ibid*. p. 98.

19 'The Mistresses of George I' from *The Letters of Philip Stanhope, Earl of Chesterfield*, ed. Lord Mahon (London, 1845–53, 5 vols) vol. 2, p. 458.

20 Macky, *op. cit.* vol. 1, p. 190.

21 Nottingham University, Portland MS PWB/79.

22 *Ibid*. 'The Duke of Argyll's Levee'. Portland MS. PWV/718.

23 Chancellor, *op. cit.* p. 134.

24 *The Letters and Works of Lady Mary Wortley-Montagu*, ed. Lord Wharncliffe (London and Philadelphia, 1837, 3 vols) vol. 2, p. 196.

25 *Ibid*. p. 198.

26 *Ibid*. p. 198.

27 *Ibid*. p. 199.

28 *Ibid*. p. 201.

29 *Ibid*. p. 183.

30 BM Add. MS 22227, f. 209.

31 Wentworth Papers, p. 479.

32 *The House*, Duchess of Devonshire (London, 1982) p. 24.

33 Ralph, *op. cit.* p. 184.

34 *Ibid*. p. 184.

35 *Ibid*. p. 184.

36 *Every One a Witness: The Georgian Age, An anthology*, ed. Arthur F. Scott (London, 1970) pp. 21, 22.

37 *The Devonshire House Circle*, Hugh Stokes (New York, 1916; London, 1917) p. 26.

38 *Country Life*, 13 November 1980, p. 1751.

39 *The English Connoisseur*, Thomas Martyn (1766, 2 vols) vol. 1, p. 28.

40 *Ibid*.

41 *London and its Environs Described* ... Anon. Publisher: Robert Dodsley (London, 1761, 6 vols) vol. 2, pp. 225–32.

42 *Some Account of London*, Thomas Pennant (London, 5th ed. 1813) p. 175.

43 *Country Life*, 13 November 1980, p. 1751.

44 Devonshire, *op. cit.* p. 24.

45 Walpole to Lady Ailesbury, 31 July 1762.

46 Walpole to Mann, 10 April 1747.

47 *Anecdotes of Painting*, *op. cit.* vol. 4, p. 228.

48 Walpole to Conway, 5 June 1764.

49 *Country Life*, 13 January 1966.

50 *Chronicles of Fashion*, Mrs Elizabeth Stone (London, 1845, 2 vols) vol. 2, p. 211.

51 Walpole to Montagu, 23 June 1750.

4. The Age of Parade

1 Quoted in 'Chesterfield House, Mayfair', H. Avray Tipping, *Country Life*, 25 February 1922.

2 *Ibid*.

3 Mahon, *op. cit.* to Madame de Monconseil, 31 July 1747.

4 *Ibid*. to Dayrolles, June 1748.

5 Strype, *op. cit.* vol. 2, bk. 6, p. 4.

6 John Cornforth MSS: 'Chesterfield House', pp. 3, 4.

7 *Country Life*, vol. 39, pp. 58, 188, 284.

8 *Ibid*. vol. 129, p. 1327, fig 4.

9 Cornforth, *op. cit.* p. 3.

10 *A Complete Body of Architecture*, Isaac Ware (London, 1756) chap. 38.

11 Chancellor, *op. cit.* p. 214.

12 Isaac Ware, *op. cit.* pp. 429–36.

13 Mahon, *op. cit.* to Bristowe, 12 December 1747.

14 Chancellor, *op. cit.* p. 211.

15 Mahon. *op. cit.* to Dayrolles, 4 November 1748.

16 *Ibid*. 24 February 1749.

17 *Ibid*. 27 April 1750.

18 *Ibid*. 19 June 1750.

19 *Ibid*. 26 December 1748.

20 *Ibid*. to Madame de Monconseil, 13 June 1749.

21 *Ibid*. to Dayrolles, 31 March 1749.

22 *Ibid*. to Madame de Monconseil, 5 September 1748.

23 *Ibid*. to Bristowe, 17 September 1747.

24 *Quarterly Review*, vol. 76, 1845, p. 484.

25 Mahon, *op. cit.* to Bristowe, 17 September 1747.

26 *Quarterly Review*, vol. 76, 1845, p. 484.

27 Chancellor, *op. cit.* p. 211. A translation is as follows: 'Now with old books and sleep and languid hours,/To taste the longed-for bliss of private life.'

28 Mahon, *op. cit.* to his son, 18 November 1748.

29 Isaac Ware, *op. cit.* p. 433.

30 Walpole to Mann, 27 February 1752.

31 *Ibid*. 23 March 1752.

32 *The Autobiography and Correspondence of Mary Granville, Mrs Delany*, ed. Lady Llanover. Series 1 (London, 1861) vol. 3, p. 409.

33 Walpole to Conway, 12 February 1756.

34 *The Norfolk House Music Room*, Desmond Fitzgerald (London, 1973) p. 49.

35 Walpole to Conway, 12 February 1756.

36 *Letters by Madame du Bocage* (1770) vol. 1, p. 7.

37 Walpole to Mann, 22 March 1762.

38 Walpole to Berry, 26 May 1791.

39 Fitzgerald, *op. cit.* p. 5.

40 *Norfolk Assembly*, R. W. Ketton-Cremer (London, 1957) p. 179.

41 Fitzgerald, *op. cit.* p. 48.

42 *Ibid*.

43 *The Dukes of Norfolk: a quincentennial history*, John Martin Robinson (Oxford, 1983) p. 155.

44 Lady Llanover, *op. cit.* p. 157.

45 Robinson, *op. cit.* p. 157.

46 *Complete Peerage*, vol. 11, p. 269.

47 *The Harcourt Papers*, ed. E. W. Harcourt (Oxford, 1880–1905, 14 vols) vol. 3, p. 67.

48 Probably Mary Wynyard, later second Countess de La Warr. She is described in *The Complete Peerage* as having been 'a remarkable beauty': vol. 2, p. 163.

49 *Letters by Madame du Bocage*, *op. cit.* vol. 1, p. 7.

50 *Elizabeth Montagu, the Queen of the Blue-Stockings: her correspondence from 1720 to 1761*, ed. Emily J. Climenson (London and New York, 1906, 2 vols) vol. 1, p. 271.

51 *Ibid*. vol. 3, p. 203.

52 *Ibid*. vol. 2, p. 30.

53 Lady Llanover, *op. cit.* Series II, vol. 4, p. 508.

54 Chancellor, *op. cit.* p. 156.

5. An Eighteenth-Century Household

1 Alnwick, *Percy Letters*, vol. 30, p. 51.
2 *Anecdotes of Painting*, Horace Walpole (London, rev. ed. 1888, 3 vols) vol. 1, p. 250, n. 1.
3 *Calendar of State Papers* (Domestic 1611–18) p. 145.
4 Information from John Cornforth.
5 *London and its Environs Described, Op. cit.* 5, p. 51.
6 Alnwick, Percy Archives, vol. 3, 3.
7 *Diary of John Evelyn*, 9 June 1658.
8 *Country Life*, vol. 52, 12 December 1931, p. 648.
9 Walpole to Lady Ossory, 27 October 1774.
10 *Country Life*, vol. 114, p. 347.
11 Walpole to Mann, 20 October 1752.
12 *The Complete Peerage*, vol. 9, p. 751.
13 *Country Life*, vol. 114, p. 348.
14 Walpole to Mann, 5 May 1757.
15 *Diary of a Journey to England, 1761–62*, Count Friedrich von Kielmansegge (London and New York, 1902) pp. 145, 146.
16 Walpole to Montagu, 8 June 1762.
17 Walpole to Duchess of Grafton, 31 January 1766.
18 Count Kielmansegge, *op. cit.* p. 147.
19 Alnwick, Duke of Northumberland's Additional MSS (1973) C.21/a.
20 Walpole to Lady Ossory, 1 June 1776.
21 *The Russells in Bloomsbury, 1669–1771*, Gladys Scott Thomson (London, 1940) pp. 197–9.
22 *Shelburne Papers*, Box S. 119/1/3.
23 *Shelburne Papers*, London Housekeeping Bills, 1781.
24 *Shelburne Papers*. Remarks on Housekeeping etc: Lansdowne House. H 137. No 20. 'Duties of a Clerk of the Kitchen.'
25 Walpole to Hertford, 7 April 1765.
26 Walpole to Montagu, 26 April 1759.
27 Walpole to Mann, 25 February 1750.
28 Fitzgerald, *op. cit.* p. 49.
29 Walpole to Montagu, 28 April 1761.
30 Walpole to Montagu, 23 December 1759.
31 Walpole to Ossory, 11 October 1788.
32 *Notes by Lady Louisa Stuart on 'George Selwyn and his Contemporaries' by John H. Jesse*, ed. W. S. Lewis (Oxford University Press, New York 1908) p. 21n.
33 *The Letters and Journals of Lady Mary Coke*, ed. Hon. J. A. Home (Edinburgh, 1889–96, 4 vols) vol. 1, p. 249.
34 Walpole 38, p. 210.
35 *Leaves from the Note-Books of Lady Dorothy Nevill*, ed. Ralph Nevill (London, 1907) p. 147.
36 Walpole to Bentley, 6 May 1755.
37 Scott Thomson, *op. cit.* p. 234.
38 Syon MSS U.1.25.
39 Scott Thomson, *op. cit.* p. 236.
40 Alnwick, Duke of Northumberland's Miscellaneous MSS (1978) H/1/11.
41 Scott Thomson, *op. cit.* p. 282.
42 *Bedford Papers*.
43 Scott Thomson, *op. cit.* p. 236.
44 *Alnwick Papers*.
45 British Museum. Add. MSS 10116, p. 210.
46 *Survey of London*, vol. 30 (1960), p. 533.
47 *Bedford Papers*.

6. The Neo-Classical Triumph

1 *Country Life*, vol. 60, p. 663.
2 *Ibid*.
3 *The Letters of Mary Lepel, Lady Hervey*, John W. Croker (London, 1821) pp. 214–15.
4 *Ibid*.
5 Lady Llanover, *op. cit.* Series I, vol. 3, p. 402.
6 *Ibid*. p. 408.
7 *The Letters and Journals of Lady Mary Coke, op. cit.* vol. 4, p. 100.
8 Walpole to Bentley, 5 January 1755: 'Lord Montfort ... consulted indirectly, and at last pretty directly, several people on the easiest method of finishing his life ... he invited company to dinner for the day after his death, and ordered a supper at Whites; where he supped the night before. He played at Whist till one in the morning; it was New Years morning: Lord Robert Bertie drank to him a happy New Year; he clapped his hand strangely to his eyes. In the morning he had a lawyer and three witnesses, and executed his will which he made them read twice over paragraph by paragraph: and then asking the lawyer if that will would stand good though a man were to shoot himself? and being assured it would; he said, "Pray stay while I step into the next room"; went into the next room, and shot himself.'
9 Lady Llanover, *op. cit.* Series I, vol. 3, p. 445.
10 *Country Life*, vol. 40, p. 703.
11 *Ibid*.
12 *Ibid*.
13 *A Six Weeks Tour through the Southern Counties of England and Wales*, Arthur Young (London, 1768) p. 110.
14 *Ibid*. pp. 110, 111, 112.
15 *Ibid*. p. 112.
16 *Ibid*. p. 113.
17 *Ibid*.
18 Arthur Young, *op. cit.* 2nd ed. (1769) pp. 359–60.
19 Chancellor, *op. cit.* p. 342.
20 *Londonderry House*, John Cornforth, p. 1.
21 *The Letters and Journals of Lady Mary Coke, op. cit.* vol. 2, p. 15.
22 *Country Life*, vol. 115, pp. 510, 590, 676, 1126, 1220.
23 *Survey of London*, vol. 29, p. 143.
24 *Ibid*.
25 *Critical Observations on the Buildings and Improvements of London*, James Stuart (London, 1771) p. 32.
26 *Survey of London*, vol. 29, p. 143.
27 *Works in Architecture of Robert and James Adam* (London, 1773, 3 vols) vol. 1, no. 1, p. 5.
28 Drawing by G. Basevi in the Soane Museum.
29 Chancellor, *op. cit.* p. 126.
30 *Survey of London*, vol. 32, p. 369.
31 *Ibid*.
32 *Ibid*. p. 371.
33 *Memoirs of Mrs Sophia Baddeley*, Elizabeth Steele (London, 1787, 6 vols) vol. 1, p. 136.
34 *Survey of London*, vol. 32, p. 371.
35 *Peace in Piccadilly: the Story of Albany*, Sheila Birkenhead (London and New York, 1958) p. 21.
36 *Georgiana: Duchess of Devonshire*, Brian Masters (London, 1981) p. 46.
37 *The Life and Letters of Lady Sarah Lennox, 1745–1826*, ed. the Countess of Ilchester and Lord Stavordale (London and New York, 1901, 2 vols) vol. 1, p. 261.
38 Birkenhead, *op. cit.* p. 23.
39 Lennox, *op. cit.* p. 36.
40 Birkenhead, *op. cit.* pp. 28, 29.
41 *Ibid*. p. 30.
42 *Georgian London*, Sir John Summerson, p. 114

7. The Clients of Robert Adam

1 *Robert Adam and his Circle in Edinburgh and Rome*, John Fleming (London and Cambridge, Mass., 1962) pp. 245–7.
2 *The Architecture of Robert and James Adam*, Arthur T. Bolton (London and New York, 1922, 2 vols) vol. 1, p. 22.
3 Fleming, *op. cit.* pp. 254–5.
4 *Ibid*. p. 253.
5 *The Letters and Journals of Lady Mary Coke, op. cit.* (1892) vol. 3, pp. 59, 60.
6 *Lady Shelburne's Journal*, Bowood, 16 September 1765.
7 Bolton, *op. cit.* p. 8.
8 *Ibid*.
9 *Ibid*.
10 *Ibid*.
11 *Ibid*. p. 11.
12 *Shelburne Papers*, Bowood.
13 *Ibid*.
14 *The historical and the posthumous memoirs of Sir Nathaniel William Wraxall, 1772–1784*, ed. H. B. Wheatley (London, 1884, 5 vols) vol. 2, pp. 62, 63.
15 *Ibid*. p. 61.
16 Sir John Summerson, *op. cit.* p. 143.
17 Robert & James Adam, *Works, op. cit.* vol. 1, Part V, Preface.
18 *Ibid*. vol. 2.
19 Duke of Northumberland, Additional MSS (1973) F/10/3.

20 *Ibid.*
21 Walpole to Ossory, 3 April 1773.
22 Walpole to Mann, 8 June 1774.
23 Lady Llanover, *op. cit.* vol. 5, pp. 1–3.
24 Coke, *op. cit.* vol. 4, p. 439.
25 Walpole, vol. 32, p. 371.
26 'Elizabeth, Countess of Home, and her house in Portman Square', Lesley Lewis, *Burlington Magazine*, vol. 109, p. 450.
27 Felice Giardini was the most celebrated violinist of his day.
28 *William Beckford*, J. W. Oliver, pp. 106, 107.
29 Historical Manuscipts Commission, 9th Rpt. Pt II. Morrison MSS. p. 480a.
30 *The Memoirs of the Life and Correspondence of Mrs Hannah More*, William Roberts (New York, 1834, 2 vols) vol. 1, p. 53.
31 H.M.C. Bath MSS. vol. 1, p. 345.
32 Walpole, vol. 33, p. 499.
33 Mrs Montagu to Leonard Smelt, 26 April 1789. Huntington Library, MO 50256.
34 *Mrs Montagu, 'Queen of the Blues', her Letters and Friendships from 1762 to 1800*, ed. Reginald Blunt (London, 1923, 2 vols) vol. 2, p. 103.
35 Montagu to Smelt, *op. cit.* 26 April 1780.
36 Roberts, *op. cit.* vol. 1, p. 241.
37 *Ibid.*
38 Blunt, *op. cit.* vol. 2, p. 112.
39 *Ibid.* p. 111.
40 Walpole to Mason, 14 February 1782.
41 Blunt, *op. cit.* vol. 2, p. 242.
42 *A Lady of the Last Century*, John Doran (London, 1873) pp. 326, 355.
43 'On Mrs Montagu's Feather-Hangings', from *The Poetical Works of William Cowper* (Oxford, 1947 ed.)
44 *The Letters of Hannah More*, p. 123.
45 Blunt, *op. cit.* vol. 2, p. 246.
46 Walpole to Berry, 14 June 1791.
47 *St James's Chronicle*, 11–14 June 1791.
48 *Diary and Letters of Madame d'Arblay*, ed. Charlotte F. Barrett (London, selected ed. 1890–91, 3 vols) vol. 3, p. 408.
49 Walpole to Mann, 18 June 1777.

8. Gilded Magnificence

1 *The Life and Letters of Lady Sarah Lennox: 1745–1826, op. cit.*, p. 291.
2 *Chatsworth Papers.* Scrapbook of news cuttings, dated 1805.
3 *Ibid.*, dated 1801.
4 *Journal of a Tour and Residence in Great Britain during the years 1810 and 1811, by a French Traveller*, Louis Simond (Edinburgh and New York, 1815, 2 vols) pp. 34–6.
5 Walpole, vol. 33, p. 499.
6 *Survey of London*, vol. 40 (1980), p. 240.
7 *Ibid.* p. 242.
8 *Bendor: Golden Duke of Westminster*, Leslie Field (London, 1983) p. 65.

9 *Survey of London*, vol. 40, p. 242.
10 *Ibid.*
11 *Country Life*, 20 November 1980, p. 1897.
12 *The Journal of Mrs Arbuthnot 1820–1832*, ed. Francis Bamford and The Duke of Wellington (London, 1950, 2 vols) vol. 1, p. 21.
13 *George IV: Regent and King, 1811–30*, Christopher Hibbert (London and New York, 1973) p. 193.
14 *Alnwick Papers*, V. I. 64.
15 *Ibid.* U. III. 8. (8).
16 Arbuthnot, *op. cit.* vol. 1, p. 311.
17. *Northumberland House: its Saloons and Picture Gallery, with a description of its magnificent Staircase* (London, 1851).
18 *The Private Letters of Princess Lieven to Prince Metternich, 1820–26* ed. Peter Quennell (London, 1937; New York, 1938) p. 167.
19 *Ibid.* p. 171.
20 *The Creevey Papers*, ed. Sir Herbert Maxwell (London, 1904, 2 vols) vol. 2, p. 80.
21 *Letters of Lady Sarah Lennox, op. cit.* p. 291.
22 *Letters from Benjamin Disraeli to Frances Anne, Marchioness of Londonderry, 1837–61*, ed. Edith, Marchioness of Londonderry (London, 1938) p. 74.
23 *Ibid.* p. 136.
24 *Londonderry House and its Pictures*, H. Montgomery Hyde (London, 1937) p. 7.
25 *Some Account of My Life and Writings*, Sir Archibald Alison, ed. Lady Alison (Edinburgh, 1883, 2 vols) p. 153.
26 *Sybil*, Benjamin Disraeli (London, 1920) p. 366.
27 *The Londonderrys*, H. Montgomery Hyde (London and New York, 1979) p. 37.
28 *The Court of London from 1819 to 1825*, Richard Rush (London, 1873) pp. 48, 49.
29 Huxley, *op. cit.* p. 59.
30 Grosvenor Office. William Croggan's accounts, April 1827.
31 Arbuthnot, *op. cit.* vol. 1, p. 14.
32 *Ibid.* vol. 2, p. 219.
33 *Wellington Archives*, Stratfield Saye. Duke to Wyatt, 4 September 1829.
34 Arbuthnot, *op. cit.* vol. 2, pp. 335, 336.
35 *Wellington Archives*, Duke to Wyatt, 24 October 1830.
36 *Ibid.* Wyatt to Duke, 23 April 1831.
37 Arbuthnot, *op. cit.* vol. 2, p. 333.
38 *The Building and Decoration of Apsley House*, J. Hardy, *Apollo Magazine*, September 1973.
39 *The Three Howard Sisters: Selections from the Writings of Lady Caroline Lascelles, Lady Dover and Countess Gower, 1825–33*, ed. Maud, Lady

Leconfield, and revised and completed by John Gore (London, 1955) p. 161.
40 *The Greville Diary*, ed. P. Whitwell Wilson (London and New York, 1927, 2 vols) vol. 1, p. 347.
41 *Wellington and his Friends: Letters of the First Duke of Wellington*, ed. seventh Duke of Wellington (London and New York, 1965) p. 98.
42 *Ibid.* p. 99.
43 *A Portion of the Journal kept by Thomas Raikes, Esq. from 1831–47* (London, 1856–7, 4 vols) vol. 1, p. 49.
44 *Treasures of Art in Great Britain*, Dr Gustav Waagen (London, 1854–57, 4 vols) vol. 2, p. 57.
45 'Stafford House Revisited', John Cornforth, *Country Life*, 14 November 1968, p. 1257.
46 *Ibid.* 7 November, p. 1191.
47 *Elizabeth, Lady Holland to Her Son, 1821–45*, ed. the Earl of Ilchester (London, 1946) p. 66.
48 *Ibid.* p. 77.
49 *Greville Diary, op. cit.* vol. 1, p. 311.
50 *The Memoirs, Journal and Correspondence of Thomas Moore*, ed. Lord John Russell (London and New York, 1853–56, 8 vols) vol. 6, p. 122.
51 'Stafford House', John Cornforth MSS p. 3.
52 *Country Life, op. cit.* 7 November, p. 1189.
53 Summerson, *op. cit.* p. 250.
54 *Journals and Correspondence of Lady Eastlake*, ed. Charles Eastlake Smith (London, 1895, 2 vols) vol. 1, p. 315.
55 *My Reminiscences*, Lord Ronald Gower (London, 1883 and New York, 1884) p. 6.
56 *Companion to the Most Celebrated Private Galleries of Art in London*, Mrs Anna B. Jameson (London, 1844) p. 167.
57 Gower *op. cit.* p. 2.
58 *Selected Correspondence of Frederick Chopin*, trans. and ed. Arthur Hedley (London, 1962 and New York, 1963) p. 332.
59 *Looking Back*, The fifth Duke of Sutherland (London, 1958) p. 36.
60 Gower, *op. cit.* p. 3.
61 *The Leviathan of Wealth*, Eric Richards (London, 1973) p. 18.

9. Echoes of Italy and France

1 Greville, *op. cit.* vol. 2, p. 201.
2 'Devonshire House, London', John Cornforth, *Country Life*, 20 November 1980, p. 1897.
3 Eastlake, *op. cit.* vol. 1, pp. 245, 246.
4 *The World*, 19 May 1875, pp. 11, 12.
5 Moore, *op. cit.* vol. 5, p. 203.
6 'Old Grosvenor House', Lady Helen Seymour, *Blackwood's Magazine*, June 1961.

7 *Survey of London*, vol. 40, p. 249.
8 *Ibid*.
9 Richard Rush, *op. cit.* p. 122.
10 *Survey of London*, vol. 30, p. 497.
11 *Country Life*, 13 May 1949, p. 1121.
12 *The Builder*, 28 August 1852.
13 Chancellor, *op. cit.* p. 250.
14 *Country Life*, 5 May 1928, p. 652.
15 *Ibid*. p. 653.
16 *Ibid*. 12 May, p. 687.
17 *Memoirs of Lady Constance Cairns* (Blacklock Farries, 1961).
18 *The Reminiscences of Lady Dorothy Nevill*, ed. Ralph Nevill (London, 1906) p. 52.
19 *The Literary Memoranda of William Hickling Prescott* (Norman, Oklahoma, 2 vols) vol. 2, p. 195.

10. The Palaces of the Plutocrats

1 *King Edward the Seventh*, Philip Magnus (London and New York, 1964) p. 73.
2 *The Letters of Queen Victoria*, 3rd Series, ed. G. E. Buckle (London, 1930-32; New York, 1930, 3 vols) p. 64.
3 *Afterthoughts*, Frances Countess of Warwick (London, 1931) p. 54.
4 Magnus, *op. cit.* p. 128.
5 *Country Life*, 30 July 1953, p. 346.
6 *The King*, 31 May 1902.
7 *The Rise of the Plutocrats*, Jamie Camplin (London, 1978) p. 197.
8 Warwick, *op. cit.* pp. 86, 87.
9 *The Rothschilds: a Family of Fortune*, Virginia Cowles (London and New York, 1973) p. 174.
10 *Ibid*.
11 *The King*, 31 May 1902.
12 *Ibid*. Jan.-April 1902.
13 *The Film of Memory*, Sir Shane Leslie (London, 1938) pp. 89-91.
14 *Ibid*.
15 *Alfred Beit*, G. S. Fort (London, 1932) p. 155.
16 Camplin, *op. cit.* p. 49.

17 *The Great Barnato*, Stanley Jackson (London, 1970) p. 164.
18 *Ibid*.
19 *Ibid*.
20 *Ibid*. p. 180.
21 *Ibid*. p. 190.
22 See *The House*, The Duchess of Devonshire, *op. cit.* p. 38. 'When some orator in the House of Lords ended a flowery speech with, "This is the proudest day of my life", he murmured to his neighbour, "The proudest day of my life was when my pig won first prize at Skipton Fair".'
23 *Ibid*. p. 37.
24 *The Reminiscences of Lady Randolph Churchill*, Mrs George Cornwallis-West (London and New York, 1908) p. 301.
25 *Ibid*. p. 302.
26 *The Duchess of Devonshire's Ball*, Lady Sophia Murphy (London, 1984) p. 79.
27 *Past Times and Pastimes*, Lord Dunraven (London, 1922) p. 203.
28 Cornwallis-West, *op. cit.* p. 303.
29 Cavendish, *op. cit.* p. 118.
30 Cornwallis-West, *op. cit.* p. 303.
31 Cornwallis-West, *op. cit.* pp. 303, 304.
32 *The Glitter and the Gold*, Consuelo Vanderbilt Balsan (New York, 1952; London, 1953) pp. 121, 122.
33 *Survey of London*, vol. 40, p. 281.
34 *The King* (journal), 22 March 1902.
35 *Grace and Favour: The Memoirs of Loelia, Duchess of Westminster* (London and New York, 1962) p. 86.
36 *Our Partnership*, Beatrice Webb (London and New York, 1948) pp. 346, 347.
37 Dunraven, *op. cit.* p. 194.
38 *English Landed Society in the Nineteenth Century*, F. M. L. Thompson (London, 1963) p. 322.
39 *Ibid*.
40 *Dear Duchess: Millicent, Duchess of Sutherland*, Denis Stuart (London and New York, 1982) p. 117.
41 *Ibid*. p. 118.

11. The Passing of an Order

1 Stuart. *op. cit.* p. 188.
2 *The Times*, 1 February 1919.
3 *Ibid*. 26 April 1919.
4 *Ibid*. 19 May 1920.
5 *Ibid*. 15 April 1920.
6 *Ibid*. 19 May 1920.
7 *Grace and Favour*, Loelia, Duchess of Westminster, p. 86.
8 *The New Devonshire House*, Bernard Darwin (Devonshire House, Ltd., London, 1925) p. 23.
9 *Ibid*. pp. 25-9.
10 *Lost London: A Century of Demolition and Decay*, Hermione Hobhouse (London, 1971 and Boston, Mass., 1972) p. 19.
11 Information from Daphne Fielding.
12 Westminster, *op. cit.* p. 86.
13 *Daily Mail*, 26 July 1924.
14 *Daily Express*, 13 July 1928.
15 *Ibid*. 10 July 1928.
16 *Ibid*.
17 *The Times*, 16 July 1929.
18 *Country Life*, 11 May 1935, p. 490.
19 *The Times*, 10 February 1938.
20 *More Memories*, Margot Asquith (London, 1933) p. 33.
21 *Laughter in the Next Room*, Osbert Sitwell (Boston, Mass., 1948 and London, 1949) p. 215.
22 *Ibid*.
23 *Ibid*. p. 223.
24 *Retrospect*, Lady Londonderry (London, 1938) p. 237.
25 *Ibid*. p. 247.
26 *The Londonderrys*, *op. cit.* p. 182.
27 *'Chips': the Diaries of Sir Henry Channon*, ed. R. R. James (London, 1967) p. 28.
28 *Ibid*. pp. 16, 17.
29 *Ibid*. p. 29.
30 *Ibid*. p. 39.
31 *Country Life*, 26 February 1938.
32 James, *op. cit.* pp. 64, 65.
33 *Ibid*. p. 349.
34 *Ibid*. p. 465.
35 From the revue, *Nine Sharp & Earlier*, by Herbert Farjeon (London, 1939).

Index

Page references and plate numbers in italics refer to illustrations.